PRACTICAL ABAP – FI/CO

A Technical Guide with Functional Perspective

SELVA LAKSHMANAN

HARIHARAN SUBRAHMANYAN

Preface

This book is a practical ABAP guide focusing on finance and controlling modules. Books on SAP generally tend to focus on either the configuration aspects or the programming aspects of the various modules within SAP. We believe that a practical ABAP guide that contains an explanation of related SAP configuration and business processes will be of great value to the developer.

From our combined experience of over 35 years in the SAP field, we are convinced that to be a highly sought after developer, you need a solid grounding of configuration concepts and master data elements that have a bearing on the ABAP objects you will be working on. The same applies to the functional consultant/configurator who should have at least a basic understanding of the various ABAP objects that influence a business process being designed.

The purpose of the book is to address the need for an integrated view of business process, configuration and ABAP code which will benefit both the configurator and the developer. The technical content of the book is intentionally kept at a beginner to intermediate level. This book is meant to be a guide for both the developer and functional analyst. This was not intended to be a step by step configuration manual or ABAP coding manual. Instead, it offers both a functional and technical perspective to the two groups that form the audience for this book. Depending on the context, we have explained underlying configuration, master data values or examples of business process throughout the book. Also, ABAP code samples have been given wherever appropriate.

An important feature of this book is the process oriented organization of topics. Developers are often asked to work across various modules of SAP. In this book we have covered the 3 main areas in ECC viz. Record to Report, Procure to Pay and Order to Cash. The Plan to Build process has been deliberately not covered as it is more geared towards manufacturing and logistics. However the integration aspects of material master and accounting have been explained.

We see that most organizations structure their SAP teams along these lines. It is quite likely that the ABAP developer will be exclusively attached to one of these teams or support all of these teams. The topics covered in this book will be very helpful to the ABAP developer by enhancing his knowledge of the business process and configuration which in turn will lead to high-quality solution whether it is a simple report, user exit or any other type of enhancements.

If you are a functional analyst/configurator, you will find references to useful ABAP objects such as BAPIs, BAdIs, User Exits and BTEs throughout the book which will be valuable guide as you implement a process in SAP to meet a business requirement.

In summary, the objective of the book is to provide direction and overview of various options available. We believe this will stimulate thought during designing simple or complex solutions with or without custom code. The organization of the topics along major business processes that influence financials will be useful to both the developer and configurator.

TABLE OF CONTENTS

1 Technical Overview

Technical development within the Finance and Controlling (FICO) component is quite different from other SAP modules like SD, MM, HR. This component primarily deals with back office functions such as general ledger, accounts payable and costing activities. There is minimal usage of Web Dynpro functionality. FI and CO are compact yet complex modules. They are highly integrated with other components such as MM, SD and PP.

SAP provides a number of technical objects which are common to all SAP modules. In this chapter, these objects are explained in relation to how they are used in the FI and CO component. This chapter covers in detail the technical objects, enhancement techniques, IDOC & Message types and other tools available.

FI enhancement techniques include user exits, BAdIs, other exits, business transaction events, substitutions and validations. The business transaction event (BTE) concept is more prevalent in FI. The activation and implementation of a BTE is discussed in detail.

Like BTEs, substitution and validation are specific to FI and CO. Substitution and validation is based on accounting document so it is highly used in FI enhancement. Substitutions and validations can be accomplished with just configuration. For more complex requirements, you may require ABAP code to enhance the substitution and validation.

The accounting interface is a tool used by FI component integrating with other components. In this chapter, the accounting interface is discussed in detail.

Business Object Repository is part of SAP workflow and BAPI technology. In this chapter, you will learn about the basics of BOR and ABAP coding involved in the usage of BOR. IDOC is used across all modules. In this chapter, you will understand the basics of the IDOC and message types and how to implement ABAP code for inbound and outbound IDOCs. SAP has delivered a number of standard IDOC message types relevant to the FI component.

There are a number of technical tools available to monitor and debug ABAP programming. In this chapter, you will learn how to trace the SQL log, application log and debug ABAP code.

1.1 Functional Perspective

Generally, a functional analyst concentrates on transaction codes, screens inputs and underlying configuration. However it is also important that they have a good understanding of technical details such as table names and field names. Such knowledge would be very beneficial when they need to work on RICEF objects which are covered later in this chapter. We believe that a skilled SAP FICO analyst should bring to the table a basic knowledge of technical aspects such as field names, table names and program names.

1.1.1 Technical Details

One of the basic steps is identifying the field beneath the screen. In the following example, we will find the technical details of the document date in the transaction FB50. You can identify the technical details by clicking F1 key on the field. When you click F1, you can see the help document popup. You can view the technical detail of the field by clicking the technical detail icon on the toolbar of Performance Assistant.

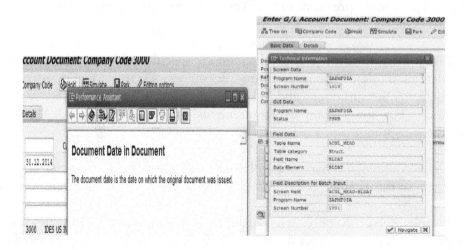

You can see four different categories viz., screen data, GUI data, field data and field data for batch input. Screen data refers to screen programming. If you see screen number 1000, it indicates an executable report program. The report program can be executed directly using the transaction code SE38. But screen programming cannot be executed from ABAP workbench. You require the transaction code to execute the screen program. You can access the screen programming using the transaction code SE51.

GUI status is combination of Menu Bar, Application Toolbar and Function Keys. You can access the GUI status using the transaction code SE41 or you can navigate from technical information help.

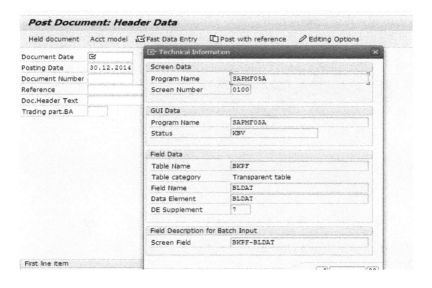

The screen uses the structure for the field and structure is not a database table. So, the data is handled by the program and stored in the code behind the program. For example, the technical detail of the document date of the transaction FB01 is as follows.

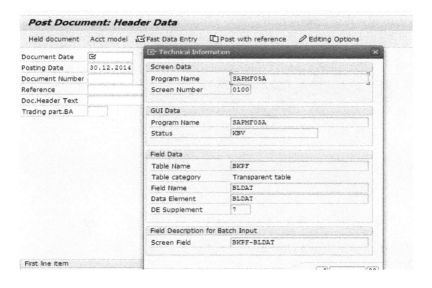

The document date is refers to a transparent table category BKPF-BLDAT. The BKPF is transparent table and you can view data using the transaction code SE16. You can notice that the help documents are same in transaction document date. The help document is associated with the data element. BLDAT of BKPF and ACGL_HEAD points to a same help document. Each program and screen of SAP behaves differently. Field data for Batch Input is related to BDC programming and it is explained in the BDC section.

1.1.2 Transaction

Transaction code is used to access functions or execute programs in the SAP application environment. It is recommended to define custom transaction codes starting with Z or Y. The details of the transaction code can be viewed using the transaction code SE93. The transaction code may point to an executable report program, screen programming, report writer reports, drill-down reporting, table maintenance or an SQL query. Note that not all custom transactions refer to a custom program or screen.

Transaction Variants and Screen Variants

Screen variant is used to hide fields, assign default values to fields or set the fields to not ready for input. Transaction variant is personalization of the SAP transaction with combination of screen variants. You can use transaction variants to tailoring some features of the transaction without any ABAP code change. You can hide fields, menu functions, screens, to supply fields with default values. You can access transaction variant using the transaction code SHD0.

Let us take transaction code FB50. You can see a number of SAP supplied transaction variants for this transaction.

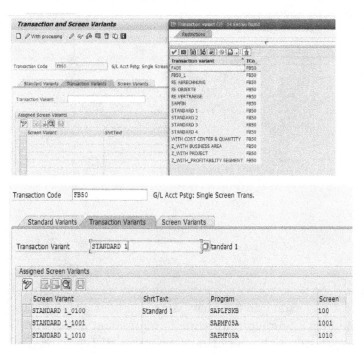

You can create a new transaction using a transaction variant. When you execute the transaction then it will execute older transaction with defined transaction variant. See screen shot showing the transaction to maintain a variant transaction.

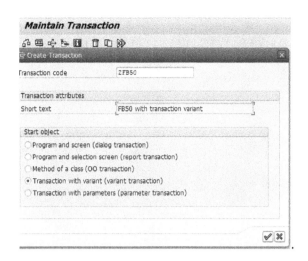

The transaction FB50 allows you to access all screen variants defined for FB50 and pick it. This feature is applicable and available for new transaction codes only.

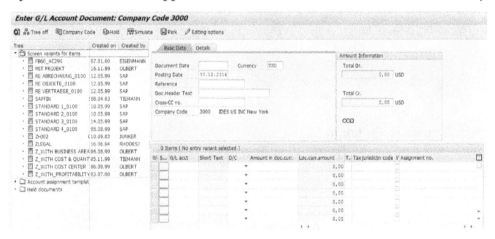

Caution: Screen variants are tremendous time savers, particularly for transactions that you regularly set up and execute in the same manner. Note that the transaction variants and screen variants are very specific to a particular business scenario.

1.1.3 Identify the programs

It is possible to identify the type of programs associated with a transaction code. For example, you can use SE93 to view the details of the transaction code. For example, you can see the attributes of the transaction code S_ALR_87009689 (Plan/Actual/Variance: Profit Center).

Transaction code	S_ALR_87013611
Package	RTTREE
Transaction text	Cost Centers: Actual/Plan/Variance

Default values for
Transaction	START_REPORT
☑ Skip initial screen	
Obsolete: Use default values for transaction	
Screen	0
From module pool	

The transaction points to the START_REPORT transaction with transaction parameters.

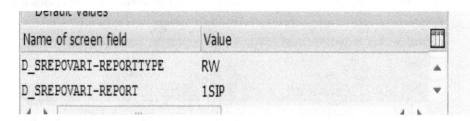

Default Values

Name of screen field	Value	
D_SREPOVARI-REPORTTYPE	RW	▲
D_SREPOVARI-REPORT	1SIP	▼

If the transaction points to the START_REPORT then transaction parameters determines the type of the report. The tranaction code S_ALR_87009689 points to the report writer (RW) and report name is 1SIP. The following are list of the parameters used by the START_REPORT transaction.

Report Type	Descrption
Blank (no value)	ABAP report program
AQ	ABAP Query
RE	Drill down report
RW	Report writer report
TR	Transaction
LS	Form
BB	Report Portfolio report

The transaction code FB50 points to the the program SAPMF05A and screen number 1099. This points to the screen module pool programing. Note that you cannot execute the screen module directly from screen painter.

The transaction code FBL1N (vendor line item) points to the report program (RFITEMAP) with selection screen 1000. The screen 1000 points to the executable report program. All other screens point to the screen module. You can execute the program RFITEMAP directly from SE38 or SA38.

1.2 RICEF

SAP offers comprehensive functionality in its finance and controlling modules. Even then, businesses often decide to undertake some level of custom ABAP development to meet their specific needs. These custom programs can be broadly classified into 5 categories.

- ➤ **R**eports
- ➤ **I**nterfaces
- ➤ **C**onversion
- ➤ **E**nhancements
- ➤ **F**orms

In most SAP implementations they are collectively referred to as either RICEF or FRICE objects. These are tracked closely in a formal manner in most new implementations or deployment projects. In this section, we will give some examples of business scenarios where custom developments may be used.

1.2.1 Reports

Custom reports can become necessary if data to be output is required to be pulled together from different areas. Many companies may decide not to give end-users access to develop their own ABAP queries. Also some reports may require complex calculation or may be interactive in nature and hence not suitable for a query or a report painter.

An example is if a controller wants to see details of invoices for a certain period along with complex calculations that pull in data from pricing condition tables, sales order and delivery related data and billing documents, it may be considered a candidate for a custom report.

From a custom report, it is possible to add drill in functionality by embedding a call transaction. Example is a material number is shown as an output row in a report along with this standard cost. If the user so chooses, he may be able to click on the material number and be taken to a display of released cost estimate for that material.

Another business scenario could be a requirement to update a custom table from a report output. The data in the custom table could then be used to feed to a custom data store object in BW to be used in multi-dimensional analytical reporting.

1.2.2 Interfaces

Interfaces within the context of FI/CO often refer processing of outbound or inbound files of different formats to/from different source. Inbound data can be received in the form of xml or flat files and through a custom program that data can be staged to update transactions in SAP.

On the inbound side, you may get a flat file from a large customer on a daily basis with details of their orders and this file is processed by a custom program that eventually calls a BAPI to create a sales order in SAP. Another example is an inbound interface from a freight carrier with estimated freight costs that updates z table which in turn may be used in another business process

On the outbound side you may collect the data from SAP sales orders and deliveries and pass it in a pre-defined format to a transportation management company. We have also seen instances in the area of accounts payable where banks insist on getting files in a specific format and layout not covered by pre-delivered SAP file formats. A common approach is to generate tab delimited or comma separated files.

In addition to data exchanged with an external partner, there are many cases where data needs to be sent internally to non-SAP systems. This could be a company B2C website, a portal or a specialized reporting tool.

1.2.3 Conversions

During a new implementation or a deployment, large volume of data will have to be migrated from legacy systems to SAP. It could be open invoices, inventory balances, chart of accounts, general ledger balances, material master, customer master, vendor master records and so on. Depending on the size and complexity of the business, this becomes a major endeavor. Often this is viewed as critical for a successful implementation and for this reason many large SAP implementations have dedicated data migration teams for a certain period of time.

Even though SAP has provided LSMW functionality, many companies tend to develop custom programs for data conversions which they are able to use in subsequent deployments. SAP provides a number of direct input programs to upload the master data. The LSMW functionality is used to map between the input file and standard SAP direct input file format.

1.2.4 Enhancements

We have covered technical aspects of custom enhancements in the form of user exits, BADIs, Substitution & Validation, BTEs and Enhancement framework. The SAP workflow is considered as a part of enhancements. The enhancements are explained detail in the later section. Some applications of custom enhancements have also been called out in different places in the following chapters.

1.2.5 Forms

This is another area in which custom development is very common. SAP has delivered several standard forms by way of SAP Script or SmartForms. However the actual look and layout of standard forms and aspects such as logo, wording of text in out of the box forms may not always meet needs of the business.

There is usually a need for custom forms especially for invoice outputs, dunning letters and remittance advice.

1.3 Technical Objects

Technical objects are referred as ABAP objects. In this section, you will go through a few important objects like dictionary objects, ABAP programs, lock objects, authorization objects, search helps, business objects and logical database. The purpose of the section is to give an introduction to technical objects especially to a functional resource. In addition, this section contains sample ABAP code and suggestions to handle special situations.

1.3.1 Table & Views

Transparent table is a database table and stores data directly. The transparent table can be Master, Transaction or Configuration data. The view is list of fields derived from one or more tables, but not stored physically. The table and view can be maintained using the ABAP workbench transaction code SE11. You can display the data of the transparent tables and views using transaction code SE16. If the table maintenance is generated for the table or view then you can view and maintain the data using the transaction code SM30. You can generate the table maintenance dialog using the transaction code SE54.

From functional perspective, you can access the table and view data using SE16 or SE16N. The transaction SE16 allows you to display the data records. The transaction code SE16 does not allow you to change or delete the record. But, you can maintain the table by activating the maintenance view of the table or view. The maintenance view is generated using the transaction code SE54. The transaction codes SM30 and SM34 are used to maintain the table, view or view cluster entries. The transaction provides you option to display, maintain or transport the entries. Most of IMG configurations use the SM30 or SM34 transaction.

There are few types of the SAP table. Pooled tables are logical tables that must be assigned to a table pool when they are defined. Pooled tables are used to store control data. A table pool is combination of several pooled tables. The data of the pooled table is sorted in a common table in the database. The example of the pool table is A005 (Customer/material) with pool table KAPOL.

Cluster tables are logical tables that must be assigned to a table cluster when they are defined. Cluster tables can be used to store control data. They can also be used to store temporary data or texts, such as documentation.

BSEG (Accounting line item table) is a clustered table (RFBLG). Note that in SQL trace, you can see the table RFBLG instead of BSEG.

Indexes are created to improve the performance of accessing the table data. The table may have one or more indexes. SAP identifies the appropriate index based on select statement's where condition. SAP delivers a number of indexes for the SAP delivered tables. SAP allows you to create your own indexes. You can use SQL trace to identify what indexes are used by the SQL statement.

RFINDEX – The report program does FI consistency check of the index tables BSIS, BSAS, BSID, BSAD, BSIK, and BSAK with line items in the table BSEG.

1.3.2 ABAP Programs

The ABAP program is the main technical objects for the SAP transaction. The user interface (UI) is handled by the screen programming and Web Dynpro applications. FICO is part of backend system and it uses little or none of Web Dynpro applications. All FICO screens are handled by the screen programming.

Each ABAP program has a program type and it is defined in program attributes. There are seven program types which are explained below.

- **Executable Program** – You can execute the program directly (without any transaction) using ABAP editor (SE38/SA38). Most reports (either standard or custom) are written in ABAP as the executable programs. The standard SAP reports are used, starting with the letter 'R'. You can associate the logical database with the report. This is elaborated upon in the logical database section. The ABAP report program is event-based programming.

  - **Initialization** – This event is triggered before the standard selection screen is called. You can initialize input fields and global variables in this event.

  - **At-Selection-Screen** – This event is triggered while the selection screen is processed. This event is between initialization and start-of-selection.

  - **Start-of-selection** – This event occurs after the selection screen is processed and before the data is read.

  - **End-of-selection** – This event is the last event called by the runtime environment. It is triggered after the data has been read from the database.

  - **At Line-Selection** – This event occurs when you click the result line item.

- **Module Pools** – The module pool can only be controlled by screen flow logic. You cannot execute the module pool directly. You must start them using a transaction code. It is appropriate to use module pools when you write dialog-oriented programming.

  You can access the screen using the transaction code SE51. The screen program uses the following events.

  - **Process Before Output (PBO)** – The event is executed before the screen output. You can read the data from the database and output the data to the screen.

  - **Process After Input (PAI)** – The screen programming uses the function code (or OK code) to process the data. By clicking buttons (processing function codes), the block of PAI code are executed.

  - **Process On Help Request** – This event occurs when you click F1 on the field.

  - **Process On Value Request** – This event occurs when you click the F4 button on the field.

- **Function Groups** – The function group is a collection of one or more function modules. You can define global variables and the values can be set and read from one or more function modules. The global variables in the function group are session level. The function module is executed using the ABAP statement CALL FUNCTION. You can access the function group using the transaction code SE80. The function module can be viewed by the transaction code SE37. You can execute the function module manually from SE37. One of the function module attribute is Remote Function Call (RFC). By enabling this, you can execute the function module from an external system. Parameter interface definition and some programming restrictions are applied for RFC function modules.

  Note that the table maintenance view (transaction code SE54) uses the function group as the base ABAP code.

- **Class Pools** – You can code an ABAP program in Object Oriented programming using the ABAP class. You can define the class globally using the transaction code SE24. Also, you can define the class locally in the ABAP program. ABAP class can be instantiated using the CREATE OBJECT statement and you can execute the method using the ABAP statement CALL METHOD. The class can be destructed using the ABAP statement FREE OBJECT. FI/CO components use fewer ABAP class objects compared to logistics components.

- **Interface Pools** – Interface is an abstract code which has no screens or separate processing blocks. You can implement the code in the interface class. The interface is implemented in the class objects.

- **Subroutine Pools** – Subroutine is a small piece of code with logical grouping. You can define subroutine between FORM and ENDFORM. You can call these subroutines from the ABAP code using the PERFORM statement.

- **Type Groups** – ABAP Type is an ABAP statement where you can define a structure for your ABAP code. You can define a set of ABAP types as a global type group. You can include this into your ABAP using the statement TYPE-POOLS.

- **Include Programs** – The include program does not represent a stand-alone program and you cannot execute the include program directly. Include programs can be used in one or more main programs. You can insert the include program using the statement INCLUDE. They merely serve as a library for ABAP source code.

Web Dynpro ABAP is the SAP standard UI technology for developing Web applications in the ABAP environment. The Web Dynpro program uses class program objects as base to handle events and methods. You can access the Web Dynpro application using the transaction code SE80.

1.3.3 Forms

SAP Script is standard SAP tool to create and maintain the business form. It allows you to display, print or email the business form using the ABAP print program. You can enhance the forms using the standard tools. The SAP script divides into two main category viz., a form painter to design the form and print program to process the SAP script form. SAP Script Form is client dependent and language dependent. You can access the form painter using the transaction code SE71.

The print program allows the user to input the parameters, retrieves the data from database, SAP Script form to be used, and type of distribution (like display, email or fax).

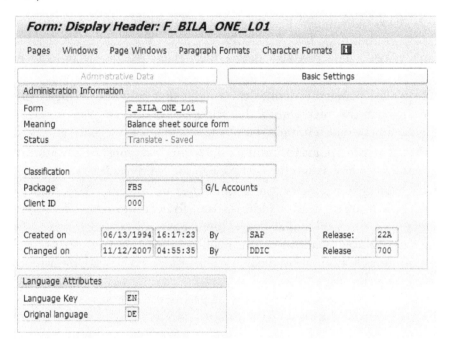

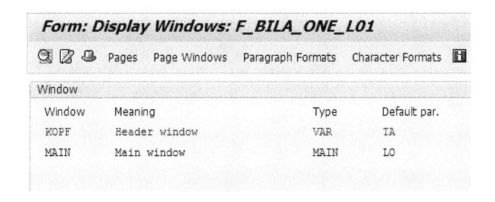

Form: Display Page Windows: F_BILA_ONE_L01

| | | | Pages | Windows | Paragraph Formats | Character Formats | |

Page Window

Page   PAGE

Window	Meaning	Left	Upper	Width	Hght
MAIN	00 Main window	2,00 CH	9,00 LN	113,00 CH	38,00 LN
KOPF	Header window	2,00 CH	2,00 LN	113,00 CH	6,00 LN

SAP Script Form Components:

- Header – It is used to control header and SAP printing information. It consists of the administration information and basic settings. You can define like the page format (e.g., LETTER, LEGAL, etc.), the page orientation and the default values. You can also define the default paragraph and the first page.
- Paragraphs – The paragraph defines the format that contains all information needed to format the text within the window. You can also define the paragraph alignment (like left, right, etc.), line spacing, font formats, etc.
- Pages – Page is starting point for printing the form. You must define at least one page for a form and assign the first page in the form header.
- Windows – Windows are the output area defined on a form. Also, Windows are individual text areas (header address, date, footer) in a page. SAP Script allows up to 99 windows. There are three types of windows viz., Main, Constant and Variable windows. The main window can flow across pages. The main window is created by default. The constant and variable windows are use only once per page.
  A page window is definition of window at page level. You can arrange the window's position and their sizes on the page.
- Character Formats – Character format allows you to format entire blocks of text within a paragraph.

Symbols

SAP script form uses symbols to insert program and system data into the form. You can declare the symbol within &<symbol>&. SAP script supports the following the type of symbols:

- Text symbol
- Program symbol
- Standard symbol
- System symbol

Control Commands

The control commands are allowed you to influence the output formatting such as apply special formats into the text, apply condition logic, assign values, etc. The control commands are indicated by the '/:' paragraph format in the format column. The editor interprets the invalid control commands as comment line (rather than stops).

Control Command	Description
ADDRESS	Formatting the address
BOTTOM, ENDBOTTOM	Define footer text
BOX, POSITION, SIZE	Boxes, Lines and shading
CASE, ENDCASE	Implement case statement
DEFINE	Value assignment to text symbol
HEX, ENDHEX	Hexadecimal values
IF, ENDIF	Implementing IF statement
INCLUDE	Include other text
NEW-PAGE	Creating a new page
PERFORM, ENDPERFORM	Implementing subroutine
PRINT-CONTROL	Insert print control characters
PROTECT, ENDPROTECT	Protect text from page-break
RESET	Initialize outline paragraph
SET COUNTRY, SET DATE MASK, SET SIGN, SET TIME MASK	Formatting set
STYLE	Change style
SUMMING	Summing the variables
TOP, ENDTOP	Set header text

You can activate the debugging in the form painter (SE71) using the menu Utilities->Activate Debugger to enable debugging. Or you can use standard program RSTXDBUG to activate the debugging.

Table	Description
STXH	SAPScript text
TNAPR	Processing programs for output
TFO01	SAPScript font families
TFO02	SAPScript system fonts
TFO03	SAPScript printer fonts

Transaction	Description
SE71	SAPScript Form

SE72	SAPScript Styles
SE73	SAPScript Font Maintenance
SO10	SAPScript: Standard Texts

Function Module	Description
OPEN_FORM	Open SAP Script form
START_FORM	Start the SAP Script form and the new layout set is opened.
WRITE_FORM	Write content to the SAP Script form
END_FORM	End SAP Script form
CLOSE_FORM	Close the SAP Script layout set

Smart Forms

SAP Smart Forms is used to create and maintain forms for mass printing in SAP Systems. As output medium SAP Smart Forms support a printer, a fax, e-mail, or the Internet (by using the generated XML output). SmartForms has easier user interface and requires no programming for UI design. You can access the smart forms using the transaction code SMARTFORMS.

Like SAP Script form, a Smart form consists of pages, output areas, graphics and data or text contents. You can use static or dynamic tables to display data or text contents in the output area.

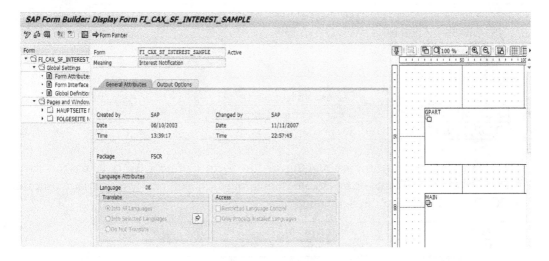

Three components:

- Navigation Window – Navigate the nodes and sub-nodes like Global settings & Pages and Windows and text elements. The Global settings support Form Attributes, Form Interface and Global definition.

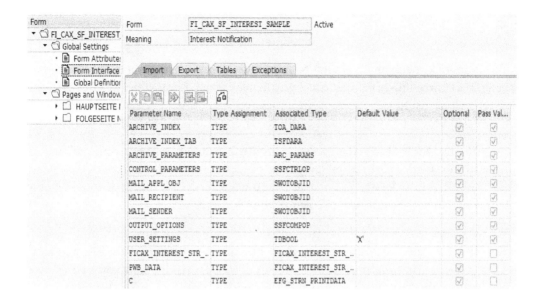

Smart form supports two types of windows viz., Main and Secondary window. You can define only one main window and multiple secondary windows for page.

- Form Definition – The maintenance information about the smart form.
- Form Painter – The UI interface to define the smart forms.

You can migrate SAP Script forms to the smart forms by using the menu path Utilities -> Migration -> Import SAPscript Form in the transaction code 'smartforms'. For mass migration, use the transaction SF_MIGRATE. It creates the Smart Forms under the names of the SAPscript forms plus the extension _SF.

The smart form creates a function module in background when it is activated. You can execute the generated function module to get the smart form output. The function module SSF_FUNCTION_MODULE_NAME can be used to get the function module for the smart forms. Note that the function module name can be different between development, test and production systems for the smart form.

You can use the function module to test your smart form.

Transaction	Description
SMARTFORMS	Smart form maintenance
SMARTSTYLES	Define smart form styles

Adobe Interactive Form: SAP FI/CO is not using any adobe interactive forms as part of standard Form printing.

1.3.4 Lock Object

The lock mechanism is vital to handling multiple users' access to the same data records. SAP provides the lock mechanism using the Lock object. You can set and release the lock using the function modules (which are generated by the lock object). You can also access the lock object using the transaction code SE11.

For the lock object, you must define the primary table & optional secondary tables and key fields of these tables. Lock object supports three types of lock mode: Write Lock, Read Lock, and Exclusive. If you want to access this lock from an external system, you can set the Allow RFC flag in the attribute.

You can see that SAP has provided a lock object for the accounting document header BKPF in the following screen shot. For the lock object EFBKPF, you can lock the object using the function module ENQUEUE_EFBKPF and you can release the lock using the function module DEQUEUE_EFBKPF.

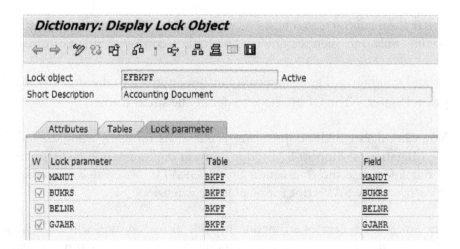

Monitor Tool

You can view the locks using the transaction code SM12. In addition, you can remove the lock entry in this transaction if you have proper authorization. Be cautious when you are removing the lock.

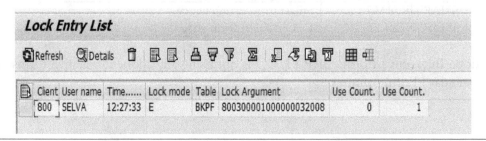

1.3.5 Authorization Object

The SAP authorization concept protects transactions, programs, and activities from unauthorized access. The SAP authorization concept is based on the basis of the authorization objects. The authorization object allows you to inspect your privileges for specific activities on the specific data object within a program.

The authorization object enables you to perform complex checks of an authorization. An authorization object supports grouping up to ten authorization fields that are checked in an 'AND' relationship.

Roles

The role is a combination of one or more authorization objects with activities. You can assign a role to a user. The user will then have all permissions defined in the role. You can assign multiple roles to a user as well. The role itself can be assigned to multiple users. The transaction code PFCG can be used to create a role.

A composite role can be created where you can assign one or more roles to a role. When you assign a composite role then all defined roles are assigned to the user. You cannot define any authorization object in the composite role. The role definition is part of the SAP security team. SAP delivers a set of standard roles for the financial components level. Custom roles can also be defined. Based on the user position, you can assign appropriate roles to them.

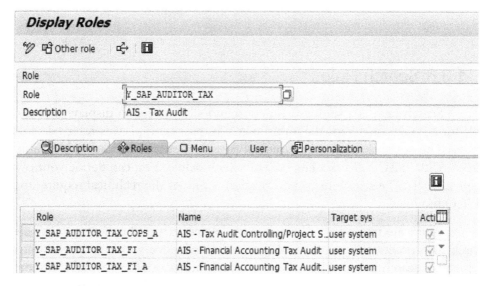

The ABAP statement AUTHORITY-CHECK is used to perform an authorization check. The following sample code is to do an authorization check on the transaction code ZFB1. The code forces users to have authorization on transaction code ZFB1. Otherwise, force the error message.

```
AUTHORITY-CHECK OBJECT 'S_TCODE'
    ID 'TCD' FIELD 'ZFB1'.
IF SY-SUBRC NE 0.
    message e077(ZB) with 'ZFB1.
ENDIF.
```

Troubleshooting

When you are accessing the program or transaction and you are not authorized to view data or execute the program, then you can view the last authorization result using the transaction code SU53. The transaction will display the last authorization check and help you identify the authorization issue. In some projects, basis/security team requires the SU53 screen to identify the authorization issue.

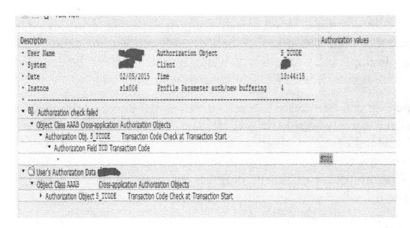

1.3.6 Search Help

Search help is a standard function and allows user to display the list of values (F4) for a screen field with the input help. In past times, it was referred as the Match Code. The search help can be attached to a data element, check table, table field or screen field. SAP delivers a large set of search helps. You can define your own search helps as well. The search help modification is one of the technical requirements in the FI/CO modules.

There are two types of search helps: elementary and collective. The elementary search help describes a search path while the collective search help combines several elementary search helps. The collective search help can offer several alternative search paths. You can access search help using the ABAP workbench transaction SE11.

You can associate the search help to a data element, a check table, a table field and a screen field. The following screenshot is collective search help (DEBI) for customer.

Dictionary: Display Search Help

Collective srch hlp	DEBI Active
Short description	Search help for customers

Attributes | Definition | Included search helps

Param. assignment

Search Help	H...	Short text	
DEBIA	☐	Customers (general)	
DEBID	☐	Customers (by company code)	
DEBIE	☐	Customers by country/company code	
DEBIL	☐	Customers by country	
DEBIP	☐	Customers by personnel number	
DEBIT	☐	Customers by Tax Information	
DEBIX	☐	Customers by Address Attributes	
DEBIY	☐	Customers by Address Attributes (Fuzzy Search)	
AFM_DEBI	☐	Customer Append Search Help for IS-PS	
APP_JVB_VPTNR	☐	JV partner in coding block	
ASH_DEBI	☐	Append Search Help for Customers	
DEBI_ES_APPEND	☐	Customer search (with Enterprise Search)	
RE_KUNNR	☐	Search Help: Customer by Real Estate Contract	

Search Help Exit

Most search helps use the transparent table or view (as a data source) as the selection method. The direct table access may not meet all customer requirements like conditional data selection or other complex data selection. SAP provides a search help exit to enhance search help to handle complex scenarios. In search help exit, the data is fetched from the defined data source. This also allows you to modify the flow in multiple steps.

The search help exit is a function module that has predefined interface parameters. In the function module, you can define your program logic to manipulate and administrate the data.

- Before displaying the dialog box for selecting the required search path.

- Before starting the F4 process for the elementary search help

- Before displaying the dialog box for input the search conditions

- Before selecting data

- Before displaying the hit list

- Before returning the values selected by the user to input template

The search help exit is a very powerful exit point and it has features such as fetching, filtering and displaying the result. The function module must have the same interface as function module F4IF_SHLP_EXIT_EXAMPLE. The exit function must have the following parameters:

```
*"-----------------------------------------------------------------
*"*"Local Interface:
*"  TABLES
*"     SHLP_TAB TYPE  SHLP_DESCT
*"     RECORD_TAB STRUCTURE  SEAHLPRES
*"  CHANGING
*"    VALUE(SHLP) TYPE  SHLP_DESCR
*"    VALUE(CALLCONTROL) LIKE  DDSHF4CTRL STRUCTURE
DDSHF4CTRL
*"-----------------------------------------------------------------
```

The CALLCONTROL-STEP carries the detail about when this function exit has been called.   Check the function module F4IF_SHLP_EXIT_EXAMPLE.

Step	Description
SELONE	Select one of the elementary search help.
PRESEL	Enter the selection criteria
SELECT	Select the values
DISP	Display the values.
EXIT	Exit the search help

Note that any wrong modification or addition of the parameters in search help exit causes a short dump. Implement the search help exit with high caution.

1.3.7 Business Object Repository

Business Object Repository (BOR) is an object-oriented repository that contains SAP business object types and SAP interface types. The object type and interface type has multiple components of attributes, methods and events. The business object type is fundamental for SAP workflow system. The BOR is used in multiple places. In this repository, the BAPIs are defined as methods.

You can view BOR information using the transaction code SWO1.

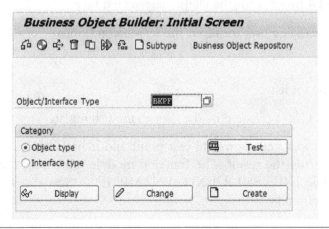

The BOR is based on the object-oriented concept and it has the following components:

- Key Fields – The key fields are a unique identification of the object. When you instantiate the object, you need to pass the key fields.

- Attributes – The attributes are part of the object attributes used in the object. You can access and update these attributes in the methods.

- Methods – You can define methods to represent the actions you take with the object and its attributes. The method can be referred to as a BAPI and ABAP code.

- Interfaces – The abstract interface object and interface methods can be implemented in the business object.

- Events – The possible events for the object. The workflow object uses the BOR events as part of triggering or terminating events. You can raise the events in the standard ABAP code.

The business object type is stored in the ABAP program.

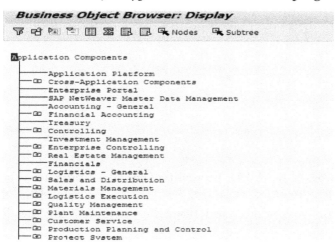

You can browse through the BOR using the transaction SWO2. SAP generates an ABAP program for each BOR object type.

Subtyping and Delegation

One of the most important features in object-oriented development is that of inheritance. This concept lets you extend core functionality by creating a child of the parent object that inherits all of its attributes and methods.

The main purpose of the subtyping is to extend the functionalities of the standard SAP object. For example, you may want to add a few methods and events to a BKPF object. You can subtype BKPF to ZBKPF and implement your changes. Now you need to inform the SAP system to use the redefined version ZBKPF and not the version that was delivered on the BKPF object. This is called delegation.

You can access the delegation customization from menu Settings->Delegate (in SWO1) or by the transaction code SWO6. You can delegate the standard business object to a custom business object. The standard SAP program will use a custom business object instead of the standard business object type.

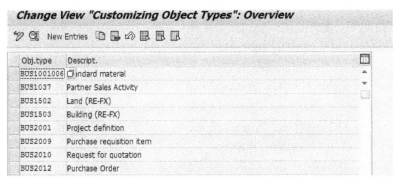

Delegate your custom object to a standard SAP object.

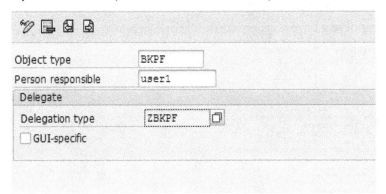

The BOR type is based on ABAP program. The ABAP program is generated automatically by the BOR definition. You can get the program name from the basic data of an object type and can be accessed from the program using the 'Program' toolbar menu.

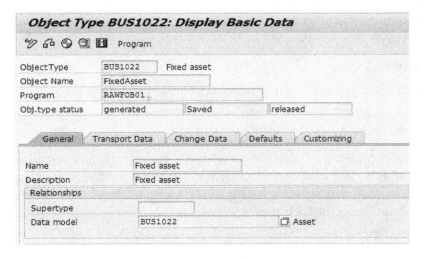

Release Status

You can define the release status at an object type and object type component (Key fields, attributes, methods and events) level. The release statuses are:

- Modeled – Signature interfaces are defined
- Implemented – Functionality is implemented and used for internal and testing purposes.
- Released – BOR Object and all of its associated methods are fully functional and the interface is complete. This would show up as an entry in the BAPI explorer or BOR, and can be invoked from an external application as well (Non-SAP).
- Obsolete – This status means the BOR and its components cannot be used.

Technical Details

Each object type is generated as an ABAP program. The include program <CNTN01> does have a number of macros and is used in all business object types program. You can use simple macros to create, invoke and raise events.

Function Module	Comments
SWO_CREATE	Create the BOR object
SWO_INVOKE	Get attribute from BOR object

There are a number of macros used in the BOR program. The following are a list of highly used macros. The macros are part of the include <cnt01>.

Macro	Description
SWC_CREATE_OBJECT	Instantiate the BOR object.
SWC_FREE_OBJECT	Free the BOR object.
SWC_GET_OBJECT_TYPE	Get object type of the instantiated object.
SWC_GET_OBJECT_KEY	Get object key of the instantiated object.
SWC_SET_ELEMENT	To set a single line variable in Container
SWC_GET_ELEMENT	To fetch a single line variable from Container
SWC_DELETE_ELEMENT	To delete the element from Container
SWC_COPY_ELEMENT	To copy the element of Container
SWC_SET_TABLE	To set a multi-line variable or internal table in Container
SWC_GET_TABLE	To fetch a multi-line variable or internal table from Container
SWC_CALL_METHOD	Invoke the method of the object.
SWC_RAISE_EVENT	You can raise the event
SWC_CREATE_CONTAINER	To create the container
SWC_RELEASE_CONTAINER	To clear the container. Both release and clear macros do same action.
SWC_CLEAR_CONTAINER	To clear the container

Sample code to create and get attribute from the BOR object BUS2119.

```
include <cnt01>.
DATA:
  lv_objtype TYPE swo_objtyp,
  lv_objkey TYPE swo_typeid,
  lo_object TYPE swo_objhnd,
  lv_status TYPE swo_verb,
  lv_return  TYPE sworeturn.

  lv_objtype = 'BUS2119'. "Payment order
  lv_objkey = '<bank_area_with_paymentno>'.
  swc_create_object lo_object lv_objtype lv_objkey.
```

Invoking the attribute value of the object is as follows:

```
* return attribute.
swc_get_property l_object 'StatusPaymentOrder'    lv_status.
```

The following sample code is used to raise the business object programmatically. You can raise the event using the macro or through the function module. The following sample code is raise event based on the function module. When you raise the event, the related workflows will be triggered.

```
CALL FUNCTION 'SWE_EVENT_CREATE'
EXPORTING
  objtype          = c_bus1001
  objkey           = v_objkey
  event            = c_event
IMPORTING
  event_id         = v_event_id
TABLES
  event_container  = container
EXCEPTIONS
  objtype_not_found = 1
  OTHERS           = 2.
```

BAPI

A Business Application Programming Interface (BAPI) is an interface providing access to processes and data in business application systems such as R/3. BAPIs start with Business Object Repository as a method. BAPI's core technology facilitates a broad development spectrum and its features as follows:

- Operates with different platforms, including UNIX and COBRA
- Uses a variety of programming languages, including C++, Java, Visual Basic and Advanced Business Application Programming (ABAP)
- Application development via any front-end client application with advanced R/3 logic
- External R/3 application layer access
- Client R/3 application access to core R/3 business logic
- Client access to all object-oriented application views

BAPI is a remote function enabled function module and it must have its own function group. You can call or execute BAPI the same way as the function module. You need to call BAPI_TRANSACTION_COMMIT after each BAPI call to finalize or commit the change. If some error occurs, you can rollback all changes using BAPI_TRANSACTION_ROLLBACK. In the following chapters, you will go through possible BAPIs or function modules based on SAP applications and business objects.

The BAPI can return the message table parameters and you identify the BAPI is successful or a failure. The BAPI return code follows the BAPIRET2 structure.

Column	Data Type	Description
Type	Char 1	Type of messages. blank or S – Success E – Error W – Warning I – Information A – Abort
ID	Char 20	Message Type
NUMBER	NUMC	Message number.
MESSAGE	Char 220	Full message text

1.3.8 Message Class

The message class allows you to communicate with users from the ABAP code. SAP used the message class mainly for a server error message or warning message to the users. The message is identified by the ID (Max. 20 characters) and the number (3 digit number). You can define a message text up to 72 characters. You can also access the message type using the transaction code SE91. All messages are stored in the table T100. The message can be raised through the ABAP statement MESSAGE. SAP provides an option to conduct the where-used search on the message number. If ABAP code uses the ABAP statement message then the where-used search will find it.

You can define variables in the message text using the character &. You can pass the variable in the keyword WITH in the MESSAGE command. For example, the message class FR is used by the finance reporting modules.

```
MESSAGE E004(FR) WITH lv_currency.
```

The above statement stops the process with the error message 'Currency <lv_currency> could not be found'.

Message class	FR	Activ

Attributes	Messages

Message	Message short text	Self-explanat'y
000	This program (&) has been replaced by &	☑
001	Automatic payment transactions are not intended for company code &	☑
002	Payer & is not defined for account & &	☐
003	Payee & is not defined for account & &	☐
004	Currency & could not be found	☐
005	Account determination for transaction &1 is missing for account &2 &3 &4	☐

Note that any dynamic creation of the message will not be included in the where-used search. One of the common practices is using a message statement in the IF statement (with a false statement) next to the dynamic message creation.

1.3.9 Logical Database (LDB)

Logical database (LDB) is a special ABAP program to retrieve data and make it available to the application program. The logical database is highly used in HR and FI components. Most FI reports use the logical databases. You need a deeper ABAP knowledge to understand the components and their applications. The logical database contains OPEN SQL statements that read data from the database tables. When you use logical database, you do not need to use the OPEN SQL statement.

As a functional consultant, you will see a number of reports that use the same selection screen interfaces and the same kind of authorization checks against the data. These are the main features of the logical database. You can identify a possible database table or structure used by the logical database. The following are a few logical databases heavily used in the FI component:

Logical Database	Description
KDF	Vendor database.

SDF	G/L Account database
DDF	Customer database
BRF	Document database
BRM	Account documents
FPMF	Payment medium framework logical database
ADA	Assets database
KLF	Historical Balance Audit Trail
FSF	Cash Management Total Records
KKF	Balance audit trail of open items
MAF	Dataset of Dunning Notices
PYF	Database for payment medium print program
PMF	Logical database for Medium
CEK	Cost centers – line items
CIK	Cost centers – actual data
CPK	Cost center – plan data
CRK	Cost center – Total
ODK	Order logical database (internal order)

You can view the logical database using the logical database builder in the ABAP workbench. The transaction code for this is SE36. The logical database provides a particular view of database tables and access in a particular way. Use the logical database, when database tables you want to read correspond largely to the structure of the logical database. The main purpose of the logical database is to reuse predefined functionalities for reading data from database. The logical database can perform the following tasks:

- **Database table access** – The individual programs do not need to know the exact structure of the relevant database tables. Instead you can use the logical database and handle the internal table using GET events.

- **User Interface** – The logical database has built-in selection screen. All programs using the logical database share same user interface.

- **Improving performance** – The logical database will take care of the performance measures.

Structure of Logical database

The logical database is divided into the following sections.

- **Table Structure** – The structure defines the data view of the LDB. The data structure is hierarchical. Multiple tables are linked to each other using the foreign key. Some data structure dependencies form a tree-like hierarchy structure. These structures are read from the database as defined. The root node is a single node at the highest level.

- **Selection** – The selection defines the selection screen of the LDB. When you link the LDB to an executable program, the selection of the LDB become a part of the standard selection (screen 1000). Note that when the LDB is executed using the function module LDB_PROCESS, the selection is filled using the interface parameters of FM.

- **Database program** – The program contains ABAP statement to read the data and pass it to the user of the LDB. The name of the database program is SAPDB<ldb> (where <ldb> is logical database name).

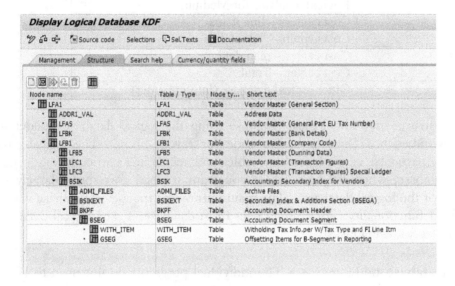

Advantages:

- Easy-to-use selection screens
- Uses centralized authorization check against database access

The following events occur when you run the program that is linked with the logical database.

- **INITIALIZATION** – The event occurs before the selection screen is displayed.
- **AT SELECTION-SCREEN** – After user input on a selection screen has been processed, but while the selection screen is still active.
- **START-OF-SELECTION** – After the standard selection screen has been processed, but before data is read from the logical database.

Runtime of Logical database to executable program

- **GET <node>** – After the logical database has read a data record from the node <node>.
- **GET <node> LATE** – After all of the nodes of the logical database have been processed that are hierarchically subordinate to the node <node> in the structure of the logical database.
- **END-OF-SELECTION** – After all data has been read by the logical database

Dynamic selection allows you to define further selections for the database access other than selection criteria defined in the logical database. The logical database can be assigned in the program attribute with its selection screen. The selection screen is from the logical database. The following example shows the usage of the KDF logical database used in the vendor line item display program RFITEMAP.

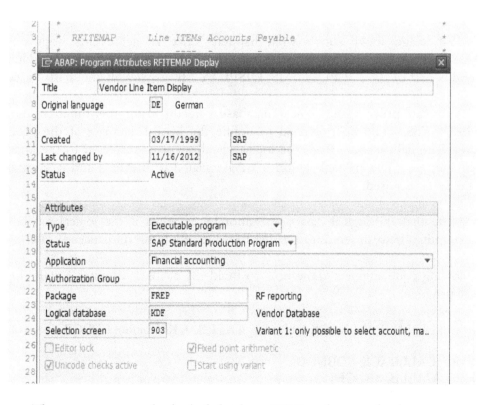

The program uses the logical database KDF and uses selection screen version 903. You can define selection screen versions in the SE36 transaction. You can access the selection screens using the menu Extras->select screen versions.

The get events of LFA1, LFB1 and BSIK are defined at start-of-selection.

```
249
250    get lfa1.
251  * general account master data:
252      perform lfa1_info_fill.
253  * perform t005_info_fill using 'K'.
254
255    get lfb1.
256  * company master data:
257      perform t001_info_fill.
258  * company account master data:
259      perform lfb1_info_fill.
260
261    get lfb1 late.
262  * customer items requested?
263 ☐   if not x_apar is initial and not lfa1-kunnr is initial.
264        perform read_customer_items.
265      endif.
266
267    get bsik.
268  * importing BKPF and BSEG data from archive
269      perform import_arch_from_memory.
270  * line items, basic fields:
271      ld_yrper(4) = bsik-gjahr.
272      ld_yrper+5  = bsik-monat.
273      check ld_yrper in so_yrper.
274      perform pos_table_fill  changing  x_stop.
275
276    end-of-selection.
277  * any branch accounts? prompt user if necessary:
278      perform lfb1_check_branch.
```

The image above shows what happens once all get events populate the required internal tables and the program calls the ALV grid to display the result. The ALV grid is part of the FM FI_ITEMS_DISPLAY. It displays all line items based on this.

You can process the logical database directly using the function module LDB_PROCESS. You do not need to define the logical database at the program attribute. The data records from the logical database are transferred to the attached callback routines. The callback routines are associated with events and it is executed when the event is raised.

Note that the logical database cannot be re-called if the logical database is already running. If so, exception LDB_ALREADY_RUNNING is raised.

The following code snippets show how to build the callback routines for the logical database program.

```
form BUILD_CALLBACK tables PT_CALLBACK structure LDBCB.

PT_CALLBACK-LDBNODE    = 'KNC1'.
PT_CALLBACK-GET        = 'X'.
PT_CALLBACK-GET_LATE   = ' '.
PT_CALLBACK-CB_PROG    = SY-REPID.
PT_CALLBACK-CB_FORM    = 'LDB_CALLBACK'.
append PT_CALLBACK.

PT_CALLBACK-LDBNODE    = 'KNC3'.
append PT_CALLBACK.
...
endform.                       " BUILD_CALLBACK
```

The callback subroutines are equivalent to GET events defined in START-OF-SELECTION. The subroutines populate the internal tables using the events.

```
form LDB_CALLBACK using PD_NODE like LDBN-LDBNODE
            PD_WORKAREA
            PD_MODE    type C
            PD_SELECTED type C.
 data: LS_KNC1  like KNC1,
     LS_KNC3  like KNC3,
     LS_LFC1  like LFC1,
     LS_LFC3  like LFC3,
     LS_SKC1C like SKC1C.
 case PD_NODE.
  when 'KNC1'.
   LS_KNC1 = PD_WORKAREA.
   clear LS_APAR_DATA.
   move-corresponding LS_KNC1 to LS_APAR_DATA.
   append LS_APAR_DATA to LT_APAR_DATA.
  when 'KNC3'.
   LS_KNC3 = PD_WORKAREA.
   clear LS_APAR_SPECIAL.
   move-corresponding LS_KNC3 to LS_APAR_SPECIAL.
   append LS_APAR_SPECIAL to LT_APAR_SPECIAL.
….
…
  endcase.
  PD_SELECTED = 'X'.
endform.
```

The logical database is processed directly by the function module. You are required to populate the selection parameters.

```
LS_PARAMS-SELNAME = 'SD_BUKRS'.
LS_PARAMS-SIGN   = 'I'.
LS_PARAMS-OPTION = 'EQ'.
LS_PARAMS-LOW    = '0001'.
clear LS_PARAMS-HIGH.
append LS_PARAMS to LT_PARAMS.

LS_PARAMS-SELNAME = 'SD_GJAHR'.
LS_PARAMS-SIGN   = 'I'.
LS_PARAMS-OPTION = 'EQ'.
LS_PARAMS-LOW    = '2014'.
clear LS_PARAMS-HIGH.
append LS_PARAMS to LT_PARAMS.
LS_PARAMS-SELNAME = 'SD_SAKNR'.
LS_PARAMS-SIGN   = 'I'.

LS_PARAMS-OPTION = 'EQ'.
```

```
LS_PARAMS-LOW    = '3300'.
clear LS_PARAMS-HIGH.
append LS_PARAMS to LT_PARAMS.
```

After the function module is executed, it will populate all internal table based on the selection. In addition, the function module will populate internal tables based on the callback routine code. You can use the internal table for further processing.

```
Call function 'LDB_PROCESS'
  exporting
    LDBNAME              = GC_LDB
  tables
    CALLBACK             = LT_CALLBACKS
    SELECTIONS           = LT_PARAMS
  exceptions
    LDB_SELECTIONS_NOT_ACCEPTED = 4
    others               = 1.
```

Dynamic Selection

Dynamic selection is not part of the selection portion of the logical database. You can access the dynamic selections in the application toolbar of the selection screen. Dynamic selections reduce the database access of logical database programs by way of a dynamic statement. Dynamic selections must be coded in the logical database program.

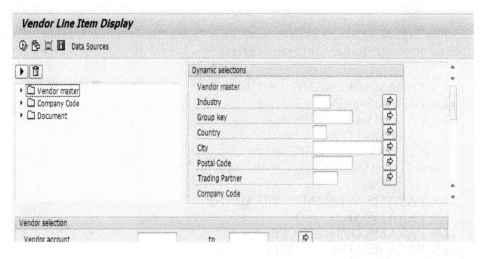

In the vendor line item display above, the dynamic selection has three sections and you can see it in selection view definition. You can add and remove the fields from the dynamic selection. The dynamic selection is part of the selection view definition. You can define the selection view using the transaction code SE36.

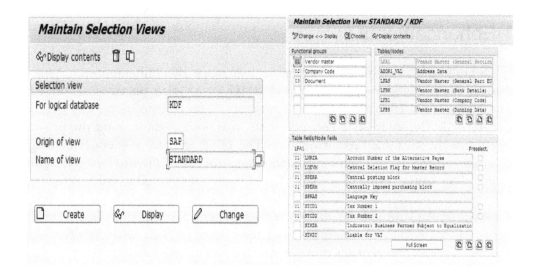

LFA1 Custom fields in dynamic selection

Copy the standard selection view to the custom view. You can add the fields from LFA1 in the Vendor master functional group. The changes are transportable.

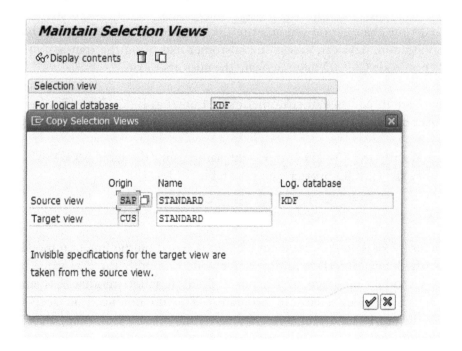

The CUS view takes precedence over the STANDARD view. You can handle dynamic selections of the customized version of the logical database.

1.4 Enhancements

SAP FI/CO is a flexible system with a range of configurations. You can implement these configurations using SAP IMG. SAP also provides a number of enhancements outside of the IMG configuration. The enhancements can be UI or process related. Before making enhancements, you need to understand the processes involved and the customer requirements. The GAP analysis and understanding of SAP business process and implementation help the developer to provide optimal solutions. This section explains some IMG configurations related to enhancements.

SAP FI/CO provides a number of enhancement techniques like User Exit, Customer Exit, BADI, Business Transaction Event (BTE) and Substitution & Validation. This section explains more standard SAP enhancements.

1.4.1 Customer Exit

The customer exit or user exit is a hook provided by the SAP standard application and handle custom development. SAP provides a set of enhancement components and you can implement your changes in the enhancement. Once you implemented your change, you can activate the component so changes will be part of the SAP application. You can access the customer exit using the transaction SMOD. The transaction code CMOD helps activate the customer exit.

There are three types of customer exits: Function Exit, Menu Exit, and Screen Exit. The user exit is always referred to by the function module (prefix with EXIT_).

You can identify the SMOD component name using the table MODSAP. You can identify any CMOD project using the table MODACT.

User Exit

The user exit is an enhancement technique based on the function module. The user exit is pre-defined interface in the source code to modify the data value based on the function module interface parameters. Each function module has an ABAP statement which includes a custom program. You do not need an access key to modify this custom include program. You can only modify exporting, changing and table parameters.

Menu Exit

Menu exits add items to the pull-down menus in standard SAP applications. You can use these menu items to call up your own screens or to trigger entire add-on applications. SAP creates menu exits by defining special menu items in the Menu Painter. These special entries have function codes that begin with a "+" (a plus sign). You can specify the menu item's text when activating the item in an add-on project

Screen Exit

Screen exits add fields to screens in R/3 applications. SAP creates screen exits by placing special sub-screen areas on a standard R/3 screen and calling a customer sub-screen from the standard screen's flow logic.

Field Conversion Exit

Conversion exit is a method that converts a field from display format to the internal SAP format and vice versa. The conversion routine is part of the data element definition. For example, the material number 123456 will be stored 000000000000123456 (18 characters length) in the database. In the UI screen and write statement, the material number will be displayed without the leading zeroes.

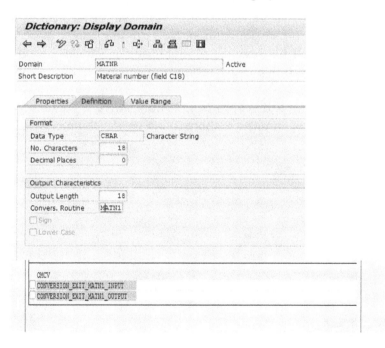

A conversion exit consists of two function modules. One module converts incoming data into the representation that will be used internally. The second is a module that converts internally represented data to that which is displayable and user friendly. Conversion exits are called automatically whenever a variable (whose domain has a conversion exit defined) is either input via a selection screen or output via a write statement.

ALPHA is one of the most commonly used conversion exit routine by SAP.

1.4.2 BADI

Business Add-In (BADI) is an enhancement technique based on ABAP objects. BADI is an anticipated point of extension or well-defined interface in the source code to do enhancements. There are two types of BADIs supported by SAP: classic and kernel-based BADIs. Kernel BADIs are highly integrated in the ABAP runtime environment. Kernel BADIs are highly flexible and faster than classic BADIs. The navigation screens are also different between classic and kernel BADIs. You can list the BADIs using the transaction code SE94.

SRM has two components BADI Definition and BADI Implementation. SAP provides the definition and you can implement the code for the standard SAP BADI. You can define your own custom BADI as well. You can access the BADI definition using the transaction code SE18 and implementation using the transaction code SE19.

The most important attributes of BADIs are their ability to be used multiple times and the BADI filter. The BADI filter is an implementation will be executed based on the filter value at the runtime environment. Thus, you can implement a separate implementation for each filter value combination. You can implement more than one implementation when the BADI has been set to multi-use flag. When you do multiple implementations, ensure that each implementation is not dependent on another.

The sequence of implementation is based on compilation. There is possibility that you can have different sequences of implementations between development and Test or Product landscapes.

Classic BADI screenshot

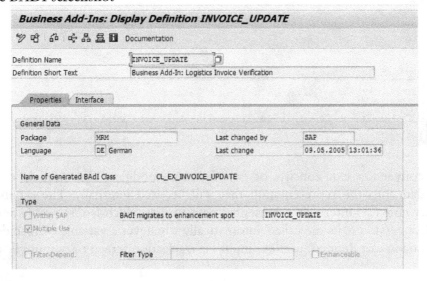

Note that the Kernel BADI interface is different from the classic BADI.

Technical Challenge: One of the challenges commonly faced by the developer is identifying the BADIs hit in a particular transaction or program. You can view the list of BADIs in the documentation. The technical challenge is that to identify what are BADIs hit by a transaction or program.

Solution: This solution is only applicable if you have debug authorization. The BADI is always checked by the ABAP class CL_EXITHANDLER and method GET_CLASS_NAME_BY_INSTANCE. You can also add a break point in the method and execute the transaction or program. The variable name EXIT_NAME refers to the BADI name. When you run the program or transaction, it stops at the BADI based on the data flow.

1.4.3 Enhancement Framework

The enhancement framework is a very powerful enhancement tool where you can modify the process flow of the code. This is an advanced ABAP development and it requires a deep knowledge of the process flow of the code. The enhancement framework brings all enhancement techniques under one roof and improves the way SAP is enhanced. This can also be switched using the Switch Framework. There are four enhancement technologies available under this framework. All these enhancements are considering enhancements but not modifying the system.

o **Source code enhancement** - Enhancement needs to be incorporated directly into the ABAP source code. This implementation technology is known as Source Plug-In. There are two types of source code enhancements:

- Implicit enhancement option
- Explicit enhancement option

Explicit enhancement options are provided at specific source code places explicitly by SAP. There are two ABAP statements ENHANCEMENT-POINT and ENHANCEMENT-SECTION. When the enhancement section is implemented, only the implementation gets executed and the original code does not get executed. Implicit enhancement options are automatically available at pre-defined places such as:

- At end of all the programs, after the last statement
- At the beginning and end of FORM subroutines
- At the end of all function modules
- At the end of all visibility areas (public, protected and private) of local class

- **Function group enhancement** - You can enhance the function module by adding parameters. These parameters must be optional. You can use source plug-in to enhance source code logic for the new parameters.

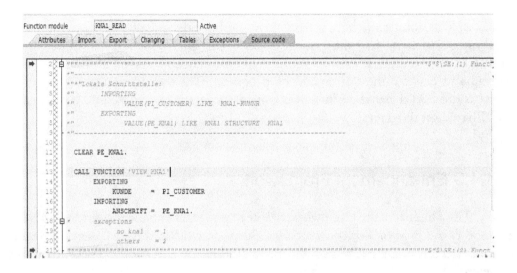

- **Class enhancement** - You can enhance the global classes and interfaces for the following options:

  - Adding new parameters to the existing methods. Parameters must be optional.

  - Adding new methods

  - Adding Pre-exit, Post-exit or Overwrite-exit to an existing method.

Kernel-BADI enhancement - is improvement of the old classic BADI and integrated into the enhancement framework. The kernel BADI is much faster than the classic BADI.

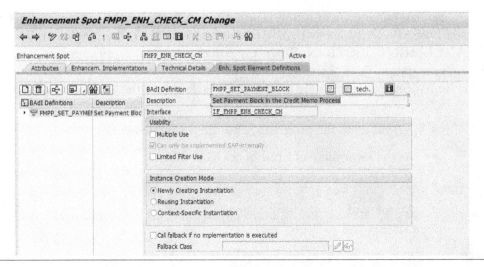

1.5 Business Transaction Event

The business transaction event (BTE) is one of the FI enhancement techniques where you can add custom business logic. BTE allows you to implement additional logical components, in the form of a function module. The BTEs are positioned strategically in transactional processes that allow enhancements to core SAP processes. The enhancements are supported with future SAP releases. The usage of BTEs is detailed in all chapters with respect to the application area.

The BTEs are typically leveraged in FI and SD transaction objects for process modifications. The BTE is identified by the event number. (In the following section, BTE_NO refers to a business transaction event number). The transaction code is FIBF and the IMG menu path is Financial Accounting -> Financial Accounting Global Settings -> Business Transaction Events.

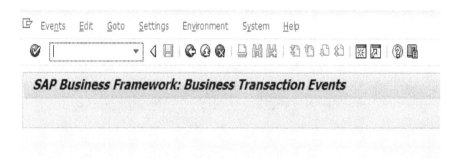

1.5.1 Definition

The BTE uses two types of Interfaces: Publish & Subscribe (P/S) and Process interfaces.

- Publish and Subscribe Modules – These interfaces inform external software that a certain event has taken place in the standard SAP application. The interface provides appropriate data. The external software cannot return any data to the R/3 system. This interface type allows you to start multiple additional operations. The multiple operations are independent of each other.

- Process Modules – These interfaces control a business process differently than the way handled by the standard R/3 system. It intervenes and returns data to the SAP application. When the event is triggered, a process can be replaced by a single custom external process using the process interface. If you are using an add-on from an SAP partner, the enhancement is processed at runtime. If you choose your own custom development, the partner enhancement is ignored and your own custom enhancement is processed at runtime.

You can view all active SAP application and partner functions in the FIBF transaction. You can access the SAP application and partner applications using the menu Settings->Identification.

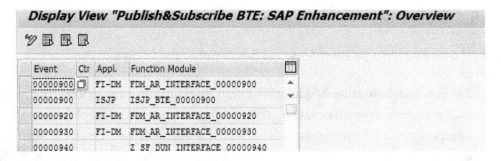

All business transaction events are defined in the SAP applications and associated with a function module. Each event is associated with a sample function module. The partner can redefine the same event with their function module. The partner function module overrides the SAP application function module. You can create custom function modules for the event and it SAP applications and partner function module.

You can access the list of events with function modules in the FIBF. The menu path is Settings->P/S modules->of sap application.

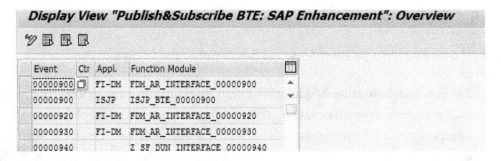

You can list out sap application, partner and customer level events for P/S modules and process modules.

1.5.2 Reports

There is a separate program for listing P/S interfaces and Process interfaces. This listing program is very powerful and you can see all interfaces, documentation and sample function module for the event.

You can view the list of P/S BTE events using the transaction BERE.

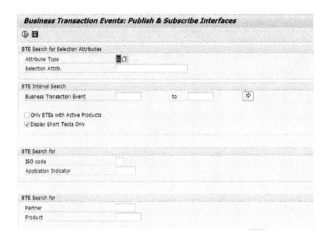

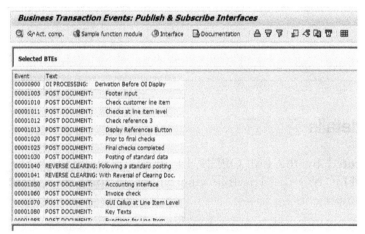

Transaction: BERP for process interfaces

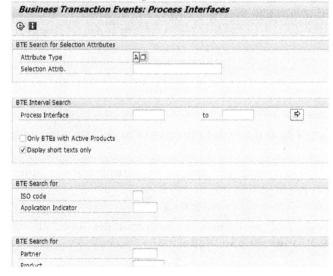

Results

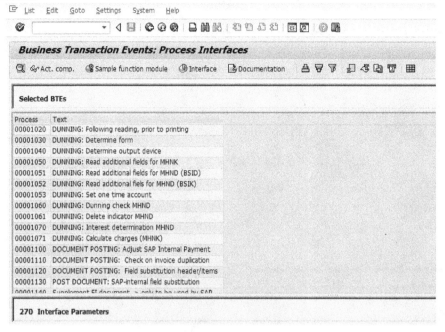

1.5.3 Technical details

The BTE is executed by the FM OPEN_FI_PERFORM-<BTE_NO> or OUTBOUND_CALL_<BTE_NO>. The following tables are some base database tables used by the BTE component.

- TPS31 – Processes BTE – alternative function modules from SAP
- TBE01 – List of the Publish & Subscribe transaction events. The table provides the sample function module for the event.
- TBE24 – Custom products
- TBE31 – Publish & Subscribe BTE: SAP Enhancement

Useful Function Modules

- BF_FUNCTIONS_FIND – List out active function modules associated with the event.
- BF_FUNCTIONS_READ – List out SAP application, partner and customer function modules for the event.

In some part of the FI standard code, SAP uses these function modules stated above instead of the OPEN_FI_PERFORM function module.

1.5.4 BTE Implementation

The applicable BTEs are explained in the following chapters. Follow the steps for implementing BTE event.

- Identify the Event number. The BTE event can be either a process interface or p/interface.
- You can get the sample function module from the transaction code BERE (publish and subscriber interface) or BERP (process interface).
- Copy the sample function module to a custom function module. One recommendation is to use event number in the function module for easy reference.
- Implement your code in the custom function module.
- Add the event in FIBF, settings->P/S Modules (or Process interfaces) ->...of a customer and add the event and try with the new function module name. This step allows your function module to be executed for the BTE event.

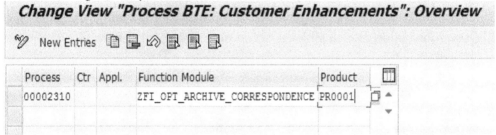

1.6 Substitution and Validation

One of the unique features of SAP FI component is substitution and validation. Using substitution, you can change the document values while posting the accounting document. Using validation, you can validate the data before the account document is posted. You do not need to change the standard system to customize your validations and substitutions. In other SAP modules like MM and SD, the validation and change data use the user exits or BADIs. You can configure rules, validations and substitutions as part of the configuration. You can also implement the advanced and complex validations and substitutions as user exits.

1.6.1 Rule Manager

The rule manager is main component of substitution and validation. You can define all your validations, substitutions and rules in the rule manager. The following components are part of Substitution and Validations.

- **Rules** – Rules refer to a Boolean logic that returns true or false. It is used to create logical rules or statements. These logical statements are then used to analyze, select, and process data that enters the FI-SL application component. The rules manager stores the Boolean rules used to analyze the data. You can use formula to create your rules as well. The Boolean rules are used like re-usable statement in the rules, validations and substitutions.

- **Validation** – Validation is used to check settings and return a message if the pre-requisite check condition is met. You can use validation to supplement additional validations to existing standard SAP logic in order to fit your business needs. A validation is a valuable tool that can be used in many of the financial and controlling modules. With validation rules, you can implement your integrity data check of the posting document. The validation will be executed after the substitutions.

- **Substitution** – Substitution is used to change (substitute) the entered value with the value that has been defined in the substitution configuration. You can use substitution to changing the accounting document data to fit your business needs.

The following table provides the list of application areas supported by Substitution and Validation.

Application Area	Validations	Substitutions	Rules
AM – Asset Management	X	X	X
CO – Controlling	X	X	X
CS – Consolidation	X		X
FI – Finance Accounting	X	X	X
GL-Special Purpose Ledger	X	X	X
GR – Report Writer			X
GS – Ledger Selection			X
GU – Rollups			X
KC – Enterprise Controlling: SAP-EIS	X	X	X
LC – Legal Consolidation	X		X
PC – Profit Center Accounting		X	X
PS – Project System	X	X	X

1.6.2 Boolean Class

The Boolean class provides dimensions that can be used in validations, substitutions and rules. Using the Boolean class, you can specify message classes for validation messages. You must assign an application area and call up point code to the validation, substitution or rule.

The Boolean class information is stored in the table GB01 and GB01C. You can maintain the Boolean class adding and deleting the dimensions. The SAP standard fields are defined in the table GB01. SAP delivers the table GB01C in order to add and exclude the fields. If the fields are not defined for a Boolean class then you cannot be used in the validations, substitutions and/or rules. You can maintain using the transaction code SM30 for the view V_GB01C. If the field is excluded in GB01, the field cannot be included in GB01C. You can add new fields and exclude fields from GB01.

The Boolean class has three types:
- B – fields in Boolean statements/rules (read only)
- S – fields that can be substituted (write only)
- A – fields for both class B & S (read and write)

The integration manager validates the data against the validation rules. The validation rules are defined as a Boolean logic and the application document will not be posted unless all related validations rules are passed.

1.6.3 Call-up Point

Call-up points determine when the validation or substitution is run. The call-up points that are available depend upon the application area that is selected.

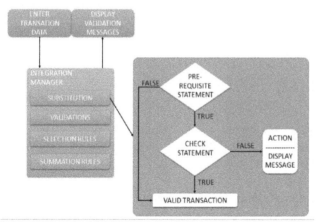

For the FI application area, the following call-up points are available.

- 0001 Document Header – Call-up point is used to validate entries at the document header level. The entries that are usually available for validation at this point are stored in the BKPF table.

- 0002 Line Item – Use this call-up point to check line item entries within a document. The entries that are usually available for validation at this point are stored in the BSEG table.

- 0003 Complete document – This call-up point is also known as Matrix validation. This validation checks the settings of the document as a whole.

1.6.4 Substitution

In other SAP components, change or save BADI (or user exit) is used to modify the document data. In the FI/CO component, this can be done by functional team using IMG configuration. Most of the substitution requirements can be implemented without any coding. Any complex substitution can be done using the substitution exit subroutine. The substitution can be assigned at the calling point like document header (0001), item (0002) or complete document level (0003). The following diagram provides the basic execution of substitution. The substitution process is done before the validation process.

You can define and view substitutions using the transaction code GGB1.

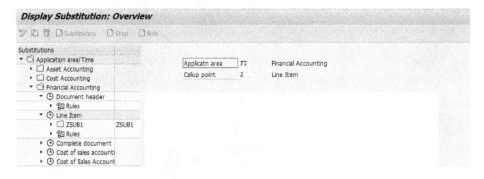

The substitution has two step processes:

- **Pre-requisite** – Provide the Boolean logic for when the substitution will take place. The logical definition can be a logical combination of table fields, rules, and exits.

- **Substitution** – In this step, you define which field's value will be updated. You can substitute the field value with a constant, Exit or Field assignment. You can substitute more than just fields in this definition. The field assignment allows you to assign a value to the other field. The exit substitution does not refer to any separate field. Substitution happens at exit subroutine.

Activation

The transaction code OBBH is used to activate the substitution at the company code level. The activation level must be 1 for activating the substitution.

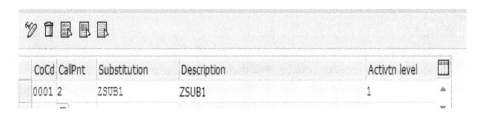

Substitution Rules

The substitution rule is a reusable logical definition. The rules can be defined at the Document header, Line Item, and Complete document. This rule is similar to the pre-requisite step of the substitution process. You can use table fields, rules and exits in the rules.

Substitution Exits

To create and maintain the substitution exits, you need the developer access. The standard SAP system handles all substitution in the include program RGGBS000. The substitution include programs are configured at the application level. You can configure the substitution include program using the transaction code GCX2. To create a user defined exits, you can copy RGGBS000 into a custom program (e.g., ZRGGBS000) and assign it in the configuration.

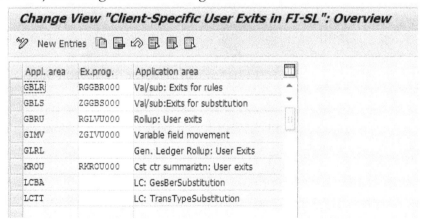

How to create an exit subroutine

You must define your user exits in the global variable 'exits'. The user exit subroutine should start with the letter U. This variable is populated using the subroutine get_text_titles. Once you define your exit name (defined as title in exits variable) in the subroutine then it is available in the substitution definition (GGB1). The exit name must be defined with the parameter.

User exit type	Description	Application	Example
1	No parameters are defined for the user exit.	Rules, validations, and substitutions (prerequisite)	See form pool RGGBR000, parameter type C_EXIT_PARAM_NONE
2	Same as user exit type 1, except one parameter (the field to be substituted) is defined in the user exit. For example, you can create a substitution routine that analyzes the cost center irrespective of the field used.	Substitution	See form pool RGGBS000, parameter type C_EXIT_PARAM_FIELD
3	All data is passed as one parameter; this exit type can only be used in matrix validations and substitutions.	Rules, validations, and substitutions (prerequisite)	See form pool RGGBR000, parameter type C_EXIT_PARAM_CLASS

Technical Challenge: Substitute the item text which must following string pattern '##bseg-zfield-bseg-awkey##'.

Solution: The standard substitution rule can be used since the item reference text is combination the values. We need to use the exit function to substitute the item text field.

Step 1: Create an exit routine 'U111' (numbering is based on existing subroutines).
Step 2: Assign the exit routine into the exit name
Step 3: Define substitution with exit.
Step 4: Regenerate the substitution rules.

Change Request Transport

The substitution changes are part of the client dependent transport. You can collect and assign it to a transport. Use SCC1, to copy the transport between clients.

Tips: Take special care while transporting the substitution configuration. You cannot transport an individual step of a substitution/validation. Because of this, ensure that all the steps in substitution/validation between your development and production environment are in sync. In some cases you may need to run the program RGUGBR00 in the target client to ensure that generated code is up to date.

Trouble Shooting:

If the substitution does not occur, make sure check the following:
- Pre-requisite follows your requirements
- Substitution is activated for the company code
- Not all fields are available for calling point 1 and 2 for the substitution in transaction like MR01, MRHR, MRHG and MR21.
- No substitution for FI reversal.
- A customer-defined field ZFELD was included in table BSEG. Such fields are not substituted during postings (from other modules) via the FI/CO interface. You must enhance the coding block so that ZFELD is substituted.

You can do debugging easily when you use substitution exit rule or substitution.

- RGUGBR19 – To check all syntax in all validation and substitution.
- RGUGBR33 – Report to analyze the validation and substitution.

1.6.5 Validation

Validation is another important aspect in the FI component. You can maintain the validations using the transaction code OB28 or the transaction code GGB0.

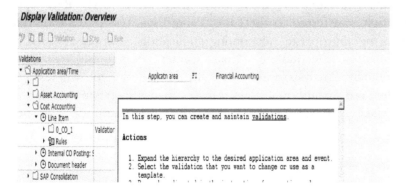

Creation of the message class is one of the basic steps when define validation. Later, the message number is associated to an individual validation step.

Tips

The function module FI_VALIDATION_DOC does validation for FI document.

Troubleshooting

If the substitution is not working properly, make sure that the substitutions are regenerated properly. You can regenerate the substitution using the program RGUGBR01. This one is common for both validation and substitution.

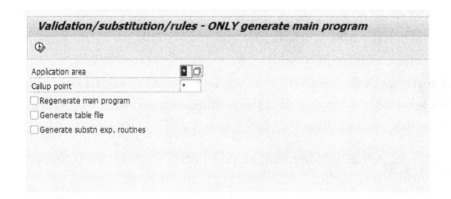

1.7 Accounting Interface – RWIN Interface

The FI/CO interface (RWIN) is the central interface for transferring postings from other application components in the SAP R/3 System to Accounting. The FI/CO interface controls updates of actual data in Accounting and carries out checks from the Accounting standpoint.

Actual data relevant to Accounting from other SAP R/3 application components are first transferred to the FI/CO interface. The FI/CO interface then sends the data to the appropriate Accounting application component (such as Asset Management, Financial Accounting, Cost Center Accounting, Profit Center Accounting, Profitability Analysis, and so on). In this section, you will learn how the RWIN interface is used in outbound data transfer from FI system to other systems. The RWIN interface is more applicable for ABAP programmer than functional consultant.

Technical Details

The outbound RWIN interface executes a set of function modules for a particular process and event. These function modules are executed sequentially and synchronous. All these function modules are stored in a standard table called TRWPR and can be maintained using the transaction code SM30. The standard SAP system provides TRWPR configuration entries. Also, the business switches control the execution of the RWIN function modules.

The function modules RWIN_CHECK and RWIN_CHECK_SUBSET execute the RWIN accounting interface. The usage of these function modules are part of the standard SAP code (based on the process and event). The RWIN accounting interface executes only installed and active components. The following tables can be maintained by SM30 to define installed and active components.

- TRWCI – Table stores installed components of the FI/CO interface.
- TRWCA – Table stores active components of the FI/CO interfaces.

You can see valid up to year in the TRWCA entry.

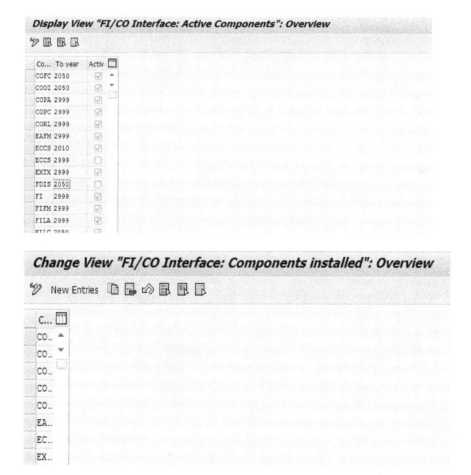

The following snippet provides the basic usage of the function RWIN_CHECK_SUBSET. In this snippet, you can get all RWIN interface function modules for the process 'DOCUMENT' and event 'RECORD'. It will then execute all function modules in the loop. Note that all the function modules defined under this process and event must follow the interface parameters.

```
DATA: lt_trwpr LIKE trwpr OCCURS 0 WITH HEADER LINE,
      ld_gjahr LIKE bkpf-gjahr.

  ld_gjahr = sy-datum(04).

  CALL FUNCTION 'RWIN_CHECK_SUBSET'
      EXPORTING
          i_event      = 'RECORD'
          i_gjahr      = ld_gjahr
          i_process    = 'DOCUMENT'
      TABLES
          t_trwpr      = lt_trwpr.

  LOOP AT lt_trwpr.
     CALL FUNCTION lt_trwpr-function
       EXPORTING
         i_awtyp       = i_awtyp
         i_awref       = i_awref
         i_aworg       = i_aworg
         i_awsys       = i_awsys
         i_awtyp_excl  = i_awtyp_excl
         i_awtyp_incl  = i_awtyp_incl
         i_bukrs       = i_bukrs
         i_valutyp     = i_valutyp
       TABLES
         t_documents   = t_documents[].
  ENDLOOP.
```

The following is the debugging screen for lt_trwpr.

Table	LT_TRWPR[]					
Table Type	Standard Table[17x6(54)]					
Line	PROCESS[C(8)]	EVENT[C(8)]	SUBNO[N(3)]	COMPONENT[C(4)]	KZ_BLG[C(1)]	FUNCTION[C(30)]
1	DOCUMENT	RECORD	010	FI		FI_DOCUMENT_RECORD
2	DOCUMENT	RECORD	015	NFSC		NFSC_DOCUMENT_RECORD
3	DOCUMENT	RECORD	020	COPC		COPCA_DOCUMENT_RECORD
4	DOCUMENT	RECORD	040	GL		G_DOCUMENT_RECORD
5	DOCUMENT	RECORD	050	RAIN		AMIN_DOCUMENT_RECORD
6	DOCUMENT	RECORD	060	RK-1		CO_DOCUMENT_RECORD
7	DOCUMENT	RECORD	063	COPA		COPA_DOCUMENT_RECORD
8	DOCUMENT	RECORD	065	EAFM		FM_DOCUMENT_RECORD
9	DOCUMENT	RECORD	067	GM		GM_DOCUMENT_RECORD
10	DOCUMENT	RECORD	068	EAFM		FM_CCF_DOCUMENT_RECORD
11	DOCUMENT	RECORD	080	RK-1		PP_DOCUMENT_RECORD
12	DOCUMENT	RECORD	090	MMML		CKML_F_DOCUMENT_RECORD
13	DOCUMENT	RECORD	110	COOI		CO_COMMITMENT_RECORD
14	DOCUMENT	RECORD	160	RK-1		FERC_DOCUMENT_RECORD
15	DOCUMENT	RECORD	300	FMCO		FM_CO_DOCUMENT_RECORD
16	DOCUMENT	RECORD	500	ISRE		RE_DOCUMENT_RECORD
17	DOCUMENT	RECORD	700	FMBD		FMKU_DOCUMENT_RECORD

The sequence of the function modules is based on the sequence number of the TRWPR table entries. You can see function modules applicable for installed and active components. The following screenshot provides the list of function modules for the DOCUMENT process and RECORD event.

Display View "RWIN: Processes": Overview

BusTran.	Time	No.	Co...	Doc	Function Module	
DOCUMENT	RECORD	10	FI	☐	FI_DOCUMENT_RECORD	
DOCUMENT	RECORD	15	NFSC	☐	NFSC_DOCUMENT_RECORD	
DOCUMENT	RECORD	20	COPC	☐	COPCA_DOCUMENT_RECORD	
DOCUMENT	RECORD	40	GL	☐	G_DOCUMENT_RECORD	
DOCUMENT	RECORD	50	RAIN	☐	AMIN_DOCUMENT_RECORD	
DOCUMENT	RECORD	60	RK-1	☐	CO_DOCUMENT_RECORD	
DOCUMENT	RECORD	63	COPA	☐	COPA_DOCUMENT_RECORD	
DOCUMENT	RECORD	65	EAFM	☐	FM_DOCUMENT_RECORD	
DOCUMENT	RECORD	67	GM	☐	GM_DOCUMENT_RECORD	
DOCUMENT	RECORD	68	EAFM	☐	FM_CCF_DOCUMENT_RECORD	
DOCUMENT	RECORD	75	ECCS	☐	FC_DOCUMENT_INTERFACE_RECORD	
DOCUMENT	RECORD	80	RK-1	☐	PP_DOCUMENT_RECORD	
DOCUMENT	RECORD	90	MMML	☐	CKML_F_DOCUMENT_RECORD	
DOCUMENT	RECORD	100	FDIS	☐	CASH_FORECAST_MM_DOCUMENT_REC	
DOCUMENT	RECORD	110	COOI	☐	CO_COMMITMENT_RECORD	
DOCUMENT	RECORD	160	RK-1	☐	FERC_DOCUMENT_RECORD	
DOCUMENT	RECORD	200	JVA	☐	GJ_DOCUMENT_RECORD	
DOCUMENT	RECORD	210	JVA	☐	CRP_DOCUMENT_DISPLAY	
DOCUMENT	RECORD	300	FMCO	☐	FM_CO_DOCUMENT_RECORD	
DOCUMENT	RECORD	500	ISRE	☐	RE_DOCUMENT_RECORD	
DOCUMENT	RECORD	590	FICA	☐	FKK_RWIN_DOCUMENT_RECORD	
DOCUMENT	RECORD	700	FMBD	☐	FMKU_DOCUMENT_RECORD	
DOCUMENT	RECORD	720	ISSR	☐	ISSR_DOCUMENT_RECORD	
DOCUMENT	RECORD	799	INV	☐	CON_FIN_DOCUMENT_RECORD	

You can add your own function module in the RWIN interface. Make sure that you have analyzed the processes, events and business requirements. Note that new custom function module must follow the event's parameters interface. Otherwise, it can lead to a possible dumping. The sequence number of the custom development is executed last. The custom development sequence number must be between 900 and 999. The following screenshot is the help document from SAP.

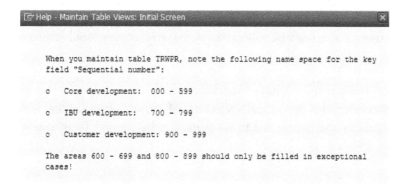

When you maintain table TRWPR, note the following name space for the key field "Sequential number":

o   Core development: 000 - 599

o   IBU development: 700 - 799

o   Customer development: 900 - 999

The areas 600 - 699 and 800 - 899 should only be filled in exceptional cases!

To summarize, you can enhance your business logic by writing custom function modules. Understanding the process and event is vital to enhance your business logic. For the functional team, you should understand the types of integration function modules executed by each business process.

Tips: This technique is considered a modification and is to be used only as a last resort.

1.8 SAP Workflow

SAP Workflow is a workflow engine that enables the design and execution of a business process within the SAP application systems. You can use a workflow as a simple release, approval procedure, or a complex business process like Multi-Step Approval associated with multiple agents. The audit trail and history of system-based workflow helps the organization in a transparent manner.

The workflow is based on the business object repository types. The workflow can be triggered and terminated by the BOR object's events. A workflow must be defined before it can be executed. When you activate a workflow definition, you automatically generate a runtime version. When the workflow is started (manually or automatically), the relevant runtime version is used for the execution.

Workflow tasks describe elementary business activities. The task always refers to a method of an object type. Tasks can also refer to automatically executable methods (background tasks) or task that need a user to execute them (dialog tasks). The workflow template is a definition of the workflow process. You can access the task and template using the transaction code PFTC.

Workflow processes are delivered as part of standard SAP. The standard SAP workflow can be enhanced and a new custom workflow can be created. The number of workflow templates and tasks has been defined for the financial accounting component.

The workflow manager is a SAP component which is responsible for controlling and managing the process. By evaluating conditions with object attributes and taking into account the results of individual steps, it determines which steps are to be processed next.

The binding definitions within a workflow definition between the workflow and the task containers of the individual steps are of central importance. The object reference to the object to be processed must generally be passed from the workflow container to the task containers.

1.8.1 Event Linkage

Event linkage is part of the SAP workflow process. The event linkage table is a database table which defines the connection between events and their associated receiver programs. The event linkage table is populated for the triggering event of the workflow. Also, you can create your own subscribe receiver type to handle the event by your own function module. This functionality provides great flexibility for the developer to provide a simple follow-on action for an event. You can activate or deactivate the linkage table.

The event linkage can be viewed using the transaction code SWE2. The event linkage supports only the events defined in the workflow business objects (defined in SWO1) and ABAP Class events. The ABAP class event linkage makes the ABAP class definition more versatile. The receiver call can be either a Function module or ABAP Class method.

The event linkage provides an option to enable use of Queue for the event processing. If the indicator is set, the event queue is active. Otherwise, the receiver is started immediately. If you define a custom function module or an ABAP class method is defined in the configuration then it must follow the event linkage interfaces.

```
*"----------------------------------------------------*"*"Local Interface:
*"  IMPORTING
*"     VALUE(EVENT) LIKE  SWETYPECOU-EVENT
*"     VALUE(RECTYPE) LIKE  SWETYPECOU-RECTYPE
*"     VALUE(OBJTYPE) LIKE  SWETYPECOU-OBJTYPE
*"     VALUE(OBJKEY) LIKE  SWEINSTCOU-OBJKEY
*"     VALUE(EXCEPTIONS_ALLOWED) LIKE  SWEFLAGS-
EXC_OK DEFAULT SPACE
*"  EXPORTING
*"     VALUE(REC_ID) LIKE  SWELOG-RECID
*"  TABLES
*"      EVENT_CONTAINER STRUCTURE  SWCONT
*"----------------------------------------------------
```

1.8.2 Troubleshooting

Event Trace - The workflow events are logged in the trace log irrespective of whether the receiver called successfully. You can activate and deactivate the event trace log using the transaction code SWELS. The event trace has a triggering object type, triggering object, event id, triggering program and date. The system logs the event only when the event trace is activated. You can view the event trace using the transaction SWEL.

Workflow Log – The runtime workflow consists of a sequence of work items which represent the individual steps. The work items are executed by the agent (dialog work item) or by the system (background work item). You can analyze the audit trail of the workflow execution using the work item log. You can access the workflow log using the transaction code SWI1.

1.9 IDOC & Message Type

Intermediate Document (IDOC) is a standard data structure for electronic data interchange (EDI) between SAP applications and an external program. IDOCs are used for transfer of messages from SAP to an external program and vice versa. The transfer from SAP to non-SAP system is done via EDI subsystems whereas for transfer between two SAP systems, ALE (Application Link Embedding) is used. You can trigger IDOC in SAP system or in EDI subsystem. There are two types of IDOC viz., Inbound and Outbound IDOCs. Inbound IDOC is triggered in EDI subsystem and sent to the SAP system. Outbound IDOC is triggered in the SAP system and sent to the external system. EDI converts the data from IDOC into XML or equivalent format and then sends the data to partner system through the Internet.

For transmission of information electronically, two widely used standards are ANSI ASC X12 and EDIFACT. ANSI ASC X12 is a committee formed by representatives of major organizations, government bodies and EDI software companies. This committee defines standards and guidelines for information interchange over EDI. You can access the IDOC area menu using the transaction code WEDI. The basics of the IDOC are as follows:

1.9.1 IDOC Type

The IDOC Types are based on the EDI standards and mostly on EDIFACT standards. Basic Types (or IDOC Type) defines the structure of an IDOC. Each basic type describes standard IDOC segments, format of data fields and their size. The basic type also defines the number of segments and fields in an IDOC. All the fields that are necessary for transmission of message for a particular business transaction are mapped in different segments. It also defines the structure and relationship of IDOC segments along with mandatory and optional segments. You can access IDOC type and extension through the transaction code WE30.

Display basic type: ACC_GL_POSTING01

🔲 🔲 🔲

```
ACC_GL_POSTING01              Accounting: General G/L Account Posting

      E1BPACHE08              Posting in Accounting: General Posting                      BAPIACHE08
      E1BPACGL08              Posting in Accounting: General Posting                      BAPIACGL08
      E1BPACCR08              Posting in Accounting: Billing Doc. (Currency Fields, Item) BAPIACCR08
      E1BPEXTC                BFA: Container for Customer Exit Parameter.                  BAPIEXTC
```

IDOC extension

IDOC extension is extension of the basic type and contains additional custom IDOC segments and fields that are not available in the standard basic type.

1.9.2 Message Type

IDOC processing involves transmission or receipt of document in the form of a message, each of which represents a document in SAP. Message type is associated with Basic IDOC Type (Basic Type) and defines the kind of data or document that is exchanged with the partner. SAP FI does have a number of a message types and that will be listed and explained further in the following section. You can define the message types using the transaction code WE81 and assign the message type to the basic type and extension using the transaction code WE82.

Display View "Output Types and Assignment to IDoc Types": Overview

🖉 🔲 🔲 🔲

Output Types and Assignment to IDoc Types

Message Type	Basic type	Extension	Release	🔲
ACC_INVOICE_PYMN	C_INVOICE_PYM...		46C	▲
ACC_INVOICE_REC...	ACC_INVOICE_REC...		40A	▼
ACC_INVOICE_REC...	ACC_INVOICE_REC...		45A	
ACC_INVOICE_REC...	ACC_INVOICE_REC...		46A	🔲
ACC_INVOICE_REV...	ACC_INVOICE_REV...		46C	
ACC_MAN_ALLOC	ACC_MAN_ALLOC01		620	
ACC_PRIM_COSTS	ACC_PRIM_COSTS01		40A	
ACC_PRIM_COSTS	ACC_PRIM_COSTS02		620	
ACC_PURCHASE_OR	ACC_PURCHASE_OR		40A	

1.9.3 IDOC segment

IDOC segments contain the actual data that is sent to or received from a partner. These segments contain the actual values and refer to a SAP data structure. You can define child segments to an IDOC segment. You can access the IDOC segment using the transaction code WE31.

Development segments: Display segment definition E2BPACHE08002

Segment type attributes

Segment type	E1BPACHE08	☐ Qualified segment
Short Description	Posting in Accounting: General Posting	

Segm. definition	E2BPACHE08002	☑ Released
Last Changed By	SAP	

Po...	Field Name	Data element	ISO c...	Ex...
1	OBJ_TYPE	AWTYP	☐	5
2	OBJ_KEY	AWKEY	☐	20
3	OBJ_SYS	AWSYS	☐	10
4	USERNAME	USNAM	☐	12
5	HEADER_TXT	BKTXT	☐	25
6	OBJ_KEY_R	AWKEY_REV	☐	20
7	COMP_CODE	BUKRS	☐	4
8	AC_DOC_NO	BELNR_D	☐	10
9	FISC_YEAR	GJAHR	☐	4
10	DOC_DATE	BLDAT	☐	8

1.9.4 Partner

Partner is the Business Partner with which the exchange of information is to take place using IDOC. It can be a vendor or customer or any other system. Depending on the direction the information is sent, the partner plays a role of either a "sending partner" or a "receiving partner". The partner type/role is used to identify partners within the sap systems. The partner type is KU for customer, LI for vendor and LS for Logical System.

The transaction code WE20 is to configure the partner profiles. In the partner profile, you can configure header and, all outbound and inbound parameters (by message type). The message type is accepted (receiving or sending) only when the partner is configured with message types.

Port

The IDOC Port contains the information about the way data is sent between the source and target system. The type of port defines the information contained within the port. For the port type "Internet", the port will contain IP address of the target system. For the port type "file", directory or file name information is maintained. The "tRFC" port contains information about the RFC destination of the target system. For IDOC transmission using ALE "tRFC" ports are used.

1.9.5 IDOC Structure

The IDOC is built based on three components viz., Control records, Data records and Status records.

Control record – Control record contains information such as IDOC number, direction, IDOC Status, Basic Type, Message Type, Partner (Sender/Receiver), date and time of creation/update, etc. The control record information is stored in the table EDIDC.

Data Record – The data record stores actual value and w.r.t. the IDOC segments. The IDOC display tool will display the data by the IDOC segment level. The data record is stored in the table EDID4. This table is one of the huge tables.

Status records – The status value determines the current state of the IDOC. The status values for outbound IDOCs are between 01 and 49 and the status values for inbound IDOCs between 50 and 99. The status is maintained in the database view V_STACUST. You can access the status maintenance using the transaction code WE47. The IDOC can have one or more status record. The latest one is considered as current status.

1.9.6 Search tools

SAP provides search tools that search the IDOC from the database.

Transaction code WE02 (WE05 also points to same program)

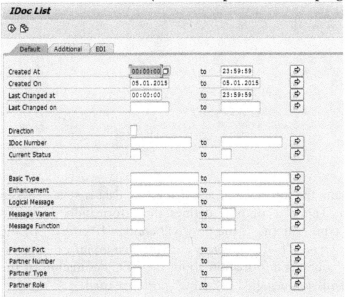

WE09 – This t-code is very powerful as it provides the ability to search for information in a specific field within the IDOC.

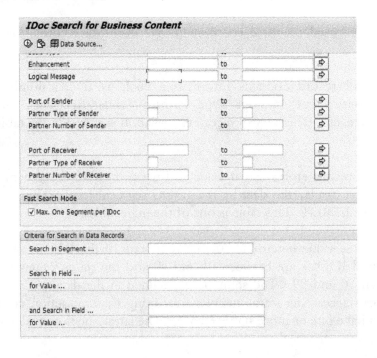

1.9.7 Processing

    IDOCs are processed immediately (automatically) as they are generated or added in the system. You need to check 'Transfer IDOC Immediately' in the Outbound and Inbound options for immediate process. For manual processing, you can set 'Collect IDOCs' in the outbound parameter options and 'trigger by background job' in inbound parameter options. IDOCs can also be manually processed using the transaction code BD87.

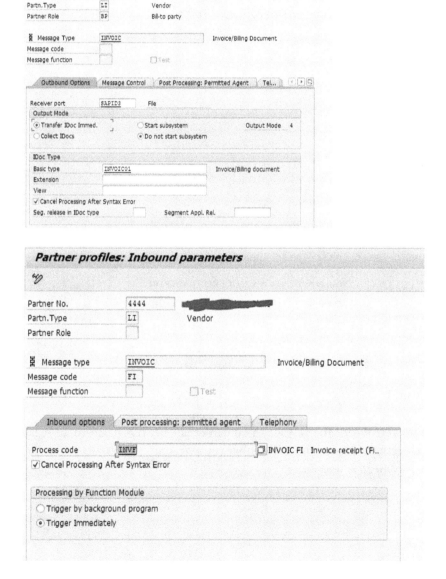

IDOC processing by background is the most preferred way of processing IDOCs. You can schedule the IDOCs processing program as a background job. The following programs are used to process the IDOCs:

- RBDAPP01 – Processing Inbound IDOCs
- RSEINB00 – Processing inbound idoc from file
- RSEOUT00 – Processing Outbound IDOCs

Documentation Tool

Standard SAP provides documentation on Basic Type, extension, and segment type and it can be accessed using the transaction code WE60.

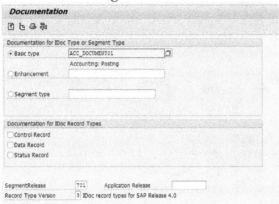

HTML document of the document screenshot

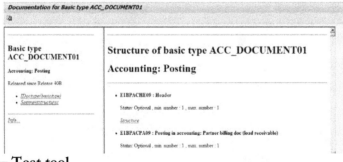

WE19 – Test tool

Test tool is a powerful tool for IDOC. You can create an IDOC from an existing document, a basic type, basic type with enhancement, etc.

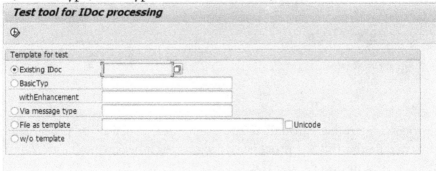

1.9.8 IDOC Types in FI/CO

The table below contains a list of IDOC types commonly used in FI/CO and their corresponding function module. Knowledge of this list will come in handy when designing any business process that involves external entities such as banks, suppliers or even internal business processes involving intercompany transactions.

Direction	IDOC Basic type	Message type	Function Module
Outbound	INVOIC01	INVOIC	IDOC_OUTPUT_INVOIC_IV_M M
Outbound	INVOIC01	INVOIC	IDOC_OUTPUT_INVOIC
Outbound	INVOIC02	INVOIC	IDOC_OUTPUT_INVOIC
Outbound	PEXR2001/ PEXR2001	PAYEXT	
Inbound	PEXR2001	REMADV	IDOC_INPUT_REMADV
Inbound	INVOIC01	INVOIC	IDOC_INPUT_INVOIC_FI
Inbound	INVOIC01	INVOIC	IDOC_INPUT_INVOIC_MRM
Inbound	FINTA01	LOCKBX	IDOC_INPUT_LOCKBX
Inbound	FINTA01	LOCKBX	IDOC_INPUT_FINSTA

1.9.9 Technical Details

To create the IDOC, you need two important variables viz., control data and IDOC segment data. You need to populate the variable lt_edidd with IDOC segment structure. Once the segment is populated then all their child segments are populated immediately.

Populating control data

```
" Get Partner Profile Information
SELECT SINGLE * FROM edp13
  INTO ls_edp13
*   UP TO 1 ROWS
  WHERE mestyp = iv_msgtyp AND
```

```
        mescod = lv_msgcod AND                                "
DLAP00137827
        mesfct = lv_msgfct.                                   "
DLAP00137827

  IF sy-subrc <> 0.
    RAISE invalid_partner_profile.
  ENDIF.

  MOVE ls_edp13-rcvprn   TO lv_edidc-rcvprn.
  MOVE ls_edp13-rcvprt   TO lv_edidc-rcvprt.
  MOVE ls_edp13-rcvpfc   TO lv_edidc-rcvpfc.
  MOVE ls_edp13-idoctyp  TO lv_edidc-idoctp.
  MOVE ls_edp13-mescod   TO lv_edidc-mescod.              "
  MOVE ls_edp13-mesfct   TO lv_edidc-mesfct.
```

Populating IDOC segment data based on three

```
LOOP AT IT_ACCHD INTO lv_acchd.
* Füllen des Kopfes
  CLEAR LS_E1ACH2.
  CLEAR lv_idoc_data.
  MOVE-CORRESPONDING LV_ACCHD TO LS_E1ACH2.
  LV_IDOC_DATA-MANDT = SY-MANDT.
  LV_IDOC_DATA-SEGNAM = 'E1ACH2'.
  LV_IDOC_DATA-SDATA = T_E1ACH2.
  APPEND LV_IDOC_DATA TO LT_EDIDD.

  LOOP AT IT_ACCIT INTO LV_IDOC_ACCIT.
   CLEAR LV_E1ACA2.
   CLEAR LV_IDOC_DATA.
   MOVE-CORRESPONDING LV_IDOC_ACCIT TO LV_E1ACA2.
   LV_IDOC_DATA-MANDT = SY-MANDT.
   LV_IDOC_DATA-SEGNAM = 'E1ACA2'.
   LV_IDOC_DATA-SDATA = LV_E1ACA2.
   APPEND IDOC_DATA TO LT_EDIDD.
   LOOP AT IT_ACCCR INTO LV_IDOC_ACCCR.
     WHERE POSNR = IDOC_ACCIT-POSNR.
     CLEAR LV_E1ACA3.
     CLEAR LV_IDOC_DATA.
     MOVE-CORRESPONDING LV_IDOC_ACCCR TO LV_E1ACA3.
     LV_IDOC_DATA-MANDT = SY-MANDT.
     LV_IDOC_DATA-SEGNAM = 'E1ACA3'.
     LV_IDOC_DATA-SDATA = LV_E1ACA3.
     APPEND IDOC_DATA TO LT_EDIDD.
   ENDLOOP.
  ENDLOOP.
```

```
ENDLOOP.
```

Creating outbound IDOC using the FM MASTER_IDOC_DISTRIBUTE.

```
CALL FUNCTION 'MASTER_IDOC_DISTRIBUTE'
  EXPORTING
   master_idoc_control       = lv_edidc
  TABLES
   communication_idoc_control   = lt_edidc
   master_idoc_data          = lt_edidd
  EXCEPTIONS
   error_in_idoc_control     = 1
   error_writing_idoc_status   = 2
   error_in_idoc_data        = 3
   sending_logical_system_unknown = 4
   OTHERS                 = 5.
```

Processing the inbound IDOC:

```
*** Read the IDOC detail from the database
 CALL FUNCTION 'IDOC_READ_COMPLETELY'
   EXPORTING
     document_number       = p_docnum
   IMPORTING
     idoc_control         = lv_edidc
   TABLES
     int_edidd           = it_edidd
   EXCEPTIONS
     document_not_exist    = 1
     document_number_invalid = 2
     OTHERS             = 3.
```

Status Change

```
*** Call the function to update the ORDCHG IDOC status
 CALL FUNCTION 'IDOC_STATUS_WRITE_TO_DATABASE'
   EXPORTING
     idoc_number          = s_edidc-docnum
   TABLES
     idoc_status          = it_edids
   EXCEPTIONS
     idoc_foreign_lock     = 1
     idoc_not_found        = 2
     idoc_status_records_empty = 3
     idoc_status_invalid    = 4
     db_error            = 5
     OTHERS             = 6.
```

1.10 Tools

SAP provides a number of tools for implementation and monitoring transactions. In this section, Batch data Communication (BDC), Legacy System Migration Workbench (LSMW), SQL Trace and Application Log are discussed briefly.

1.10.1   BDC

Batch data communication is a technique for mass input of data by simulating the user input of the existing transactional screen via an ABAP program. It follows all checks and authorization by the standard SAP transaction. BDC is transaction oriented and screen flows.

Why BDC

Even though BDC is an older technique, it is very handy in the Financial accounting side. There are a number of BAPIs provided to create the master data and transaction data. FI implements a lot of enhancements through BTE, Validation and Substitutions. Also, some business logics use the transaction screen programming logic. BDC is a better option than BAPI.

Mapping between BDC and Screens

The BDC_OK code indicates what action is to be executed on the screen. The OK code can be an action on the screen like Save, Park, etc. or it is used to flow to next screen. The BDC recording will record all OK code information. The code BDC_CURSOR contains the cursor position. It points to a field where cursor will be.

The BDC can be executed in two methods:
- Session method
- Call transaction method

There is one more BDC method that using the ABAP statement CALL DIALOG. However, SAP recommends against using this method unless necessary. The CALL DIALOG method is outdated and more complex and less comfortable to use than the other techniques. It uses same BDC data like session and call transaction methods.

BDC Structure

- PROGRAM - Program name

- DYNPRO   - Screen (DynPro) number
- DYNBEGIN – Screen (Dynpro) start
- FNAM   - Field Name
- FVAL   - Field Value

BDC recording

SAP provides a tool to record the BDC flow for a transaction.   You can access ths tool using the transaction code SHDB.

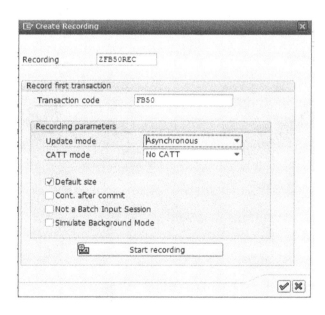

Commands

Command	Description
/n	Terminates current batch input transaction
/bend	Terminates current batch processing and set the session to failed
/bdel	Deletes the current batch input transaction
/bda	Switches from display errors only to Foreground processing
/bde	Switches from foreground process to display errors only

1.10.2 LSMW

Legacy System Migration Workbench (LSMW) is a tool that supports data transfer from non-SAP to SAP systems. The LSMW is a cross-application component and it is used widely in all SAP applications. LSMW is a very powerful tool that may not require any ABAP code development. But it still, you need to understand technical structures of the object data. Also, the LSMW provides options to developer to enhance the LSMW code.

LSMW supports multiple import techniques for migrating data:

- BAPI – The BAPI will be executed when the mapping between the LSMW input file and BAPI import parameters are set.
- IDOC Message – The inbound IDOC message will be processed when the input LSMW data is mapped into the IDOC structure.
- Batch Input Recording – The recording is stored in the SM35 batch recording transaction.
- Direct Input – This is a standard SAP program to upload the data directly into the database.

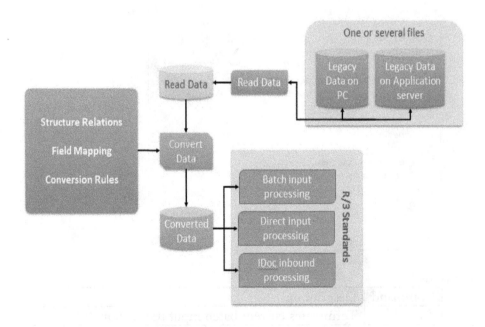

The main functions of the LSMW:
- Import data – Import data from legacy data (spreadsheet data, sequential file)
- Convert data – Convert the source format data into target format data (which is used in the import data)

- Import data – Import the data into the R/3 database using the import techniques.

The LSMW object can be defined using the following hierarchy.
- Project
- Subproject
- Object

ABAP Coding

Sometimes, the LSMW standard functions cannot cover all customer requirements. You can write ABAP code and reusable form routines in the conversion rules. You can also use ABAP coding in LSMW events to fulfill your requirements. The LSMW supports a number of events where you can implement your code. The events are as follows:
- _GLOBAL_DATA_ - In this event, you can define all your global data and types and the variable can be used in all events.
- _BEGIN_OF_PROCESSING_
- _BEGIN_OF_TRANSACTION_ - This event is triggered when a transaction begins. For example, you can implement any validation against the transaction. Based on the validation, you can skip the transaction using the LSMW function SKIP_TRANSACTION. Every transaction can have one or more records and the following the events for specific for record.
  - _BEGIN_OF_RECORD_ - This event is triggered beginning of the record that is before applying the conversion rules for the source structure.
  - _END_OF_RECORD_ - This event is triggered after the record is applying the conversion rules for the source structure.
- _END_OF_TRANSACTION_ - This event is triggered after the event is processed.
- _END_OF_PROCESSING_ - This is the last event and triggers after all transactions are converted. You can use it for writing process log on this event such as successful and failed records.

Global functions

The LSMW allows you to define your own form routines so you can use it in the events. Also, the LSMW provides a number of functions which can be used in your ABAP coding. The following functions are supported by the LSMW.

Global Function	Description

TRANSFER_RECORD	Transfer the current record to the output buffer
TRANSFER_TRANSACTION	Writes the current transaction to an output file.
SKIP_RECORD	The current records is not transferred to the output buffer
SKIP_TRANSACTION	The current transaction is not transferred to an output file.

These functions are stand-alone and do not have any parameters. The LSMW generates the ABAP program and you can view the conversion program by checking the 'Display Conversion Program' check box in the user menu. Then the display conversion program is part of the process steps.

You can transport the LSMW by generating a change request or export and import the LSMW object.

1.10.3   SQL Trace

SQL Trace is a powerful tool to test the performance of the database. You can use this to identify what tables are used for a transaction. Always switch off the trace after you are finished with the task. Bigger trace files are difficult to open and sometimes may cause abnormal termination. You can access the SQL trace using the transaction code ST05.

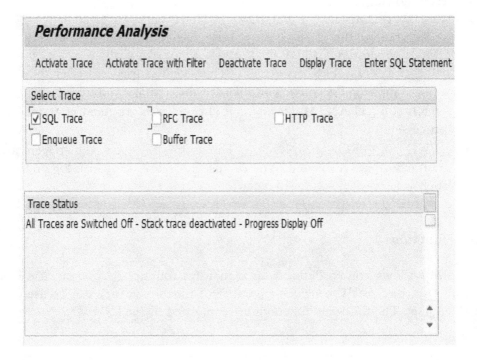

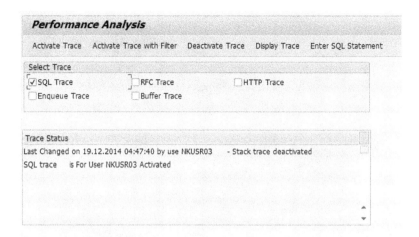

Combined table results

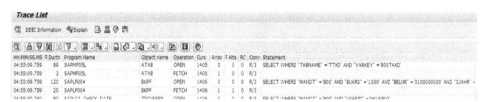

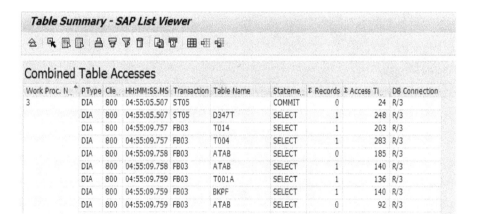

Runtime Analysis

The runtime analysis provides you an overview of the duration of your source code from individual statements up to complete transactions. Using the runtime analysis, you can identify the following:

- Excessive or unnecessary usage of modularization units
- CPU intensive program codes
- Inefficient and redundant database access
- User-specific functions that could be replaced with ABAP statements

You can do runtime analysis using the transaction code SE30.

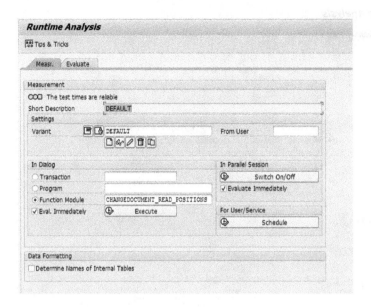

The sample result for MM03.

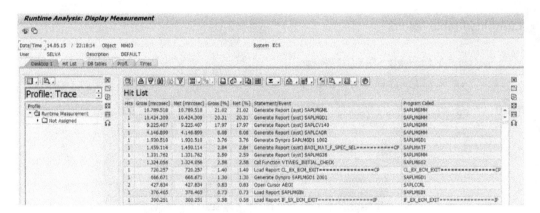

1.10.4   Application Log

The application log is one of the common logs used by SAP applications. Application logging records the progress of the execution of an application so that you can refer to it later if necessary. The application log has the following advantages:

- System-wide uniform event logging
- ALV display support
- Analysis of Log data

Analyse Application Log

Object	BBP_EXTREQ	⊡ External Requirement
Subobject	*	⊡
External ID	*	

Time Restriction

From (Date/Time)	03/12/2009 ⊡	00:00:00 ⊡
To (Date/Time)	03/23/2009 ⊡	23:59:59 ⊡

Log Triggered By

User	*	⊡
Transaction code	*	⊡
Program	*	⊡

Log Class
- ○ Only very important logs
- ○ Only important logs
- ○ Also less important logs
- ◉ All logs

Log Creation
- ◉ Any
- ○ Dialog
- ○ In batch mode
- ○ Batch input

Log Source and Formatting
- ◉ Format Completely from Database
- ○ Format Only Header Data from Database
- ○ Format Completely from Archive

The transaction SLG1 allows you to analyze the application log. You can use the transaction SLG0 to define entries for your own applications in the application log. Using the transaction SLG2, you can delete the log. The application log uses several tables to store the log information. There are function modules to read the application log shown in the table below.

Function modules

Function Module	Description
BAL_LOG_CREATE	Creating application log
BAL_LOG_MSG_ADD	Adding the message to the application log
BAL_DSP_LOG_DISPLAY	Display the application log

You can use the application log in your custom programs and enhancements. The following sample code provides option to create and add log to the application log.

```
data: ls_log          TYPE bal_s_log,
      lv_log_handle    TYPE balloghndl.

ls_log-object     = 'FS_PROT'.
ls_log-subobject  = 'INFO'.
MOVE 'BP Testing' TO ls_log-extnumber.
ls_log-aluser     = sy-uname.
ls_log-alprog     = sy-repid.

CALL FUNCTION 'BAL_LOG_CREATE'
  EXPORTING
    i_s_log      = ls_log
  IMPORTING
    e_log_handle = lv_log_handle
  EXCEPTIONS
```

```
    OTHERS    = 1.

IF sy-subrc <> 0.
  MESSAGE ID sy-msgid TYPE sy-msgty NUMBER sy-msgno
      WITH sy-msgv1 sy-msgv2 sy-msgv3 sy-msgv4.
ENDIF.
```

Adding the message to Application Log.

```
    ls_msg-msgty     = sy-msgty.
    ls_msg-msgid     = sy-msgid.
    ls_msg-msgno     = sy-msgno.
    ls_msg-msgv1     = sy-msgv1.
    ls_msg-msgv2     = sy-msgv2.
    ls_msg-msgv3     = sy-msgv3.
    ls_msg-msgv4     = sy-msgv4.

    CALL FUNCTION 'BAL_LOG_MSG_ADD'
      EXPORTING
        i_log_handle  = lv_log_handle
        i_s_msg       = ls_msg
      EXCEPTIONS
        log_not_found = 0
        OTHERS        = 1.
```

1.11 Summary

This chapter explained how a functional resource can identify the database table associated with a screen field and identifying the program associated with a transaction. Using the transaction variant and screen variant, you learned how to change the screen flow without changing the code. Also, you have been introduced to the list of technical ABAP objects involved in the FI/CO development.

SAP and FI/CO related enhancements such as customer exit, BADI, enhancement framework, business transaction events, Substitution & Validation, and RWIN Accounting interfaces were discussed in detail. You have gone through the basics of IDOC message types and how to handle the inbound and outbound IDOCs in the ABAP programs.

You have learned about the ABAP development tools like BDC, LSMW, and SQL tracking. Also, you have learned about the logging tool Application log.

2 Record to Report

The organizational structure in the SAP system generally is guided by the legal entity. The organization unit company code usually represents the legal entity for which financial statements are to be prepared. In some cases organizations represent a business unit or a division as a company code rather than a legal entity but that is an exception. Such scenarios usually involve multiple instances of SAP or consolidation done in other systems such as Hyperion.

In our experience, we have seen many companies declare SAP to be the 'system of record' and therefore make available data from the SAP system to all manner of auditors both from federal and state governments as well statutory auditors.

The term Record to Report has been used to cover all transactions that eventually reflect financial statements of the legal entity. So any transaction that hits the General Ledger of the organization can be termed as a Record to Report event. Even sub-ledger transactions such as receivables, and payable ultimately flow through to the general ledger.

In this chapter, you will get a functional overview of various components that make up a broad business process commonly referred to in SAP circles as 'Record to Report'. In addition, you will also be given code examples, list of important tables and valuable tips.

This chapter briefly covers the following sub-components of FI and CO modules.

- FI- General Ledger
- FI – Special Purpose Ledger
- CO- Cost Center Accounting
- CO-Product Costing
- CO –Profitability Analysis
- Custom Development
- Reporting Tools

2.1 Organizational Units

The main organizational unit within the financial module is the company code. As mentioned before, the company code generally represents the legal entity. The company code in turn is assigned to a controlling area. The CO area is a concept specific to SAP. CO area enables several entities within a corporate structure to be reported in a consolidated manner both from a management reporting and external reporting perspective. The assignment of different company codes to one CO area enables cross company code allocations, seamless reporting based on group currency at a transactional level. In addition all the company codes within a controlling area share the same chart of accounts.

There are also some organizational units such as profit centers that lend themselves to reporting in a different dimension than just at a company code level.

2.1.1 Company Code

Company code is a very basic and smallest organizational unit of financial accounting module. In this section, we cover only technical information related to company code. The company code is stored in the base table T001. BOR Object type is BUS0002.

IMG Configuration path: Financial Accounting->Financial Accounting Global Settings->Company Code->Enter Global parameters. You can see company code 0001 (SAP A.G.) in the following screenshot.

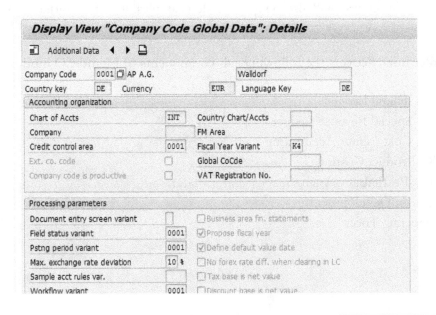

BAPIs

BAPI	Description
BAPI_COMPANYCODE_EXISTENCE	Check whether company code exists
BAPI_COMPANYCODE_GETDETAIL	Get company code detail
BAPI_COMPANYCODE_GETLIST	Get list of company codes defined in the system.
BAPI_COMPANYCODE_GET_PERIOD	Converting posting date to period for the company code

Fiscal Year & Posting Period

Fiscal year is determined by a company's accounting period for financial statements to be presented to statutory authorities. The fiscal year may correspond exactly to the calendar year but mandatory. The fiscal year is divided into posting periods. Each posting date is defined by the start and end date. In additions to the posting periods, you can define special periods for year-end closing. In G/L, a fiscal year has 12 posting periods and four special periods. In the special purpose GL, you can define up to 366.

You can maintain the fiscal year variants in IMG configuration. You can access this using IMG menu path Financial Accounting->Financial Accounting Global Settings->Fiscal Year->Maintain Fiscal year Variant or transaction code OB29. The fiscal year variants are stored in the table T009. You can assign the fiscal year to a company code using the transaction code OB37 or IMG menu path Financial Accounting->Financial Accounting Global Settings->Fiscal Year->Assign Company Code to a Fiscal Year Variant.

Some companies also follow a 4-4-5 calendar such that the start date and end date of the fiscal year is still Jan 1 and Dec 31, but the individual periods shift by a week every 3 months. This is defined in the IMG while defining fiscal year and it is associated periods.

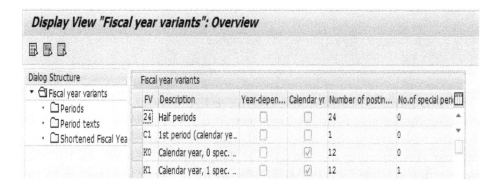

Below is an illustration of non-calendar fiscal periods:

Month	Day	Period	Year shift
2	1	1	0
3	1	2	0
4	5	3	0
5	3	4	0
5	31	5	0
7	5	6	0
8	2	7	0
8	30	8	0
10	4	9	0
11	1	10	0
11	29	11	0
12	31	12	0

This can be seen in table T009B. Another variation of this is a non-calendar fiscal year where a period shift is defined. In this case, the individual months are calendar months but the periods span across a calendar year

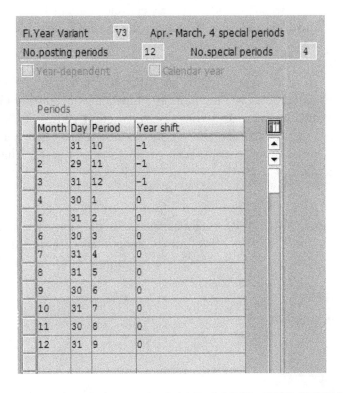

The BAPI BAPI_COMPANYCODE_GET_PERIOD will return the fiscal year and period for the given date and company code. If you know the fiscal version (defined in the table T009), you can determine the fiscal year and period for the date and fiscal year version using the FM DATE_TO_PERIOD_CONVERT. There is one more function module DETERMINE_PERIOD to determine the period for the date and fiscal year variant.

Transaction code OB52, to open and close the periods based on the company code.

A	From acct	To account	From per.1	Year	To period	Year	From per.2	Year	To period	Year	AuGr
. +			2	2015	2	2015					
. A		ZZZZZZZZZZ	2	2015	2	2015					
. D		ZZZZZZZZZZ	2	2015	2	2015					
. K		ZZZZZZZZZZ	2	2015	2	2015					
. M		ZZZZZZZZZZ	2	2015	2	2015					
. S	40320100	40320100	2	2015	2	2015					
. S	42010100	42010100	2	2015	2	2015					
. S	42510000	42529999	2	2015	2	2015					
. S	45100100	47000200	2	2015	2	2015					
. S	49020100	49020100	2	2015	2	2015					
. S		ZZZZZZZZZZ	2	2015	2	2015					
! +			1	2001	12	2003	13	2000	16	2009	
! D		ZZZZZZZZZZ	1	2001	12	2003	13	2000	16	2000	
! K		ZZZZZZZZZZ	1	2001	12	2003	13	2000	16	2000	
! M		ZZZZZZZZZZ	1	2001	12	2003	13	2000	16	2000	
! S		ZZZZZZZZZZ	1	2001	12	2003	13	2000	16	2000	

The function module FI_PERIOD_CHECK will validate whether the period is open for the fiscal year and posting period. The permitted fiscal year and posting periods are stored in the table T001B. Use parameter KOART as + for general G/L check. There is a BADI FAGL_PERIOD_CHECK that provides extended check for open posting period. This BADI is executed in the FI_PERIOD_CHECK function module. Using the BADI, you can add extra check on the period. The following values are allowed in the parameter ch_subrc.

- 0 –Posting allowed
- 4 – Period & is not opened for posting
- 6 – No authorization for posting period

Name: FAGL_PERIOD_CHECK		Multiple Use: Yes	Filter: No
Description: Posting Period check			
Method: PERIOD_CHECK			
Description: Post period check			
Name	Type	Data Type	Description
IM_BURKS	Importing	BURKS	Company Code
IM_OPVAR	Importing	OPVAR	Posting period variant
IM_GJAHR	Importing	GJAHR	Fiscal Year
IM_KOART	Importing	KOART	Account Type
IM_KONTO	Importing	KONTO	Account
IM_MONAT	Importing	MONAT	Posting Period
IM_RLDNR	Importing	RLDNR	Ledger
IM_GLVOR	Importing	GLVOR	Business Transaction
CH_SUBRC	Changing	SYSUBRC	Return value 0 – posting permitted, 4 – not allowed
Sample code: ch_subrc = 4. IF <cond>. "Implement your condition ch_subrc = 0. Endif.			

You can configure the default fiscal year at company code level. You can use transaction code OB68 to set this up. Many companies use the 'Park Document" functionality. In some cases the document may be in 'parked' and the accounting period may be closed when the document is attempted to be posted. Those documents will not post unless posting date. This can be defaulted to be the system date by a setting specific to each company code with transaction code OBD1. For each company code, you can set the posting date is to remain unchanged or can be overwritten with the system date by selecting from the available options

- posting date is not changed during posting (blank)
- posting date is set to the system date during posting (1)
- posting date is set to the system date if the posting period is closed (2)

Few interesting BAPI to get first and last day of the fiscal year defined at company code.

BAPI	Description
BAPI_CCODE_GET_FIRSTDAY_PERIOD	Get first day of fiscal year and period based on company code.
BAPI_CCODE_GET_LASTDAY_FYEAR	Get last day of fiscal year based on company code.

2.1.2 Business Area

Business area corresponds to a defined business segment or area of responsibility. It is used in both internal and external reporting. With some special processes it is possible to generate full financial statements at a business area level. The business area is part of FI IMG configuration (Transaction code is OX03). The business area is stored in the table TGSB. Like profit center business areas exist independently of company code. Business areas are often linked other organizational units such as cost center, division, and distribution channel. Many companies set up their configuration in such a way that business area is derived automatically for most transactions.

The reliance on business area has been declining in recent years. The business object type is BUS0003.

BAPI	Description
BAPI_BUSINESSAREA_GETLIST	Get list of business areas
BAPI_BUSINESSAREA_GETDETAIL	Get business area detail
BAPI_BUSINESSAREA_EXISTENCECHK	Validate existence of business area

2.1.3 Profit Center

Profit Center is a sub unit of a company responsible for revenues and costs. Often a division or business unit of a company is defined as a profit center because it is measured by its costs and revenues. A lot of companies rely very heavily on profit centers to support both external and internal reporting. Companies that do not have segment reporting with SAP's New General Ledger rely on profit center to a very large extent.

Profit center is also derived automatically in both financial and logistics transactions by a process of assignment. For example, cost centers are assigned to profit centers, material masters are assigned to profit centers, internal orders are assignment to profit center. Companies take this one step further and implement custom enhancements such as BAdIs/user exits and substitutions and to influence the profit center posting at the line item level in sales order, invoices and accounting documents.

The profit center is tied to the controlling area and this makes it possible for business unit reporting across company code. The business object types are BUS0015 (profit center) and BUS1116 (profit center group).

Table	Description
CEPC	Profit Center master data
CEPC_BURKS	Assignment of profit center to a Company code
CEPCT	Text for profit center master data
T8A00	Account determination for profit center accounting

List of transactions:

Transaction	Description
KE51, KE52, KE53	Create, Change and Display profit center
KE54	Delete profit center
KE55	Mass maintenance for profit center

BAPIs

Function Module	Description
BAPI_PROFITCENTER_CREATE	BAPI for Create profit center
BAPI_PROFITCENTER_CREATE	BAPI for Create profit center
BAPI_PROFITCENTER_GETDETAIL	BAPI for profit center detail
BAPI_PROFITCENTER_GETLIST	BAPI for profit center list
KE_PROFIT_CENTER_READ	Read the profit center master data
KE_PROFIT_CENTER_BUKRS_CHECK	Profit center validation against company code

2.1.4 Cost Elements

Cost element plays a vital role in reconciliation and alignment of costs and posting between financial accounting and controlling.

- Primary cost elements – cost or revenue-relevant item in the chart of accounts for which a corresponding general ledger exists in the financial accounting. Examples are Material cost, Personal costs and Energy costs.

- Secondary cost elements – created and maintained by the controlling component. It portrays internal value flows like internal activity allocation, overhead calculation and settlement transactions.

- Revenue elements

You can group Cost elements into a cost element group. Cost element groups are used to group GL Accounts in different ways to meet various business needs. Some examples are summarized reporting of expenses, allocation of costs at summarized level. All wages and benefits can be grouped in one cost element group.

One should also pay attention to cost element category as it influences how certain transactions are recorded in the system. The business object type for cost element is BUS1030 and for cost element group is BUS1113.

Table	Description
CSKA	Cost element master record
CSKB	Cost element based on controlling area
CSKU	Cost element texts
COKA	CO Objects: control data for cost elements
CSSK	Cost center/Cost elements

List of transactions:

Transaction	Description
KA01, KA02, KA03	Create, Change, and display cost element
KA04	Delete cost element
KA05	Cost element – display changes
KA06	Create secondary cost element
KA23	Cost elements master data report

List of BAPIs:

BAPI	Description
BAPI_COSTELEM_GETLIST	Get list of cost elements
BAPI_COSTELEM_GETDETAIL	Get detail of cost element
BAPI_COSTELEM_CREATEMULTIPLE	Create multiple cost elements
BAPI_COSTELEM_CHANGEMULTIPLE	Change multiple cost elements

2.2 Account Assignment Objects

The concept of account assignment objects is very important in all SAP financial modules. This term is used to refer to logical entities to which costs and revenues are posted within SAP. The most common example is a cost center.

The main difference between an account assignment object and an organization unit is that they exist within or in addition to an organization unit such as a company code or profit center. For example a cost center is assigned to one and only one company code and profit center. An internal order is attached to a company code and profit center.

Some common account assignment objects are cost center, internal order, WBS element, production order and CO-PA segment. Generally account assignment objects represent a certain logical unit within a business. In the case of internal orders, one company may use it exclusively for tracking capital expenditure but in another company it may be used to track costs related to a marketing campaign. The CO-PA segment which is a combination of characteristics such as product, customer etc. may be configured differently depending on the needs of a business. The business process and reporting needs of an organization influences how various account assignment objects are defined.

Account assignment objects such as cost centers and internal orders also lend themselves to hierarchies such as cost center group and internal order group which make them very useful for reporting. Account assignment objects further delineate the business transactions posted in the SAP system, thereby facilitating more detailed analysis and reporting.

It is also useful to be aware of the distinction between 'real' and 'statistical' cost objects. For a line item in a document SAP will recognize only one object as a real object and will tag the other object as statistical by assigning it a different value type. A common example is when both cost center and internal order are posted in a line item, the internal order is the 'true' object and cost center becomes 'statistical' object. We can easily figure this out by looking at the value type field in the line item detail.

At the end of this chapter we would have gained a good understanding of different ways in which account assignment objects are used by companies. We would get an idea of enhancements possible in this area.

2.2.1 Cost Center

Cost Center Accounting (CO-OM-CCA) is often used in the first phase of implementation, together with the main areas of Financial Accounting (General Ledger (FI-GL), Assets Payable (FI-AP), Assets Receivable (FI-AR)) and Overhead Orders (CO-OM-OPA).

Cost centers in one company may represent a department such as engineering, safety, human resources. In another company, cost center may represent a business unit or a region such as Mid-West region. In practice, most companies use cost centers in multiple ways.

Once costs are recorded in the system, we can use methods of activity allocation, assessment or distribution to allocate costs to other cost centers or to other cost objects such as an internal order or a PA-segment. Many organizations use several of these techniques at the same time.

It is to be noted the cost centers can both send to and receive costs from other account assignment objects. A company may allocate the selling and general administrative expenses based to their product divisions using the cost center assessment technique. The same company in another instance may allocate from a cost center to a CO-PA segment if it needs to transfer costs to different dimension within their organization. A cost center may receive costs as part of a settlement transaction carried out on an internal order or a maintenance order. A cost center can also send costs to a production order through the process of activity allocation during a production order confirmation.

Master data of a cost center plays an important role in how cost centers interact with other units within the CO module. When creating or changing cost centers we need to pay attention to validity dates, cost center category and profit center.

You can maintain cost center master data with time dependencies. You can make changes at any time for any given time interval. The data will be stored with a time reference. Master data maintenance includes an automatic check for each field's time-based consistency, resulting in individual time-based maintenance for each field.

You can group cost centers into a cost center group. You can use the cost center group to build a cost center hierarchy. The lowest hierarchy level is individual cost center. There must be at least one cost center group that contains all cost centers. The cost center group is stored in the FI set tables.

You can configure this using the transaction code OKEG.

🔲 ⬇ 🔲 🔲 | ℹ 🔲 Information...

Field Name	Name	Day	Period	Fiscal Yr	No
KHINR	Hierarchy Area				X
BUKRS	Company Code			X	
GSBER	Business Area			X	
FUNC_AREA	Functional Area	X			
WAERS	Currency			X	
PRCTR	Profit Center		X		
Address					
ANRED	Title	X			
NAME1	Name	X			
NAME2	Name 2	X			
NAME3	Name 3	X			
NAME4	Name 4	X			
STRAS	Street	X			
ORT01	City	X			
ORT02	District	X			
LAND1	Country Key	X			
TXJCD	Tax Jurisdiction	X			
PFACH	PO Box	X			
PSTLZ	Postal Code	X			
PSTL2	P.O. Box Postal Code	X			
REGIO	Region	X			
Communication					
SPRAS	Language Key	X			
TELF1	Telephone 1	X			
TELF2	Telephone 2	X			
TELBX	Telebox number	X			
DRNAM	Printer destination	X			

Below are some useful tables when dealing with cost center related master or transaction data.

Table	Description
CSKS	Cost center header
CSKT	Cost Center text
COSP	CO objects: cost totals for external posting
COEP	CO Objects: Line items by Period
COBK	CO Objects: Document Header
COST	CO Objects: Price Total

Helpful Transaction codes

Transaction	Description
KS01, KS02, KS03	Cost center: Create, change and display
KAH1, KAH2, KAH3	Cost center group: Create, change and display
KS12, KS13, KS14	Mass processing of cost centers
KSB5	Display Actual cost documents

BAPIs

BAPI	Description
BAPI_COSTCENTER_CREATEMULTIPLE	Create multiple cost centers
BAPI_COSTCENTER_GETDETAIL	Get cost center detail
BAPI_COSTCENTER_GETLIST	Get list of cost center
BAPI_COSTCENTERGROUP_GETDETAIL	Get cost center group detail
BAPI_COSTCENTERGROUP_GETLIST	Get cost center group list
BAPI_COSTCENTERGROUP_CREATE	Create the cost center group

Enhancements

- **COOMKS01** – You can enhance the CSKS (cost center) structure with custom fields. Use or create CI_CSKS structure with your additional fields. You can enhance cost center master data by adding the custom fields in the structure CI_CSKS. You can implement the SAP enhancement COOMKS01 to handle custom fields.
  - EXIT_SAPLKMA1_001 - CO-OM customer exit at PBO event in custom sub-screens 0399/3399 in SAPLKMA1.

  - EXIT_SAPLKMA1_002 - CO-OM customer exit at PAI event in custom subscreen 0399 in SAPLKMA1.
    Function code +CU1: Appears in the menu for the master data transactions for cost centers under "Goto" and "Additional fields..." and leads to the tab index for user-defined additional fields.

- **COOMKS02** –You can use the COOMKS02 enhancement only with enhancement COOMKS01. You can use COOMKS02 for programming additional checks for custom and standard fields.

  - EXIT_SAPLKMA1_003 – Function exit to additional data check on the cost center update structure (CSKSP). You can raise message and the exception 'ERROR' for any inconsistency.

2.2.2 Internal Order

An internal order is a widely used cost object. Internal Orders provide a way to present another view of expenditure and serves as a useful complement to other forms of expenditure tracking and reporting at cost center and GL Account level. For example, all the expenses associated with a project can be assigned an Internal Order number. A report can then be executed for that Internal Order displaying all the expenses, posted to multiple G/Ls, across multiple cost centers, for that project.

Internal order has some special features that distinguish it from other cost objects in CO.

- Order budgets with availability control
- Statistical orders
- Integration with FI-Fixed assets through settlement to Asset under Construction and Final Asset

Internal orders are divided into the following categories:

- **Overhead orders** - For short-term monitoring of the indirect costs arising from jobs. They can also be used for continuous monitoring of subareas of indirect costs. Overhead orders can collect plan and actual costs independently of organizational cost center structures and business processes, enabling continuous cost control in the enterprise.

- **Investment orders** - Monitor investment costs that can be capitalized and settled to fixed assets.

- **Accrual orders** - Monitor period-based accrual between expenses posted in Financial Accounting and accrual costs in Controlling.

- **Orders with revenues** - Monitor the costs and revenues arising from activities for partners outside the organization, or from activities not belonging to the core business of the organization.

The business object type is BUS2075.

Table Name	Description
AUFK	Order master data. Note that this table is common for all orders. For internal order, AUTYP = 01.
AUFP	Order line items.
TKO01	Control parameters for order type
TKO03	Order status

Transaction	Description
KO01, KO02, KO03	Internal Order: Create, change and display

The following are some function exits available for internal orders

BAPI	Description
BAPI_INTERNALORDER_CREATE	Create internal order
BAPI_INTERNALORDER_GETDETAIL	Get internal order detail
BAPI_INTERNALORDER_GETLIST	Get list of internal orders

Enhancements

You can extend the internal order header table AUFK by adding custom fields in the 'include' structure CI_AUFK. You required implementing COOPA002 enhancement to populate the custom fields.

- **COOPA_01** – The enhancement allows you to do additional check on the internal order record. This enhancement is applicable for processing internal orders with order category (01 to 03) and CO production order with order category (04 to 05). The enhancement has the following exit functions.

- o EXIT_SAPLKOAU_002 – You can do additional authorization check on the internal table record. The customer exit is executed for authorization check on internal orders in master data maintenance, planning, budgeting and reporting.
- o EXIT_SAPLRKIO_001 – The exit function is triggered while running an order report in master data maintenance. You can implement additional data check based on your requirements. The exit function processed on the following places:
    - Creating an internal order with reference
    - Creating or displaying an internal order
    - Creating or changing an order
    - Executing an order report in informational system
    - Order selection by classification
- o EXIT_SAPLRKIO_002 – The exit function is triggered when the business transactions like Release, G/L account posting on the order. You can implement own check and you raise error message and/or returning e_result = 4.

- **COOPA002** – You can use this implement to handle the customer defined fields. The function code +CUS is part of the enhancement. The exit function module is EXIT_SAPLKAUF_001.

- **COOPA003** – The enhancement enables you transferring user defined fields to the AUFK table. This is applicable for the internal order transactions KO01, KO02 and KO03. The enhancement has the following the exit function modules:
    - o EXIT_SAPLKAUF_002 – The exit function is part of PBO event where you can get the data from AUFK and transfer data to screen.

Name	Type	Data Type	Description
I_AUFK	Importing	AUFK	Master data fields
I_KAUF	Importing	KAUF	Control data for internal order
SUBSCREEN	Exporting	DYNNR	Displayed group (sub-screen)

    The I_KAUF is administrative data for the internal order screen. The field PAR_ACTVT of the I_KAUF has the following activities:
    - 01 – Create
    - 02 – Change
    - 03 – Display

    - o EXIT_SAPLKAUF_003 – The exit function is part of PAI event where you can transfer data from sub-screen fields to the AUFK data.

- **COOPA004** – You can use this enhancement to implement new SAP script form to print master data and settlement rules. When you are implementing new custom fields then print form may need the custom field information also.

In standard application, SAP uses the SAP script form CO_ORDER for printing. The enhancement has exit function EXIT_SAPLKAUF_004.

2.2.3 WBS Element

If project systems module is implemented, there is standard integration with the CO through WBS –Work Breakdown Structure. A WBS is a model of the work to be performed in a project presented in a hierarchical structure. The WBS elements represent activities within the WBS. These can be tasks or work packages. WBS element is represented as a cost object in CO.

Like cost centers – cost planning is possible for WBS elements. Also a project and all its WBS elements can also be settled in t-code CJ88. This is similar to how an internal order is settled. However, WBS elements have some additional features such as Result Analysis, Automatically Generated Settlement Rules and Multi-level settlement.

Many companies use either WBS elements or internal orders to meet requirements specific to their business. There are companies that use both depending on the underlying business process.

The WBS element's BOR type is BUS2054.

Table	Description
PRPS	WBS Element master data
PROJ	Project Definition

BAPIs

BAPI	Description
BAPI_PROJECTDEF_CREATE	Create project definition
BAPI_PROJECT_MAINTAIN	Edit Project (including networks)
BAPI_PROJECT_EXISTENCECHECK	Check the existence of the project
BAPI_PROJECT_GETINFO	Get the project details
BAPI_PROJECT_SAVEREPLICA	Copy the project

2.2.4 Business Process

This cost object is an integral part of the CO-OM-ABC Activity Based Costing component. The business process represents a cross-functional structure within the organization. It consumes resources and can cross internal organizational boundaries such as a cost center.

The business process is a master record in the CO module. Some of the fields in a business process master record are company code, currency, cost center, profit center, plant, sales organization, and object currency.

CO-Activity based costing is not as widely implemented as cost centers or internal orders. The business object types are:

- BUS1036 – Business process
- BUS1114 – Business process group
- BUS1137 – Business process structure CO

Table	Description
CBPR	CO-ABC: Business Process Master Table
CBPT	Business Process Text table
CBAR	Business process type

Transactions:

Transaction	Description
CP01, CP02, CP03, CP04	Business process: Create, change, display and delete
CP05	Display changes

BAPIs

BAPI	Description
BAPI_PROCESS_CREATEMULTIPLE	Create business process
BAPI_PROCESS_GETLIST	Get list of Business process
BAPI_PROCESS_GETDETAIL	Get detail of business process
BAPI_PROCESS_DELETEMULTIPLE	Delete one or more bus. Processes
BAPI_PROCESS_SETSTRUCTURE	Set the template for the bus. process
BAPI_PROCESS_CHANGEMULTIPLE	Change one or more bus. processes
K_BUSINESS_PROCESS_UPDATE	Business process update
K_BUSINESS_PROCESS_POST	Posting business process

2.3 General Ledger

The General Ledger in SAP serves as the complete record of all business transactions. It is the centralized up-to-date reference for the rendering of accounts. The GL in SAP is the basis of an organization's financial statements.

The GL is fully integrated with other operational areas of a company such as logistics and billing. Inventory movements, invoice verification and billing transactions all flow to the GL through the process of account determination consisting of transaction keys and account keys.

The classic GL in SAP had some inherent limitations which were subsequently addressed in the New GL. Historically, companies used other mechanisms such as profit center accounting and special purpose ledger to meet their needs for tracking and reporting business events in different dimensions such as alternate fiscal year, divisions, business units, geographical segments etc.

But the introduction of New General Ledger (New GL) as of mySAP ERP 2004 (ECC 5.0) extended the functionality of GL in a very significant way. Some of the key features of new GL are:

- Parallel accounting/ledgers
- Segment reporting
- Document splitting
- Fully reconciled cross entity postings
- Integration of legal and management reporting
- Profit center accounting is integrated within New GL

The business object type for General ledger is BUS1028.

2.3.1 G/L Account Master

The general ledger master record is a key element within the GL module. The GL master record is set up within the chart of accounts. It is common for the GL numbering to follow a certain grouping logic representing a broad type of transactions. For example numbers between 100000 to 101000 could be cash/bank accounts, 400000 to 499999 could be revenue accounts and so on.

At the outset a GL Account is defined to be a P&L or Balance Sheet account. P&L Accounts are tied to retained earnings account. At year end, the balances in P&L Accounts are automatically transferred to the retained earnings and balances are carried forward to next year through execution of a special transaction at year end.

Some important settings in a GL account are account currency, sort key, open item management, line item display, reconciliation account type and field status group. These settings control how transactions are posted, how balances and detail line items are stored and output in reports.

You want to put in place controls to ensure that GL account maintenance is done in a consistent manner by a well -trained person. Poor governance in this area can lead to problems several years down the road. One example is accumulation of thousands of line items in GL accounts incorrectly set to open item managed resulting in inability to archive old documents. An incorrect field status group setting can result in documents not posting to CO-PA or to profit center ledger.

In some cases, it may be required to restrict the ability to post to some specific GL Accounts. It is possible use authorization groups in conjunction with authorization object F_SKA1_BES to achieve this.

In New GL, master data comprises the following:

- GL account master data
- Profit center master data
- Segment

SAP recommends that if New GL is implemented, profit center accounting should be integrated in the GL application component. This means that the traditional GLPCA, GLPCT, GLPCP for profit center ledger would no longer be applicable. All transactions will instead be captured in FAGLFLEXA, FAGLFLEXP, FAGLFEXT tables.

Many large companies have successfully migrated from classic GL to new GL. SAP's System Landscape Optimization (SLO) Group offers paid services for such projects.

2.3.2 Integration of GL with other modules

The GL is integrated with all application components of SAP that generate posting data relevant to financial accounting. For example from the logistics component, inventory movements from production or from order fulfillment are automatically recorded in the GL. Customer invoices generated from sales and distribution are posted automatically to receivables sub-ledger. This happens through the process of account determination consisting of transaction keys and account keys.

Here is an example of account determination for inventory movements.

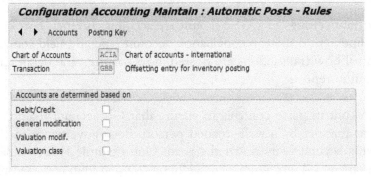

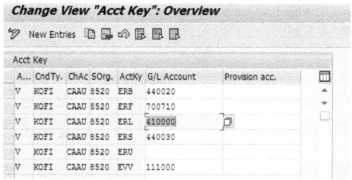

Change View "Acct Key": Overview

A...	CndTy.	ChAc	SOrg.	ActKy	G/L Account	Provision acc.
V	KOFI	CAAU	8520	ERB	440020	
V	KOFI	CAAU	8520	ERF	700710	
V	KOFI	CAAU	8520	ERL	410000	
V	KOFI	CAAU	8520	ERS	440030	
V	KOFI	CAAU	8520	ERU		
V	KOFI	CAAU	8520	EVV	111000	

Even though companies use other modules such as profit center accounting, CO-PA for their internal analysis and reporting at a more granular level, the GL still remains critical because it is considered the basis for legal financial statements.

In the SAP system the sub-ledgers automatically post to the GL through the reconciliation account maintained in the master record. You can see this in asset, vendor and customer master record. This ensures that the GL and sub-ledgers are always in synch and there is no need for an explicit transfer to GL that may be required in other ERP systems.

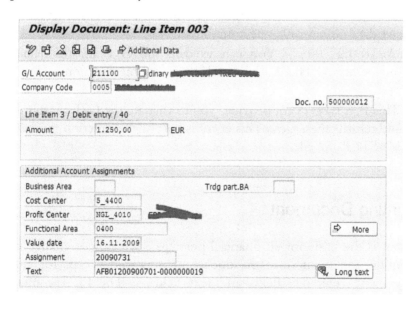

The business object type is BUS3006.

Below are some tables that contain transactional or master data in GL

Table	Description
SKA1	General Ledger master (Chart of Accounts)
SKB1	General Ledger master (Company code)
SKAT	General Ledger master (Chart of Accounts Description)
GLT0	GL Account totals by period
FAGLFLEXA	New GL Actual line items

FAGLFLEXP	New GL Plan line items
FAGLFLEXT	New GL totals

BAPIs:

BAPI	Description
BAPI_GL_ACC_GETLIST	Get G/L account list
BAPI_GL_ACC_GETDETAIL	Get G/L detail
BAPI_GL_ACC_EXISTENCECHECK	Check the existence of GL account
GL_ACCT_MASTER_SAVE	Save GL account master data
BAPI_GL_GETGLACCBALANCE	Closing balance of G/L account for chosen year
BAPI_GL_GETGLACCPERIODBALANCES	Posting period balances for each G/L account
BAPI_GL_GETGLACCCURRENTBALANCE	Closing balance of G/L account for current year
BAPI_GLX_GETDOCITEMS	Line item of document for ledger with summary table GLFLEXT

Enhancements

- **SAPMF02H** – This SMOD enhancement provides the function exit for G/L account master data. It has only one component.
  - EXIT_SAPMF02H_001 – You can validate the G/L master data and returns the messages. The BTE event 2310 does same function.

- BTE 2310 – This P/S BTE event provides you to validate the G/L master data information and returns messages. This event is part of the function module GL_ACCT_MASTER_SAVE.

2.3.3 Accounting Document

Accounting document is the basis for all financial postings. We cannot change most fields in the accounting document once the document is posted except for certain fields such as assignment, reference fields and text fields.   The FI document is categorized into:

- Document Header – Identifies the document like company code, posting/creation date, etc.
- Line Items – details of the accounting posting like G/L account, posting key, credit/debit amount

You can view the accounting document using the transaction code FB03.

Display Document: Data Entry View

| Menu ◢ | | ◀ Back | Exit | Cancel | System ◢ | | Change Display/Change Mode | Display Another Document | Select Individual Object | Display Document Header | Displa |

Data Entry View

Document Number	1500000123	Company Code	0001	Fiscal Year	2014
Document Date	30.06.2014	Posting Date	30.06.2014	Period	6
Reference		Cross-Comp.No.			
Currency	USD	Texts exist ☐		Ledger Group	

Co..*	Item	PK	SG	Account	Description	Amount	Curr.	Text	Material	WBS elem...	Profit Ctr	Trs	Network	OpAc	Purch.Doc.
0001	1	50		113550	BOA - USD-Account	1.000,00-	USD								
	2	25		75000007	German Drilling services Ltd	1.000,00	USD								

You can view the list of accounting document by executing the program RFBUEB00.

Document Header

The document header is stored in the table BKPF. There are few important date fields in the header viz., document date, posting date and entry date. The document date in most cases a business event such as the date of the vendor's invoice, or a date when an expense report was submitted. The posting date is the date on which the transaction is recorded into the general ledger. Posting date is the date for legal entity reporting and in most cases management reporting as well.

Often the posting date and document dates are seen to be different because of inherent time lag between an external event and an SAP transaction. The entry date is set automatically based on system date.

The Accounting document is identified by company code (BUKRS), document number (BELNR) and fiscal year (GJAHR). We suggest not using ONLY BELNR in your select statement to fetch accounting document. Because in some installations number range can be year-dependent causing a non-unique and potentially incorrect match.

It would be beneficial to note the relationship between the FI document and the source document also known as the original document. The original document of the accounting document is stored in the following BKPF fields. The original document indicates the underlying business event such as an SD invoice, MM Vendor invoice, an inventory movement. In multiple system scenarios it may also provide information of the source system.

- AWTYP – The original document type e.g., RMRP – Invoice, VBRK – SD Billing document
- AWKEY – The original document number
- AWSYS – The logical RFC destination of the original document.

The list of the original document type is listed in the table TTYP. The table lists all original document types and corresponding function modules to access the original document.

Document Type

The document type determines which account type (G/L, customer, vendor, etc.) a document is to be posted to, it also indicates the type of transaction as to invoice, payment, credit memo, etc. In addition document numbering is controlled by document type through the document number range. With document type configuration, you can define number range and account types. The document type information is stored in the table T003. It is common for most companies to create their own document types to suit their business needs.

Long Text

Long text is used to capture detailed information in text form. The long text can be associated to business objects. Long text is also referred as SAP Script text or text object. The long text is widely used in all SAP modules. Text object are identified by the object name and id.

You can configure Text IDs for long text at document header level. The SAP standard system delivers Note, Correspondence and Payment Advice. You can view text information in the financial document (FB03).

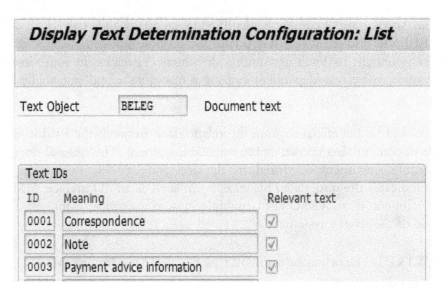

The text Object for the document header is BELEG. The following example of ABAP code is provided as a guide to read a correspondence note from an accounting document.

```
CONCATENATE '<Comp code>' '<A/c Number>' '<year>' into lv_name.
CALL FUNCTION 'READ_TEXT'
  EXPORTING
    id              = '0001'
    language        = sy-langu
    name            = lv_name
    object          = 'BELEG'
  TABLES
    lines           = i_tline
  EXCEPTIONS
    id              = 1
    language        = 2
    name            = 3
    not_found       = 4
    object          = 5
    reference_check = 6
    wrong_access_to_archive = 7
    OTHERS          = 8.
```

Tips: You can use SAVE_TEXT to update the text.

Line Items

A line item is made up of a document number (BELNR), line item (BUZEI), posting key, amount and additional details such as tax code, cost or profit center, business area and segment. Each document will have at least two line items except a clearing document that has only header information. The line items are stored in the table BSEG (except parked document). SAP would allow only a 'complete' document to post in the system, with debits equaling credits, in addition to all basic validations such as date formats, valid values for company code, currency, gl accounts, and account assignment objects such as cost center, profit center etc. being satisfied.

You can automatically enable the system to automatically (by IMG configuration) create some of the line items such as

- Tax on sales or purchases while entering customer/vendor invoice
- Payables and receivables between company codes when posting cross-company code transactions
- Gains or losses from exchange rate differences between invoice and payment (customer/vendor)
- Cash discount paid/received during payment postings
- Residual items or bank charges while posting a customer or vendor payment and clearing open items
- Tax adjustment posting for a down payment when entering special G/L transactions

Posting Key

You cannot post a document without entering a posting key, the posting key controls the entry as well as the processing of a line item in a document. It determines the account type such as vendor/customer or GL as well as whether the posted amount will be a debit or credit. The posting key defines what fields will be displayed on the document entry screen and the field status of these fields. The posting key is stored in the table TBSL. It is important to note that the field status defined for a posting key will override the field status entered in a particular general ledger account.

Parked Document

Document parking allows you to enter and park (store) incomplete documents in the system without extensive entry checks. You can call up the parking document at a later time to process further or to post.

The posting date derivation for parking document is based on the configuration of company code. You can configure using the transaction code OBD1. For enjoy transaction, you can change the posting date at any time.

Parked documents can be identified in BKPF when BSTAT = 'Z'. But the item level data will not be stored in the BSEG table. Instead, the details of parked document are in the following table.

Table	Description
VBSEGA	Assets parked document detail
VBSEGD	Customers parked document detail
VBSEGK	Suppliers parked document detail
VBSEGS	General ledger parked document detail

The business object type for the parked document is FIPP.

Open Item management

This is an important concept in SAP and is used in all 3 basic modules of SAP, viz FI, AR and AP. Transactions posted to sub-ledgers are by default open item transactions. However on the GL side, it is recommended that only some specific accounts such as GRIR Clearing, Bank clearing and Deposit account are defined as open item managed. It would be prudent to consider the nature of transactions being posted to a GL account before setting the open item flag in the master record. This is important because documents with open items cannot be archived. Typical examples of an open item are a vendor invoice or a customer invoice posted to the sub-ledger.

A cleared item is generated when an open item is cleared by an accounting transaction such as a payment or reversal. With a view to manage performance and for modularization, FI has separate tables for the open and cleared items. There are separate tables for Customer (BSID, BSAD), Vendor (BSIK, BSID) and G/L accounts (BSIS, BSAS).

The business functions that cover open items are:

- Account maintenance – Allows you to clear or partially clear posted open items. It can be done by manually or automatic account maintenance.
- Payment program – All items paid by the payment program are cleared
- Post a payment lot - A posting document is created for each payment in a payment lot or a check lot.
- Reversing a document
- Posting a return
- Resetting clearing
- Posting a document

Document Change Rules

You can configure fields that can be modified after document is posted. The document change is at header level and item level. The header level change rules is accessed by the IMG menu path Finance Accounting->Financial Global Settings->Document->Document Header->Document Change Rules, Document Header. Or you can use the transaction code OB32.

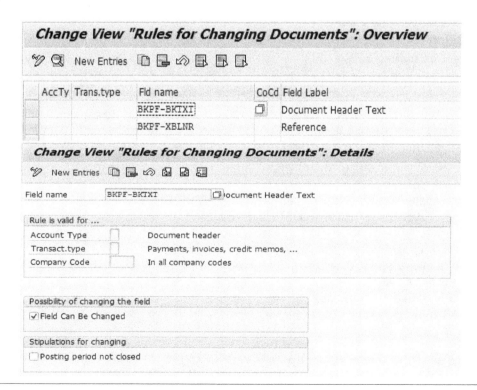

The item level change's IMG menu path is Finance Accounting->Financial Global Settings->Document->Line Items->Document Change Rules, Line Items.

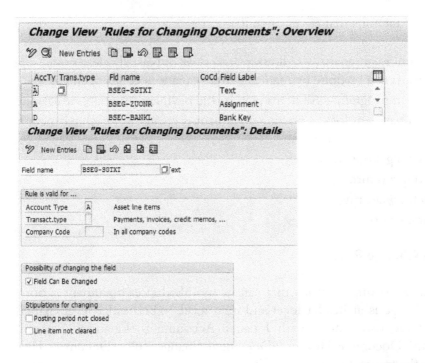

A couple of practical examples where document change rules are used in business situations are as follows:

- Reason code values – BSEG-RSTGR need to be changed in hundreds of line items en masse
- Payment method or line item text need to be changed for many line items.

The function module FI_ITEMS_MASS_CHANGE is used to change FI items. The function module uses call transaction FB02. The following is sample code for the mass change function module.

```
* Include type-pool TPIT
 DATA: lt_buztab    TYPE tpit_t_buztab WITH HEADER LINE,
    lt_fldtab    type tpit_t_fname  WITH HEADER LINE.

* Populate lv_bseg with values and list of fldtab and lt_buztab
  lv_fldtab-fname = 'SGTXT'.
  lv_fldtab-aenkz = 'X'.
  APPEND lv_fldtab TO lt_fldtab.
  LOOP AT lt_bseg INTO lv_bseg.
* Populate lt_buztab

  ENDLOOP.
```

```
* Make sure that use FM for each document
 CALL FUNCTION 'FI_ITEMS_MASS_CHANGE'
    EXPORTING
       s_bseg   = lv_bseg
    IMPORTING
       errtab   = it_errtab[]
    TABLES
       it_buztab = lt_buztab
       it_fldtab = lt_fldtab
    EXCEPTIONS
       bdc_errors = 1
       OTHERS   = 2.
```

Technical Structure

Accounting document is stored in multiple database tables. The following tables are important tables used in the FI/CO.

Table	Description
BKPF	Accounting documents
BSEG	item level
BSID	Accounting: Secondary index for customers
BSIK	Accounting: Secondary index for vendors
BSIM	Secondary Index, Documents for Material
BSIP	Index for vendor validation of double documents
BSIS	Accounting: Secondary index for G/L accounts
BSAD	Accounting: Index for customers (cleared items)
BSAK	Accounting: Index for vendors (cleared items)
BSAS	Accounting: Index for G/L accounts (cleared items)
VBKPF	Document Header for Document Parking
VBSEG A	Document Segment for Document Parking - Asset Database
VBSEG D	Document Segment for Customer Document Parking
VBSEG K	Document Segment for Vendor Document Parking
VBSEGS	Document Segment for Document Parking - G/L Account Database
BSEC	One time account
BSET	Tax documents
BSEGC	Credit card detail

The key element for the account document is BELNR (Document number), GJAHR (Fiscal Year) and BUZEI (Line item number).

ABAP Tips

The table BSEG tends to be a very large volume table. Make sure that you use proper WHERE conditions so it uses indexes. Use caution to use JOIN statement with BSEG table, try to get the accounting document numbers as an internal table and use 'FOR ALL ENTRIES' statement. Make sure that before you use FOR ALL ENTRIES, the internal table is not empty. The empty internal table used in FOR ALL ENTRIES will try to fetch all records. Also, use the tables BSID, BSIK, BSIS, BSAD, BSAK and BSAS for open and cleared items instead of BSEG.

Search Helps:

Search Help	Description
GL_ACCT_CA	G/L accounts in chart of accounts
GL_ACCT_CA_NO	G/L account no. in chart of accounts
GL_ACCT_CA_TEXT	G/L account description in chart of accounts
GL_ACCT_CA_FLAGS	G/L account with delete/lock flag in chart of accounts
GL_ACCT_CA_KEY	Keywords

BAPIs

BAPI/Function Module	Description
BAPI_ACC_DOCUMENT_CHECK	Check Accounting document
BAPI_ACC_DOCUMENT_POST	Posting Accounting document
BAPI_ACC_DOCUMENT_REV_POST	Posting Reverse Accounting document
FI_DOCUMENT_LIST_DISPLAY	Listing Account document items in ALV display
AC_DOCUMENT_CRATE	Create accounting document
AC_DOCUMENT_POST	Posting accounting document
AC_DOCUMENT_DELETE	Delete accounting document
AC_DOCUMENT_REVERSE	Reverse the accounting document
BAPI_ACC_GL_POSTING_POST	General ledger accounting post
BAPI_ACC_GL_POSTING_CHECK	Validate G/L accounting posting
BAPI_ACC_BILLING_POST	Accounting posting for billing document
BAPI_ACC_BILLING_CHECK	Accounting posting check for billing document
BAPI_ACC_INVOICE_RECEIPT_POST	Accounting post for Invoice receipt
BAPI_ACC_INVOICE_RECEIPT_CHECK	Accounting check for invoice receipt
BAPI_ACC_GOODS_MOVEMENT_POST	Accounting post for Goods movement
BAPI_ACC_GOODS_MOVEMENT_CHECK	Accounting check for Goods movement

Display document

The FB03 uses the function module FI_DOCUMENT_LIST_DISPLAY to display the values. This function module REUSE_ALV_LIST_DISPLAY to list out the line item information and header information is done using TOP_OF_PAGE subroutine.

Enhancements

- **ACBAPI01** – The SMOD enhancement is used in a number of BAPI where FI document is created as a reference. For example, the function module BAPI_ACC_BILLING_POST is used to create accounting document when billing document is posted in SD module. This enhancement is triggered before creating the accounting document. The enhancement has only one component EXIT_SAPLACC4_001 and it allows you to change the accounting header parameter.

- **BTE 1005** – This P/S event is triggered when you entering the account key and account number while posting an accounting document. You can do additional checks on the data already entered on this line item. For example, if the account entered is blocked for a payment run or dunning run, you can have some kind of further action triggered at this point.

- **BTE 1010** – This event is replaced by 1011. Do not use this event.

- **BTE 1011** – You can use this P/S BTE doing additional checks on the line items while posting the document. The event is triggered both at adding or changing the line items.

- **BTE 1012** – You can use this P/S event to do check on the country specific field BSEG-XREF3 at the time of entry. Parameter I_AKTYP contains the current activity type of the transaction ('H' = add, 'K' = adjust (correct), 'V' = change, 'A' = display). The OKCODE tells you which key was pressed.

- **BTE 1013** – This Event enables you to enter additional reference data through the inclusion (display on screen) of a button. You can show only customer specific fields.

- **BTE 1020** – This P/S event triggers before completing the document. You can do your checks prior to posting. This Event is accessed once per standard posting process and is similar to validation at document level (Event 0003). A document number has not yet been assigned when this Event is reached.

- **BTE 1025** – This P/S event is called up after final checks and prior number assignment. Following this Event, no further error messages may be sent. The document is complete at this point, and no further changes can be made to it prior to posting.

- **BTE 1030** – This P/S event triggers prior to FI posting module (POST_DOCUMENT). The parameter X_VBUP is used for information purpose only. Make sure that you are not using any commit in this event.

- **BTE 1040** - This Event is reached following callup of the update function module for FI (REVERSE_CLEARING).

- **BTE 1050** – This is P/S BTE event and it is executed after POST_DOCUMENT. You can use this BTE to add-on activities after POST_DOCUMENT. Note that the post document is executed in UPATE TASK. The indicator I_XVBUP informs you that the SAP standard system posts asynchronously.

- **BTE 1060** – This Event is reached following call-up of the update function module for FI (POST_DOCUMENT) when entering an invoice during invoice verification. At this point you can introduce your own tables for which an update posting is to be carried out at the same time as the tables.

- **BTE 1070** – Using this event, you can set PF-STATUS.

- **BTE 1080** -The event is released for SAP internals only. It can only be released for partners after consultation with SAP. The event is executed when you set the PF (GUI) status for event 00001070.

- **BTE 1085** – The event is released for SAP internals only. It can only be released for partners after consultation with SAP.

- **BTE 1110** – This P/S BTE is triggered during document change. This Event is accessed after calling the update module for change documents when saving in transaction FB02 (or FB09). It is reached before the CHANGE_DOCUMENT function module is called up. Make sure that you are not using any commit in this event. If you need to do database activities then use UPDATE TASK. The sample code is provided for the event 110. The sample code raises the event ZCHANGED of the object BKPF.

```
FUNCTION ZF_BTE1110_BKPF_CHANGED.
*"----------------------------------------------------------------
*"    IMPORTING
*"       VALUE(I_XBKPF) LIKE  BKPF STRUCTURE  BKPF
*"       VALUE(I_YBKPF) LIKE  BKPF STRUCTURE  BKPF
*"    TABLES
*"       XBSED STRUCTURE  FBSED
*"       YBSED STRUCTURE  FBSED
*"       XBSEG STRUCTURE  FBSEG
*"       YBSEG STRUCTURE  FBSEG
*"----------------------------------------------------------------
DATA: BEGIN OF LV_ACCKEY.
DATA:  BUKRS LIKE BKPF-BUKRS.
```

```
DATA:  BELNR LIKE BKPF-BELNR.
DATA:  GJAHR LIKE BKPF-GJAHR.
DATA: END OF OBJKEY.
DATA: LV_OBJKEY LIKE SWEINSTCOU-OBJKEY.
MOVE-CORRESPONDING I_XBKPF TO LV_ACCKEY.
MOVE LV_ACCKEY TO LV_OBJKEY.
* Raising Z events
CALL FUNCTION 'SWE_EVENT_CREATE'
   EXPORTING
      OBJTYPE            = 'BKPF'
      OBJKEY             = LV_OBJKEY
      EVENT              = 'ZCHANGED'
   EXCEPTIONS
      OBJTYPE_NOT_FOUND      = 1
      OTHERS             = 2.
*if sy-subrc <> 0.
* MESSAGE ID SY-MSGID TYPE SY-MSGTY NUMBER SY-MSGNO
*       WITH SY-MSGV1 SY-MSGV2 SY-MSGV3 SY-MSGV4.
*endif.

ENDFUNCTION.
```

- **BTE 1120** – This Event is reached directly from the R/3 System menu (at line item level: Environment -> Additional components).

- **BTE 1130** – This Event is reached when setting the function key status relating to Event 00001120.

- **BTE 1135** – You can use this event to function codes to Line Item.

- **BTE 1140** – The event is in the PBO part of the FI posting transactions (FB60, FV60, FB01, and so on). Here you can determine which pushbuttons or menu options are to be deactivated on a user-specific basis.

- **BTE 2215** – This P/S BTE is allowed to determine the user who is recorded in the parked document. If the user is not determined, then it is defaulted with the user who entered the parked document.

BADIs

- **AC_DOCUMENT** - You can implement this BADI for postings using the AC interface. The BADI has two methods and both are executed from the function module AC_DOCUMENT_CREATE. This BADI allows the field contents of the general accounting document (AC document) to be enriched or changed. In this way, the AC document contains complete posting information for all accounting components (such as FI, CO, and SL).
  o CHANGE_INITIAL - FI/CO Document Prior to Calling AC Components

- o CHANGE_AFTER_CHECK - FI/CO Document after Addition of AC Components
- o IS_SUPPRESSED_ACCT - Do Not Update ACCT* Tables (SAP Note 48009)
- o IS_COMPRESSION_REQUIRED - TABLE_COMPRESS on Internal Tables (SAP Note 320959)
- **ACC_DOCUMENT** – This BADI is triggered within the function modules BAPI_ACC_DOCUMENT_CHECK and BAPI_ACC_DOCUMENT_POST.
  - o CHANGE - Change the Accounting Document
  - o FILL_ACCIT - Fill Internal Table IT_ACCIT from GS_BAPI_ACCIT
- **FI_AUTHORITY_ITEM** – You can use this BADI enhancing additional check for the document display. You cannot change standard authority check but you can further check only. The BADI has only one method FI_AUTHORITY_ITEM. You can set the parameter C_RCODE as 0 (Authorization exits) and 4 (no authorization exits). Also, you can pass the error message information. The parameter I_BERACT does have the activity and its values are:
  - o 02 – Change
  - o 03 – Display
  - o 77 – Park
- **VATDATE_VALUES** – You can use this BADI that the system proposes a value for the tax reporting date field during document entry. The method VATDATE_DETERMINE determines the default value proposed on the screen, for example, during document entry in the dialog box for taxes.
  - o The method VATDATE_DETERMINE proposes the posting date, the document date, or another value according to customer-defined rules.
  - o The method VALIDATE_CHECK validates the tax reporting date.
- FI_DOC_DISP_LI - This BADI can be used to replace the display of individual line items with a program outside FI document display, with the purpose of representing specific details for these line items. The parameters I_BKPF and I_BSEG are transferred to the BADI from FI. For navigation purposes, the BADI returns OK codes within document display: There is only one method DISPLAY_LINE_ITEM.
- AC_QUANTITY_GET - Transfer of Quantities to Accounting - Customer Exit. You must activate /SAPCEM/QUANTITY_SD if you want to be able to convert units of measure. The switch is /SAPCEM/ECO_ETM.
- ADJUST_NET_DAYS - Change to Net Due Date. The switch is /SAPCEM/ECO_ETM.

Technical Challenge: Add custom fields at document header and add it in document header screen.

Solution: This requires implicit enhancement. This solution may not be supported by all in-house ABAP development teams. The function module FI_DOCUMENT_LIST_DISPLAY points to the form KOPF_ANZEIGE of the include LF064F01 for the TOP_OF_PAGE event.

The solution provided here is that enhance the subroutine as per your requirement. If you are adding the custom fields at end of the header, enhance the end of form. When you are changing total screens then implement change at top of the subroutine and exit before going to the standard program. Make sure that it does not impact any of your applications.

2.3.4 Coding Block

Adding the custom fields in the accounting item level is not straight forward. You cannot add custom fields in the table BSEG by append structure. SAP warns that do not add custom fields directly in the BSEG. You always use Edit coding block IMG activity. You can access the IMG activity by the transaction OXK3.

When you add a customer field to the coding block, the structures CI_COBL and CI_COBL_BI (for batch input) are created or enhanced. Using the customer include ensures that the customer field is automatically included in BSEG and other important tables.

For G/L reporting purpose, it is necessary and logical to add the custom fields to the totals table in the new G/L accounting. You can add customer fields to the totals table using the customer include CI_FAGLFLEX04. It will automatically add custom fields in leading standard totals table FAGLFLEXT.

Note that customer fields can significantly increase the data volume in the totals table. For this reason, before you use customer fields productively in the totals table in new General Ledger Accounting, you should ensure that the data volume in the totals table does not attain a critical level. You cannot include any fields in the totals table if they have the potential of acquiring a very large number of characteristic values. You should only use such fields as coding block fields in the document. SAP strongly recommends that defining the possible characteristic values of a customer field in the form of a customer-specific value table (check table).

Defining the Coding Block

You can add custom fields in the coding block using the transaction code OXK3. To add the custom fields, you need the development access. You can do configuration in basic mode or expert mode (you can turn in the menu Account Assignment).

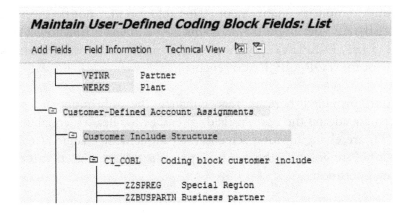

The fields are populated in the BSEG table.

Field	Key	Ini...	Data element	Data Type	Length	Deci...	Short Description
AUGGJ	☐	☐	AUGGJ	NUMC	4	0	Fiscal Year of Clearing Document
PPA_EX_IND	☐	☐	EXCLUDE_FLG	CHAR	1	0	PPA Exclude Indicator
ZZSPREG	☐	☐	ZREGION	CHAR	5	0	Special Region
ZZBUSPARTN	☐	☐	ZZBUSPARTN	CHAR	10	0	Business partner

Cluster Table: BSEG   ☐tive
Short Description: Accounting Document Segment

Attributes | Delivery and Maintenance | Fields | Entry help/check | Currency/Quantity Fields

Srch Help | Predefined Type

Custom screens

Use the transaction code OXK1 or you can access this from OXK3 (sub-screens from Environment menu). You can pick the fields and position from the account assignment fields. The coding block screen picks associate the sub-screen based on the entry fields and optional fields and priority of the coding block screens.

Maintain Coding Block Subscreens: Detail

⊕ Generate

Subscreen: 9004 New Account Assigment Screen
Priority: 9   ☐ Active

Field Name	Position	With Tex
Accounting Indicator		☐
Activity Type		☐
Asset		☐
Business Area		☐
BUSINESS LINE		☐
Business partner		☐
Business Process		☐
City		☐
Commitment Item		☐
Company Code		☐

Use the transaction code OB14, you can define the field status variant with new custom fields. The custom fields are available in the account assignment group.

Assigning Customer Fields to Ledger

You can use substitution to derive the custom fields based on your requirements. Or you can use BTE event 1120 populating the custom fields. The BTE is applicable for SD and MM integration. Also, you can use the BADI AC_DOCUMENT to enrich the customer fields. The customer fields are available for the FI validation process.

2.3.5 Line Item Display

Line layout is a handy tool that allows personalization of information displayed in line item detail. It allows user to select and re-arrange columns being displayed. The settings for line items display include:

- Line item sorting for line items
- Line layout: the information that is to be available on the screen when displaying line items
- Special fields for selecting/finding/sorting data
- Selection fields: the fields the user may specify, via which the system is to select assets, customers, vendor, materials or G/L accounts.
- Totals variants: the fields by which the line items are to be totaled
- Standard line layout and standard totals variant: the information that is to be available as standard when displaying line items
- Additional fields
- Search fields: the fields the user may specify, via which it is possible for the system to find individual items
- Sort fields: the fields the user may specify, via which it is possible for the system to sort items
- Total fields: the fields the user may specify, via which it is possible for the system to total items
- Work list for line item display

There are three important reports to display accounting line item for G/L accounts (FB3LN), Vendor (FBL1N) and Customer (FBL5N). The function module FI_ITEMS_DISPLAY is used in line items display. This is a powerful function module that uses ALV concept and user commands to access the corresponding documents.

Two structures RFPOS and RFPOSX are used to display the line item fields. To display the line items in the line items display program, the fields must be in these structures. The custom fields can be included in the structure RFPOS and RFPOSX. The special fields can be defined in the table T021S using the IMG configuration (Or use SM20 on the view V_T021S). The fields should be in the structure RFPOSX. You can use the program RFPOSXEXTN which extends the structure RFPOSX from the table T021S.

2.3.6 Enhancements

BTEs

- **BTE 1610** – This is P/S BTE event and is triggered from GUI menu (Environment->Additional components) in the line item display result. Based on the item selection, you will have Customer, Company code, Document number, line item and fiscal year. You can call your GUI screen.
- **BTE 1620** – This event is associated with the event 1610. You can change the function key status (menu text).
- **BTE 1630** – You can this event to do additional check before displaying the account line item data.
- **BTE 1640** – This P/S BTE event allows you to add additional header line information prior to standard document header.
- **BTE 1650** – You can use this event to populate the user-defined custom fields in the line item data. The event is discussed in the following technical challenge to adding custom fields in the line item display.

BADIs

- **FI_ITEMS_MENUE01** – The BADI is equivalent to the event 1610. You can activate the menu enhancements in the ALV list view. The BADI is more flexible than the event 1610. You can modify the exclude function code for the screen and define follow up actions up to four menu items.
- **FI_ITEMS_CH_DATA** – This BADI is equivalent to the event 1650. The main purpose of the BADI is populating custom fields. Also, you can modify the line item data.

Technical Challenge: How to add a custom field in the Customer Line Item Display.
Solution: Follow the steps:
- Make sure that the custom fields are extended in the structure RFPOS and RFPOSX. Uses append structure to extend the structures.
- Run the report RFPOSXEXTN make sure that structure is synchronized with T021S.

- There are two solutions to populate the custom fields of the structure. The solution one is by implementing the BADI FI_ITEMS_CH_DATA and the method CHANGE_ITEMS. The other option is by implementing the BTE 0001650.

Name: FI_ITEMS_CH_DATA		Multiple Use: Yes		Filter: No
Description: Change Line item				
Method: CHANGE_ITEMS				
Description: Change Line data				
Name	Type	Data Type		Description
CT_ITEMS	Changing	IT_RFPOSXEXT		FI Items Line display

Sample code: The sample code is for technical solution.

```
FIELD-SYMBOL: <ls_item> TYPE rfposxext.

LOOP AT CT_ITEMS INTO assigning <ls_item>.
CALL FUNCTION 'ZF_GET_CUSTVALUES'
   EXPORTING
     bukrs      = ls_item-bukrs
     gjahr      = <ls_item>-gjahr
     belnr      = <ls_item>-belnr
   IMPORTING
     field1   = <ls_item>-field1
     field2   = <ls_item>-field2
   EXCEPTIONS
     belnr_not_found = 01.
ENDLOOP.
```

Recurring Entries

Recurring entries are business transactions that are repeating regularly such as rent and insurance. You can create a recurring entry document that serves as reference and run it every period and have the same financial effect.

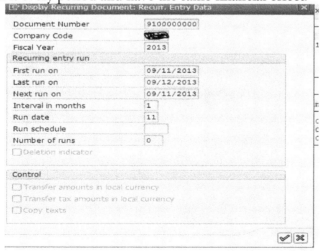

The recurring entry document itself does not update any transactional figures. Only when it is executed through transaction code F.14, it creates postings to the general ledger according parameters defined in the source document. The following data never change in the recurring entry viz., Posting Key, Account, and Line item Amounts. You can create the recurring entry using the transaction FBD1. You can list out all the recurring entries by executing the report RFDAUB00.

- BKDF – Table stores Header information about run dates and frequency of the run

If the BKPF-TCODE = 'FBD1' is the t-code to create a recurring document. The recurring entries can be entered manually using the transaction FBD5. Or you can use F.14 to create more than one recurring entries for given schedule period. You need to provide BATCH session name and you can process the batch session.

2.3.7 Accounting Editing Options

The accounting edition options are user-specific settings for:
- Document Entry
- Document display
- Open Items
- Line Items
- Credit management
- Payment Advice
- Cash Journal

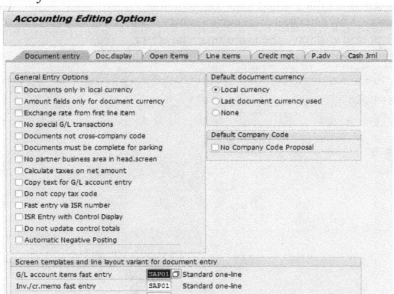

You can access accounting editing options using the transaction code FB00. All editing options are stored in table USR05 with parameter information. For each tab, there are number of user parameters stored in the USR05. For screen one, the following parameters are handled:

- FOP - Financial accounting options
- FO2 - Accounting options / Part2
- FO3 – Accounting user options (Single-screen transactions)
- FZ1 – Fi: Invoice/Credit Memo Fast Entry Line Layout
- FZ2 – FI: G/L Account Items Fast Entry Line Layout
- FZ5 – FI: Document parking Fast Entry
- KME – FI Account Assignment Model: Screen Template Variant
- FBZ - Line Layout variant for posting document – Doc. Overview

Technical Challenges: How to copy a user's accounting options of a user to one or more users.

Solution: You need to write a custom program and direct update to the table USR05. The solution is just proposed only and use with your own discretion. The following sample code provides the base code.

Populate the parameter ids used for the accounting editing options.

```
r_par-sign = 'I'.
r_par-option = 'EQ'.
r_par-low = 'FOP'. append r_par. " Document Entry
r_par-low = 'FO2'. append r_par. " Document Option 2
r_par-low = 'FO3'. append r_par. " Document Option 3
r_par-low = 'FZ1'. append r_par. "
r_par-low = 'FZ2'. append r_par. "
r_par-low = 'FZ5'. append r_par. "
r_par-low = 'KME'. append r_par. "
r_par-low = 'FBZ'. append r_par. "
r_par-low = 'LLD'. append r_par. "
r_par-low = 'LLK'. append r_par. "
r_par-low = 'LLS'. append r_par. "
r_par-low = 'LZV'. append r_par. "
r_par-low = 'LZE'. append r_par. "
r_par-low = 'FKM'. append r_par. "
r_par-low = 'DAV'. append r_par. "
r_par-low = 'KAV'. append r_par. "
r_par-low = 'SAV'. append r_par. "
r_par-low = 'LLV'. append r_par. "
r_par-low = 'FBA'. append r_par. "
```

```
r_par-low = 'ICA'. append r_par. "
r_par-low = 'REF'. append r_par. "
r_par-low = 'FR1'. append r_par. "
r_par-low = 'FR2'. append r_par. "
r_par-low = 'AVE'. append r_par. "
r_par-low = 'AVZ'. append r_par. "
r_par-low = 'FCJ'. append r_par. " Cash Journal option
```

Get the USR05 for the source user with the parameter id list and replace USR05 for the target user.

```
SELECT * INTO it_usr05
  FROM USR05
 WHERE parid in r_par.
```

You can update USR05 of the target users using the value from it_usr05.

```
LOOP AT IT_USR05.
UPDATE USR05 SET PARVA = IT_USR05-PARVA
WHERE BNAME = T_BNAME
    AND PARID = IT_USR05-PARID.
ENDLOOP.
```

The editing options uses most of options are stored in parameters and variants are stored in the ALV program itself. If the variant is user specific then you need to copy the user specific user from one user to another user.

```
** get ALV default layouts:
 ls_variant-report   = 'RFITEMAR'.
 ls_variant-username = lv_usr1.
 call function 'REUSE_ALV_VARIANT_DEFAULT_GET'
  exporting
   i_save      = 'A'
  changing
   cs_variant  = ls_variant
  exceptions
   wrong_input = 1
   not_found   = 2
   program_error = 3
   others      = 4.
```

You can copy the variant information for the target user.

```
select * into table lt_ltdx from ltdx
         where report = 'RFITEMAR'
            and username = sourceuser.
select * into table lt_ltdxt from ltdxt
         where report = 'RFITEMAR'
            and username = sourceuser.
loop at lt_ltdx.
```

```
lt_ltdx-username = targetuser.
  modify ltdx from lt_ltdx..
endloop.
loop at lt_ltdxt.
  lt_ltdxt-username = targetuser.
  modify ltdxt from lt_ltdxt..
endloop.
```

Custom Program to Post Accounting Documents

Most companies have a requirement to upload journal entries from user's local machine or interface from external or legacy systems. In recent years, BAPI_ACC_DOCUMENT_POST is widely used to accomplish this. The following section explains step-by-step the usage of BAPI_ACC_DOCUMENT_POST to efficiently post large volume documents.

Populate account document header

Object type, Company code, fiscal year, posting date (make sure that posting period is open).

```
lv_header-obj_type  = 'ZAA'.
lv_header-obj_key   = ref_key.
lv_header-username  = sy-uname.
lv_header-header_txt = 'BAPI Test'.
lv_header-comp_code = '0001'.
lv_header-fisc_year = '2015'.
lv_header-doc_date  = sy-datum.
lv_header-pstng_date = sy-datum.
lv_header-bus_act   = 'RFBU'.
```

Populating G/L Line items – ensure account assignment objects such as order, cost center etc. are correctly populated.

```
CLEAR lt_item_gl.
  lt_item_gl-itemno_acc  = 2.
  lt_item_gl-gl_account  = '0000400000'.
  lt_item_gl-tax_code    = 'V1'.
  lt_item_gl-item_text= 'BAPI Test G/L line item'.
  Append lt_item_gl.
```

Populating Amounts

Make sure that itemno_acc has proper sequence.

```
CLEAR lt_item_curr.
lt_item_curr-itemno_acc  = 1.
lt_item_curr-curr_type   = '00'.
```

```
lt_item_curr-currency    = 'USD'.
lt_item_curr-amt_doccur  = '100'.
APPEND lt_item_curr.
CLEAR lt_item_curr.
lt_item_curr-itemno_acc  = 2.
lt_item_curr-curr_type   = '00'.
lt_item_curr-currency    = 'USD'.
lt_item_curr-amt_doccur  = '100'.
APPEND lt_item_curr.
```

Populating custom fields in the extension internal table

```
CALL FUNCTION 'BAPI_ACC_DOCUMENT_CHECK'
   EXPORTING
      documentheader= lv_header
   TABLES
      accountgl       = lt_item_gl
      currencyamount = lt_item_curr
      return          = lt_return.
```

Before doing posting, check the accounting document has any validation error.

```
CALL FUNCTION 'BAPI_ACC_DOCUMENT_CHECK'
   EXPORTING
      documentheader= lv_header
   TABLES
      accountgl       = lt_item_gl
      currencyamount = lt_item_curr
      return          = lt_return.
```

```
CALL FUNCTION 'BAPI_ACC_DOCUMENT_POST'
   EXPORTING
      documentheader = lv_header
   IMPORTING
      obj_type     = g_obj_type
      obj_key      = g_obj_key
      obj_sys      = g_obj_sys
   TABLES
      accountgl     = lt_item_gl
      currencyamount = lt_item_curr
      return       = lt_return.
```

Make sure that when document post is successful, commit the work.

```
CALL FUNCTION 'BAPI_TRANSACTION_COMMIT'
   EXPORTING  wait = c_x.
```

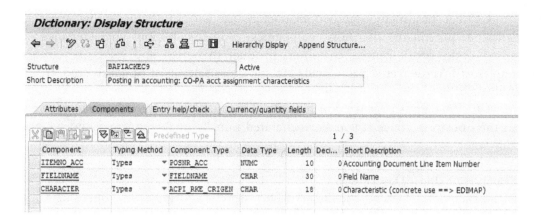

Note that the accounting interface may not populate the characteristics into CO-PA. You can populate the account assignment characteristics BAPIACKEC9 and force to use the characteristics.

2.4 CO-Profitability Analysis

. The CO-Profitability Analysis (CO-PA) is a major application area within the Controlling Application. CO-PA is a powerful tool that enables analysis of profitability at a much more granular level not generally available in other application areas such as the GL or profit center accounting

In CO-PA it is possible to evaluate profitability according to products, customers, even individual orders. CO-PA is based on a foundation of characteristics and value fields which make up the lowest level at which data is captured and stored. Postings in CO-PA are primarily inherited from other areas such as sales and distribution, production or general ledger.

The main organizational unit in CO-PA is an operating concern. An operating concern can have one or more control areas. The operating concern data is stored in the table TKEB. The business object type of operating concern is BUS0017.

2.4.1 Data Structure in CO-PA

The structure of operating concern consists of 'characteristics' and 'value fields'. This is a very important decision that has wide implications in regard to how the profitability can be reported at the level of customer, region, product or a combination of these.

CO-PA has many standard characteristics and value fields that meet the analytical requirements of most companies. Some common characteristics are company code, profit center, customer, product (material) and sales organization. Examples of SAP delivered value fields include gross sales ,cost of goods sold, freight, quantity sold

CO-PA data is organized in 3 levels. These tables are automatically generated when the operating concern is either generated initially or re-generated under certain circumstances.

Structure/Table	Description
CE1xxxx	Actual line items table where xxxx represents operating concern
CE4xxxx	Segment table where segment numbers are assigned to combination of characteristics
CE3xxxx	Segment level table exists between the line item and the segment table
CE2xxxx	Plan line items

2.4.1 Type of profitability analysis

When you define the operating concern you decide the type of profitability analysis viz. costing based or account based. Even though both types of profitability analysis can co-exist it is not common.

Companies that have sales and distribution module implemented tend to have costing based CO-PA where the value fields are posted from pricing conditions of the billing document. This is supplemented by mapping of cost elements in PA transfer structure for postings that happen only in FI. A common issue in costing based PA is that it is not always reconciled with financial accounting.

In account based CO-PA the valuation is determined by cost and revenue elements and hence it is permanently reconciled with financial accounting. In costing based CO-PA you need to complete the mapping of SD conditions to CO-PA value fields in the IMG.

Choose Activity

Activities

Perf	Name of Activity
	Maintain Assignment of SD Conditions to CO-PA Value Fields

2.4.2 Value Flow to CO-PA

The concept of flow of actual values is very important in CO-PA. CO-PA is fed by transactions from SD, MM and FI by way of value field mapping either to pricing conditions or assignment structure. In addition values are posted to CO-PA through internal processes within CO such as cost center assessments or order settlements.

It must be noted that CO-PA generally stores all values as positive and negative values are usually posted by reversals, credit memos and returns.

You have to ensure that SAP recommended cost element categories are used so that values flow correctly into CO-PA. For example, revenues would post to cost element category 11 and sales deductions to cost element category 12.

Data in CO-PA is usually stored only in operating concern currency (currency type B0). This is the global (group currency). It is also possible to store data in company code currency but it is not recommended.

2.4.3 Characteristics

In CO-PA, a combination of characteristics values will form a profitability segment. An example of this is a combination of company code/customer/material/profit center. SAP has pre-delivered a set of standard characteristics such as those listed above.

Characteristic Derivation

Often there is a need to define additional characteristics which in turn would have to be defined based on some business rules. SAP has provided the functionality of Characteristic Derivation that contains flexible derivation strategies.

Derivation Strategy – The derivation strategy has a number of derivation steps which derive the characteristics value from other characteristics. By default, SAP generates system derivation rules for all known dependencies between characteristics. The standard derivation consists:

- Steps to deriving fixed characteristics
- Steps to deriving the characteristics from SAP tables
- Steps for determining UOM of the quantity fields

A derivation step consists of group of targeted fields that can be populated with values derived from a group of source fields. You have to define the 'step type' which identifies whether it is a table look up, move, enhancements or derivation rule.

For example, you have defined a characteristic called vendor. It is possible to derive this characteristic by looking up the source list for that material (product) and always pick up the first vendor in that source list. In this case the step type within derivation strategy would be 'table lookup'. The same result can also be accomplished by implementing custom code within enhancement COPA0001 - EXIT_SAPLKEDRCOPA_001-

Characteristics hierarchy

Characteristics Hierarchy is a logical grouping of individual characteristic values which can be used in reporting. There will be hierarchy nodes and end nodes. The concept is similar to a cost element group or a cost center group used extensively within controlling.

If you have several operating companies it is possible to group the company codes in a hierarchical structure such as North America, Asia, Europe, etc. Hierarchies are particularly useful in drilldown reporting which will be covered elsewhere in this book.

Realignment

Realignment enables you to make organizational changes in the product structure, customer structure or sales structure for data that has been already been posted. You can also use realignment in reporting to represent past data in the most recently assigned organizational change.

The realignment changes the characteristic values of profitability segments. The original characteristic values can be seen only in line item reports.

2.4.4 Valuation

Valuation is a functionality offered in CO-PA as a periodic activity. Two methods of valuation are offered.

➢ Valuation using material cost estimate
➢ Valuation using conditions

If you have cost components in the cost estimate which you need to post into own value fields at the line item level, you would use the valuation method using material cost estimate. In the IMG the point of valuation is defined.

Valuation using conditions is typically used for percentage based calculations such as commissions, discounts that have already been set up in SD price determination

2.4.5 Top Down Distribution

Companies often post some value fields only at a higher level such as company code. An example would be an allowance accrual posted by a journal entry in FI. At the end of the period, the requirement is to make that information available at the customer and product level

In top-down distribution it is possible to 'distribute' that value based on reference data such as gross sales value or quantity that already exist for that period down to a customer and product level. SAP performs the proportional calculations automatically based on the reference data.

Tables:

Table	Description
TKES	CO-PA Basis Field Catalog (fixed fields)
TKEMDM	Table for Jump to CO-PA Master Data Maintenance
TKEF	Characteristics
TKEFE	Field catalog, assignment to operating concern
TKEBB	Management for Operating concerns
TKCHH	SAP-EIS: Hierarchy header
TKCHHT	SAP-EIS: Hierarchy header Text
TKECCU	CO-PA: Conditional Usage of Segment-Level Characteristics

Both characteristics and value fields are stored in the table TKEF. The column USGFL is used to differentiate between characteristics and value fields.

2.4.6 Posting

Generally, CO-PA ledger is populated automatically by business transactions originating in other modules such as SD, MM and FI. For example, the billing documents from SD in addition to posting to the general ledger would also post to CO-PA ledger through the mapping of pricing conditions to value field. Occasionally, there may be a business need to post a transaction directly only to the CO-PA ledger. This may be done in two ways. One method is a completely manual process where you use transaction code KE21N to post a CO-PA transaction and key in details of posting date, company code, characteristics and value fields. The other method is to develop your own custom program that creates these postings.

You can post actual posting using the transaction code KE21N. The actual posting uses the business object type BUS1169 and planning data update uses BUS1167.

This custom program may use a BDC based approach and call the KE21N transaction. You can use the BAPI_COPAACTUALS_POSTCOST_DATA instead of BADI. You can collect data to be posted in a structured manner within your program and pass it to BAPI_COPAACTUALS_POSTCOSTDATA

Important Programs

- COPA_BAPI_TEST - SAP provided a good test the CO-PA BAPIs to read and write CO-PA planning and actual data.
- COPA_COPY – Copying the CO-PA from existing CO-PA data.
- COPA_COPY_PLAN –Copy the CO-PA planning data

BAPI	Description
BAPI_COPAPLANNING_POSTDATA	Write Planning Data for CO-PA
BAPI_COPAACTUALS_POSTCOSTDATA	Write Actual Data for CO-PA
BAPI_COPAPLANNING_GETDATA	Get planning data
BAPI_COPA_DERIVE_GET_DETAIL	Get Derivation rule details
BAPI_COPA_DERIVE_GET_RULES	Get all rules associated to an operating concern
BAPI_COPA_WW_GET_DETAIL	Get characteristics detail for CO-PA
BAPI_COPA_WW_GET_VALUES	Get characteristics values
BAPI_COPA_WW_GET_CHAR	Get characteristics of an operating concern
BAPI_COPA_WW_GET_UDEF_CHAR	Get user defined characteristics of an operating concern

Enhancements:

- **BADI_AUTH_CHECK_KE21** – This BADI allows you to check on the current user profile for a user defined authorization object for the line item entry. You can additional authorization than the standard authorization object K_KEI_TC. It has only one method CHECK_AUTHORIZATION.

- **COPA0001** – You can use this enhancement to enhance the derivation steps. The enhancement has one component EXIT_SAPLKEDRCOPA_001 that provides you operating concern, derivation date, step id, COPA item and global variable. You can return COPA Item, Global, exit active flag and failure flag. Also, you raise the DERIVATION_FAILED exception. You can see some sample code for the enhancement.

* indicate that exit is active for this operating concern

```
E_EXIT_IS_ACTIVE = 'X'.
ITEM = I_COPA_ITEM.
CASE I_STEP_ID.
 WHEN 'RSOP'.
*    find the record which is valid for the derivation date
    SELECT PRGRP MIN( DATUM ) UP TO 1 ROWS
                INTO WORK_AREA
                FROM PGMI
                WHERE NRMIT = ITEM-ARTNR
                 AND WEMIT = ITEM-WERKS
                 AND DATUM >= I_DERIVATION_DATE
                GROUP BY PRGRP.
ENDSELECT.
IF SY-SUBRC = 0.
 ITEM-WWSOP = WORK_AREA-PRGRP.
ELSE.
 E_FAILED = 'X'.
ENDIF.
ENDCASE.
*  return derived item !
E_COPA_ITEM = ITEM.
```

- **COPA0002** – The enhancement enables you to enhance valuation in profitability analysis. The enhancement has four components and explained as below.
    - o EXIT_SAPLKEAB_001 – The user exit for Actual data valuation
    - o EXIT_SAPLKEAB_002 – The user exit for Planned data valuation
    - o EXIT_SAPLKEAB_003 – The user exit for valuation using conditions
    - o EXIT_SAPLKEAB_004 – Flexible assignment costing key

- **COPA0003** – The enhancement gives you greater flexibility in assigning postings to profitability segments. It has EXIT_SAPLKEAK_001 component that allows you to change or determine the characteristics group for manual posting to profitability segments.

- **COPA0004** – You can use this enhancement to modify foreign currency translation in the profitability analysis. The FM EXIT_SAPLKECU_001 is the only one component.

- **COPA0005** – Enhancement allows you to modify the actual data from Sales and Distribution (SD), Financial Accounting (FI) or Material Management (MM) to profitability analysis via FI/CO interface. Use the enhancement with very cautious. The enhancement has two components.
    - o EXIT_SAPLKEII_001 – The exit function is called when you create a line item in CO-PA from FI/CO document.

- o EXIT_SAPLKEII_002 – The exit function is called after the line item has been created in CO-PA.

- **COPA0006** – You can modify the planning data using this enhancement.

- **COPA0007** – This enhancement enables you to modify the transfer of external data to Profitability Analysis. The enhancement has two components.
  - o EXIT_SAPLKEA4_001 – The exit function is called whenever a line item is created from the external file.
  - o EXIT_SAPLKEA4_002 – The exit function is processed after the line item is created.

2.4.7 Reporting

The transaction KE30 is run the profitability analysis reports. The reports are based on the operating concern. The reports are using the operating concern table CE0<operating_concern>.

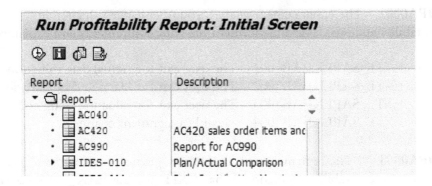

Transaction KE31 is to create CO-PA report. The CO-PA uses the report painter form and painter report.

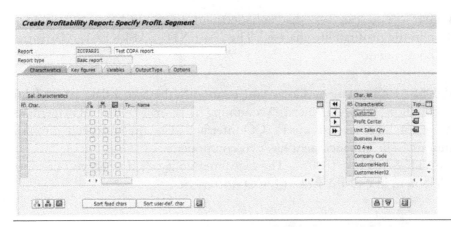

136

2.5 CO-Product Costing- CO-PC

Costing of materials is organized in three components within the Controlling application. They are Product Cost Planning, Cost Object Controlling and Actual Costing/Material ledger. Expert level knowledge of product costing is a valuable skill for both the developer and functional consultant. This component also requires a good understanding of master data in MM and PP. Some companies choose to implement any one or two of the 3 components of Product Cost Controlling

Product Cost Planning involves creation of material cost estimates which provide the detail behind the standard price set for a material. For facilities that do not have manufacturing or assembly activities, only product cost planning is sufficient. That gives them the ability to track and report costs at a more granular level than just the total standard cost a given item.

The next step would be Cost Object Controlling which involve production orders, process orders, WIP calculation, Results analysis, variance calculation and settlement. This is a fairly complex area with a great deal of integration with PP and MM modules.

The third component is Actual Costing/Material ledger. Material ledger provides functionality to manage multiple valuations for inventory. In addition the material ledger collects price and exchange rate differences relating to material movements. At the end of the period, a periodic unit price is calculated and used as basis to revalue inventory.

2.5.1 Product Cost Planning- CO-PC-PCP

Product Cost Planning is an area within the CO-PC component where material costs are planned. The total cost of an item which is frequently referred to as standard price is broken into its components such as base cost, freight, duties, overheads etc. Such a breakdown of standard cost enables analysis of product costs possible.

The main components of product cost planning are:

- Material cost estimate with quantity structure
- Material cost estimate without quantity structure
- Price update

Material cost estimate depends on values being set up correctly in material master, bill of material (BOM) and routing. Some companies use the technique of unit costing to create lower level cost estimates for situations where there is no quantity structure. This is done with transaction code CK74N.

You have to be familiar with the concepts of costing variant, valuation variant and strategy sequence to gain a good understanding of how a standard of price of a material is eventually set in the system.

Most companies execute a Costing Run for costing a large number of items. The costing run is started with transaction code CK40N. It starts with the selection of materials and finishes with the setting of standard price in the material master. At that point a 'released cost estimate' becomes the standard price in material master and can be seen in both accounting 1 and costing2 views in the material master

The screen shot below shows an example of a typical costing run:

Create Cost Estimate

Flow Step	Authorization	Parameter	Execute	Log	Status	Materials	Errs	Still Open
Selection		▷▢▸	⊕		▢	206	0	
Struct. Explosion		▷▢▸						
Costing		▷▢▸	⊕	⚒	▢	206	0	0
Analysis		▷▢▸						
Marking	🔓	▷▢▸	⊕	⚒	⬤	206	1	0
Release		▷▢▸						

An individual material is costed with the CK11N transaction and released as the new standard price in CK24 transaction.

Many companies tend to build their own custom programs that facilitate mass creation of cost estimate. These custom programs may be for creation of unit cost estimates using a BDC based approach. In recent years there is also a trend to use BAPI_COSTESTIMATE_CREATE_SPLIT to create cost estimates. You have to be aware that if this BAPI is used, cost itemization will not be created.

2.5.2 Cost Object Controlling-CO-PC-OBJ

Cost object controlling is applicable where PP module is implemented. The cost object is generally the production order or product cost collector. This area within CO-PC is broadly divided into following components:

Product cost by period – uses product cost collectors and cost object hierarchies

Product cost by order - uses manufacturing order or a sales order. In this case the cost object is the production order or the sales order item.

Cost object controlling enables analysis of costs at a more detailed level. It is possible to perform analysis of costs in different ways viz. planned vs actual costs and target vs actual costs at the level of each cost component

At the end of the period, it is required to calculate variances and settle variances to accounting. In some cases, work in progress calculation (WIP) is carried out on unfinished orders and subsequently settlement process posts an accounting document that moves the value of WIP to a pre-defined balance sheet account.

The table below lists some key programs related to cost object controlling.

Program name	Description	Related transaction code
RKAZCO43	Overhead Calculation	CO-43 Collective processing of overheads
SAPKKA07	WIP Calculation	KKAO- Collective processing of WIP
RKKS1N0	Variance calculation	KKS1- Collective processing variance calculation
RKO7CO88	Settlement	CO88- Collective processing settlement
RKKRCO00	CO Summarization	KKRC – Summarization

2.5.3 Technical Details

Tables:

Table	Comments
KALA	Costing Run: General Data/Parameters
KALD	Costing Run: Low-Level Codes
KALV	Costing Run: Costing variants
KALS	Costing Run: Costing Levels
KALF	Costing Run: Error Log Header
KALSTAT	Costing Run: Statistical Info for Separate Steps
KEKO	Product Costing - Header Data
KEPH	Product costing – item cost componet
KNKO	Assignment of cost est. number to config object
KNOB	Assignment of Cost Est. Number to Config. Object
CKHS	Header: Unit costing (Control + Totals)

CKIP	Unit Costing: Period Costs Line Item
CKIS	Items Unit Costing/Itemization Product Costing
CKCM	Costing Model
KALAMATCON2	Selection List for Costing Run – Material List

2.5.4 Enhancements

- CK_KALAMATCON2_CI – BADI for CI fields for table KALAMATCON2.
- **DATA_EXTENSION_CK** – This BADI enables you to move additional data from non-standard data to the product costing database. The additional data can be used to influence the product costing process or downstream business processes. You can extend the product costing header data table KEKO using the custom include CI_KEKO. Using this BADI, you can populate the extended custom fields. You cannot modify the header data in this BADI.

- **DYNPRO_EXTENSION_CK** – This BADI is for interface enhancement in costing
- **SUR_STOCK_TRANSF_CK** – Overhead on Materials with stock transfer between plants
- **SAPLXCKA** – You can use this SMOD enhancement to define and implement your own reports to display itemization or cost components for cost estimates with quantity structure. The enhancement supports 3 components as follows:
    - EXIT_SAPLCKAZ_001 –Display/print itemization. The example report is defined in the include ZXCKAU01. You can modify or activate example program code
    - EXIT_SAPLCKAZ_002 – Cost components report. The example report is defined in the include ZXCKAU02. You can modify report per requirements.
    - EXIT_SAPLCKAZ_003 – can be implemented to display and print itemization and cost component include ZXCKAU03. No sample program code has been provided.

2.6 Special Purpose Ledger

The special purpose ledger is a user-defined ledger for reporting purposes. Account assignment objects in special purpose ledger can be standard SAP dimensions such as cost center, profit center or user-defined dimensions derived based on your own business rules.

Note that the special purpose ledger functions only as recipient of data from other SAP components. It is also possible to load data directly into special purpose ledger from an external system though such usage is not common.

Some key features of special purpose ledger are listed below:

- Flexible data structure with the ability to combine standard and non-standard dimensions
- Selective population of data
- Alternative fiscal year
- Parallel accounting with different ledgers
- Controlled data capture into special ledgers using validation and substitution
- Flexible management of detailed line items from other applications
- Allocations and Roll Ups

2.6.1 Special Purpose Ledger – Practical Applications

You tend to see usage of special purpose ledger in situations where companies have complex reporting needs involving dimensions that are not directly mapped to standard SAP organization units such as profit center, sales organization, cost center etc. These non-standard dimensions could be sales territory or line of business which may be determined based on a combination of standard SAP dimensions. In such situations custom fields were created in special purpose ledger to meet that requirement.

Your company has overseas subsidiaries that need to prepare financial statements for a different fiscal year. The parent company may follow a January-December year whereas a subsidiary in Asia may need report for April-March fiscal year to meet their statutory reporting obligations locally.

Since the introduction of New General Ledger functionality, experts have held the view that many of the features of special purpose ledger are now available in new general ledger. However many mature SAP implementations especially those classic GL continue to rely heavily on special purpose ledger.

2.6.2 Database Tables

In special purpose ledger, database tables are created in the form of a table group.

- **Object tables** – The object tables are for receiver/sender and transaction attributes. Each object table has fixed and variable dimensions. Fixed dimensions are pre-defined and you cannot them. The variable dimensions are the key dimensions of the coding block. The object receiver/sender supports 15 variable dimensions including the local company code and global company. Two of the dimensions are reserved for SAP's internal use which leaves 13 variable dimensions available for customer definition. You can use the variable dimensions of the object 1 table in the summary table. The object table 2 is transaction attributes and it supports 15 variable dimensions. The table does not have any a sender and receiver relationship with the dimensions. The receiver object number is referred by the column ROBJNR and SOBJNR refers to the sender object number. Note that Object (receiver) dimensions must begin with R, and partner (sender) dimensions, must begin with S.

- **Summary tables** – The summary table contains summarized transaction data across documents for business transactions that enter the FI-SL System. The data is summarized for each period. The summary table has fixed and variable dimensions.

Summary table structure

  - **Fixed dimensions** – You cannot change fixed dimensions like client, ledger, record type, version, fiscal year, object numbers, quantity and maximum period.
  - **Variable dimensions** – The variable dimensions must be part of the object table 1 and 2.
  - **Derived fields** – Derived fields are those fields that you do not want to include as key fields, but that you want to include in the data part of the database table (for example, Controlling Area (KOKRS) that is derived from the company code). Derived fields can only be used for reporting purposes; you cannot use derived fields in allocations or in other FI-SL functions.
- **Actual line item tables** – It stores the actual line items. The actual line item can be used in drill down reporting and rollup values. The actual line item table has the fixed, variable, derived and additional dimensions. The variable dimensions are part of the summary table. The additional fields are optional fields that you can define the additional information for a document.
- Plan line item tables – It stores the plan line items.

Table group is to define database tables and store them in the ABAP dictionary. A table group is a group of interdependent tables defined above. You can access table group using the transaction code GCIN.

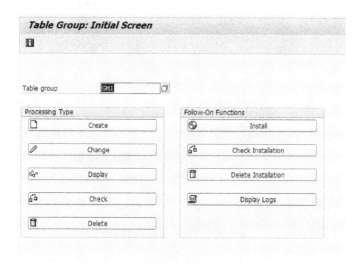

The following screenshot is for displaying GMI table group.

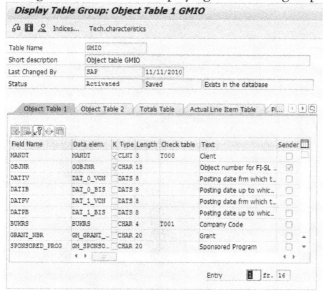

2.6.3 Activity and Field Movement

Through a combination of activity and field movements, the data entered in other SAP application areas is transferred to special purpose ledger. You can access this IMG menu or transaction code GCV3.

Note that once a ledger is defined, the company code is assigned to the ledger and the activities are assigned to the ledger. It is useful to remember that receiver table depends on the ledger and sender tables depend on the activity. You will see below an illustration of how the sender table and receiver table are connected through the definition of activity and field movement.

Display Activity: Master Data

Transaction	RFBU	Text	FI Postings
Acty Grouping Code	FI00	☐ Write line items	

Sender tables

ACCHD	Interface to Accounting: Header Information
ACCIT_GLX	FI: Interface to Accounting: Item Information
ACCCR	Accounting Interface: Currency Information

Activity type and record type

Activity type	1 ☐ sting to G/L transaction figures compulsory
Record Type	0 Actual

Currencies
- ☑ Activty wth grp cum.
- ☑ Second currency
- ☑ Store third currency
- ☑ Transaction currency

Quantities
- ☑ Store quantities
- ☑ Store add.quantity

Additional settings
- ☐ Post in period 0
- ☐ Activity blocked
- ☐ Doc.line req. in SL
- ☐ Post rollup ledger

Field movement	FIG0	Movements from FI-GLX to global ledgers		
Receiver Table	GLT2	Consolidation totals table		
Sender table	ACCHD	ACCIT_GLX	ACCCR	
Usage	Direct posting from FI, AM, MM, SD			

Receiver field	Description	Sender table	Sender field	Description	Exi	Editc
KOKRS		ACCIT_GLX	KOKRS	Controlling Area		
RACCT	Account Number	ACCIT_GLX	HKONT	G/L Account		
RASSC	Trading Partner	ACCIT_GLX	VBUND	Trading Partner		
RBUSA	Business Area	ACCIT_GLX	GSBER	Business Area		
RCNTR		ACCIT_GLX	KOSTL	Cost Center		
RMVCT	Transaction Type	ACCIT_GLX	RMVCT	Transaction Type		
SBUSA	Trading Part.BA	ACCIT_GLX	PARGB	Trading Part.BA		
UMSKZ		ACCIT_GLX	UMSKZ	Special G/L ind.		

2.6.4 Actual Posting

Actual postings in special purpose ledger happen in one of 3 ways:

- From other SAP application components such as FI, MM and SD
- Direct input into FI-SL – with t-code GB0
- From external systems

Data Transfer Program

There is a sample program RGUREC00 that loads data from an external source to the FI-SL system. The program reads data from a sequential file and transfer data to the user defined special ledger. You can copy the program and modify based on your requirements.

- The program RGUREC10 is to transfer data from FI to FI-SL. Transaction code is GCU1.
- Use transfer program RGUREC20 CO actual data to transfer data from Controlling. (GCU3)
- Use transfer program RGUREC30 MM to transfer data from Materials Management. (GCU4)
- Use transfer program RGUREC40 to transfer the opening balance of statistical key figures from CO into FI-SL. (GSTA)
- Use transfer program RKEPCU40 SD actual data to transfer data from Sales and Distribution. (GCU5).

With program RGUDEL00 (t-code GCDE) you can delete all transaction data from FI-SL ledger. These programs are usually used only in special cases such as during production start-up.

Enhancement

FI_SL_BADI_RGUREC10 – This BADI is triggered while transferring the accounting document to FI-SL data in the transfer program RGUREC10. You have access to data from BKPF and BSEG in table IT_ACCHD and CT_ACCIT. The BADI has only one method PROCESS_SUBSTITUTION. You can enhance the line item data by the table parameter CT_ACCIT.

2.6.5 Period-End Activities

Period end activities are critical in FI and CO modules as they contribute to accurate and timely statutory and management reporting. This section will go over common period end transaction, programs and report. There are only a few additional steps performed only at year end such as carry forward of balances, closing of fixed assets. For this reason, month-end and year end activities will be covered together in this section. The transactions/programs mentioned in this section are only intended to be indicative list of some common month-end processes.

As mentioned earlier in this chapter, the concept of fiscal year variant and fiscal periods is critical not only in FICO but also in other modules. If your company operates on a non-calendar fiscal periods, you would have to adjust your period-closing activities accordingly.

2.6.6 List of Useful Programs/Transactions

The list of transactions/programs in the table below is intended to be a quick reference. It is not in any particular sequence. Many period end activities need not be in a sequential order, although the opening and closing of MM, CO and FI periods is usually the starting point of all period end activities.

In this table some activities are listed as period closing related even though it may be scheduled in more frequent intervals such as weekly or even daily. This is because the system considers the activity for the entire period and posts the resulting document with the posting date of last date of fiscal period.

Transaction	Description	Program	Remarks
MMPV	Close Period for material master	RMMMPERI	
OB52	Posting periods (FI) –Specify time intervals		
OB08	Currency exchange rates		
OKP1	Change Period Lock (CO Period)		
AFAB	Depreciation Run	RAPOST2000	
CO43	Overhead calculation	RKAZCO43	
KKS1	Variance calculation	RKKKS1N0	
KKAO	Work in Progress calculation	SAPKKA07/ SAPKKA07BG	
CO88	Actual settlement – manufacturing/ process orders	RK07CO88	
KO8G	Actual settlement -Orders	RKO7KO8G	
KSV5	Cost center distribution		
KSU5	Cost center allocation		
KALC	Reconcile CO with FI		Not applicatble if new GL is implemented
KEU5	CO-PA Assessment		
KE27	CO-PA Periodic valuation		
KE28	CO-PA Top down distribution		
3KE5	Profit center assessment		
4KE5	Profit center distribution		

F.05	Foreign currency valuation	SAPF100	Classic GL
F.13	Automatic Clearing	SAPF124	Used for GRIR, Cash clearing accounts
FAGL_FC_VAL	Foreign currency valuation New GL	FAGL_FCV	
F.16	Carry forward GL balances	SAPFGVTR	Year end
F.07	Carry forward Receivables/Payables	SAPF010	Year end
GVTR	Balance carry forward special purpose ledger	SAPFGVTR	Year end
F.03	Financial accounting analysis	SAPF190	
AJRW	Asset fiscal year change	RAJAWE00	Year end
AJAB	Year end closing asset accounting	RAJABS00	Year end

In addition to executing standard SAP programs or transactions, many companies have their own desk procedures that contain several custom reports that form part of their month end closing processes. It is also likely that data in summarized form is sent at the end of each period to other SAP or non-SAP systems such as BPC and Hyperion. The key point to note is that period closing is a collection of update transactions, standard and non-standard reports and in many cases even interfaces to and from other systems.

2.6.7 Period End Reports

There are several reports that provide information relating to period end activities. A representative list of only standard reports is provided here just to give an idea of how users in finance area look at data during month end. Most of the reports listed here can be run any time during the month. However they could be more meaningful if they are reviewed as detailed information that support period end balances in both the general ledger and sub-ledgers such as AR, AP, GL and even inventory ledger.

Transaction	Description	Program	Area	Remarks
F.01	Financial statements	RFBILA00	GL	Output varies based on FS version definition
F.01	Financial statement	RFBILA00	GL	Trial balance by choosing Structured balance list

				option
S_ALR_8701 2394	Record of Use and Sales Tax (USA)	RFUTAX00	GL	
S_ALR_8701 2357	Advance Return for tax on Sales and purchases	RFUMSV00	GL AR/ AP	
S_ALR_8701 2277	GL account balances	RFSSLD00	GL	
S_P00_0700 0134	Generic Withholding Tax Reporting	RFIDYYWT	AP	
S_ALR_8701 2082	Vendor balances in local currency	RFKSLD00	AP	
S_ALR_8701 2172	Customer balances in local currency	RFDSLD00	AR	
S_ALR_8701 1963	Asset balances by asset number	RABEST_AL V01	FA	
S_ALR_8701 2018	Depreciation and interest with cost center	RAKAFA_AL V01	FA	
S_ALR_8701 0175	Posted depreciation by cost center		FA	
S_ALR_8701 2039	Asset transactions	RABEWG_AL V01	FA	
MB5L	List of stock values:balances	RM07MBST	logist ics	
S_ALR_8701 3611	Cost centers:Actual/Plan		CO-CCA	
S_ALR_8701 3611	Cost Centers: Actual/Target		CO-CCA	
S_ALR_8701 3127	Order Selection-totals by period		CO-PC	
KKBC_HOE	Order Summarization Target/Actual comparison		CO-PC	
S_ALR_8701 3603	CO/FI reconciliation in Company code currency		CO-CEL	

2.7 Reporting Tools

SAP has provided some very useful reporting tools such as report writer, report painter and ABAP queries. A functional consultant and a power user with an intermediate level knowledge can leverage these tools to develop even complex reports.

2.7.1 ABAP Queries

If you have a basic understanding of some key tables in SAP it is easy to create an ABAP Query. The query uses an Infoset within which table joins are defined. The results of a query are presented in an ALV list and can easily be downloaded. If you have expert level knowledge you can write some code within the infoset. Simple reporting needs are often met with ABAP queries.

Transaction	Description
SQ01	Maintaining queries
SQ02	Maintaining info sets
SQ03	Maintaining user groups
SQ07	Language comparison
SQVI	SQL Query quick viewer

Technical Challenges: Need to associate a SQL query to a custom transaction.
Solutions: Follow the steps:
- Create a transaction a transaction with parameters transaction using transaction code SE93.
- Enter START_REPORT in the transaction code
- Check the skip initial screen checkbox
- Enter the following values in the Default values (table control) at the end of screen
   - D_SREPOVARI-REPORTTYPE = AQ
   - D_SREPOVARI-REPORT = <User group>
   - D_SREPOVARI-EXTDREPORT = <Query Name>

2.7.2 Report Painter

Report painter is a powerful tool heavily used in especially within Controlling. Profit center accounting and cost center accounting are two major areas where report painter reports are used extensively. SAP has provided libraries, row/column models and standard layouts.

SAP encourages the use of report painter as it already incorporates most of the functions available in a report writer. In report painter, the graphical user interface helps in quick definition of the report layout. It is also possible to use sets that combine characteristics such as company codes, cost centers and GL accounts. Report painter reports lend themselves to easy formatting for amounts, usage of different colors, calculated rows and columns, amount formatting, expand and collapsing of characteristics. Below is an example of a report painter report with standard layout. In addition several reports can be grouped together and executed as a report group. In some cases a receiver report can be defined so one can transition seamlessly from totals level to line item level if required.

```
Report           1STD-001    Actual/Plan/Prev.Yr
Section           0001
Standard layout   1-BTC2


Format group:            0            0            0            0

Cost Elements         Actual, Per. 1 - & Plan, Per. 1 - &1P   Variance    Prev. Year, Per. 1 .

* Total               XXX,XXX,XXX.XX   XXX,XXX,XXX.XX   XXX,XXX,XXX.XX   XXX,XXX,XXX.XX
```

Transaction codes

Transaction	Description
GRR1, GRR2, GRR3	Create, Change and Display report
GR51, GR52, GR53	Create, Change and display report group
GR55	Execute report group

Use the function module GRW_JOB_SUBMIT_PREPARE to get the ABAP report program name for given report group. You can use the program RGRWSUBMIT to execute the report writer report. This is applicable for both report painter and report writer reports.

2.7.3 FI Sets

Sets are used in many components and subcomponents of the SAP R/3 System such as reporting, and planning. The sets are

- **Basic sets** – The set contains a specific value such as account number and cost center number

- **Key figure sets** – It contains specific basic key figures. You can combine a basic key figure with one or more dimension to create your own key figures.
- **Single dimension sets** – The set is used to set hierarchies by combining basic sets and other single-dimension sets that use the same dimension. You can

combine the basic sets ASSETS and LIABILITIES because they use the same dimension - "Account".

- **Multiple dimension sets** – The sets are used to create set hierarchies with sets that use different dimensions. You can create a multi-dimension set (called CC-ACCT) that contains the basic set CENTERS (dimension Cost Center) and the basic set OHD-ACCT (dimension Account). This multi-dimension set contains cost centers 100, 200, 300, and 400, and accounts 3000010, 3000020, and 3000030 (see the following graphic).

The sets are used in special ledger components like Boolean logic, Report writer, Allocations, Planning, Rollups and currency translation. You can create a set using the transaction code GS01. The sets can be transported between the system and clients. Within the set, you can use formulas to perform calculations.

Technical Details

Transactions

Transaction	Description
GS01, GS02, GS03	Create, Change and Display set

Tables

Table	Description
SETHEADER	Set Header and directory header information
SETLEAF	Values in the Set
SETNODE	Lower-level sets in set
T802G	Variables information
T802GU_SET	Variables used in the set
T802GU_VAR	Variables used in formula variables
T804B	Report writer: key figures

The following code provides how to convert the values in basic set into a range and use it in your selection.

```
DATA: lv_setid LIKE sethier-setid,
      it_vlaues TYPE STANDARD TABLE OF rgsbv.

CALL FUNCTION 'G_SET_GET_ID_FROM_NAME'
  EXPORTING
   shortname = p_setname      "Set Name
  IMPORTING
   new_setid = lv_setid
  EXCEPTIONS
   OTHERS   = 1.
```

```
IF sy-subrc NE 0.
  WRITE 'Invalid Set'.
ENDIF.

CALL FUNCTION 'G_SET_FETCH'
  EXPORTING
   setnr        = lv_setid
  TABLES
   set_lines_basic = it_vlaues
  EXCEPTIONS
   OTHERS       = 1.
```

Important Reports:

Reports	Description
RGUSI100	The report is used to find values in Sets.
RGSSTE00	The report is used to export the sets to a presentation server file.
RGSSTI00	The report is used to import the sets from a presentation server file.

The variable is supported by report writer and report painter. There are three types of variables viz., value, formula and set variable. The following enhancement used in the set and formula variable.

G_SET_FORMULA_EXIT – You can use this BADI to enhance for set formula variable. This is single use and filter based BADI. The filter value is based on the SET_EXIT domain. The filter value is based on the table SETEXITS. The BADI has two methods GET_TYPE and EVALUATE. The EX_VALUE of EVALUATE method returns the value. The method GET_TYPE returns the data type of formula variable.

2.7.4 Drilldown Reporting

Drilldown reporting is a dialog-oriented reporting system and it is capable of analyzing a dataset according to all defined characteristics. You can categorize any key figures in the analysis. This is primarily developed based on the special ledger G/L accounting key figures. It can generate both simple report (lists) and complex formatted list (using form reports).

Report	Description
▾ 🗀 Report type	
▸ 🗀 001	Financial Statement Analysis
▸ 🗀 002	Financial Statement Key Figure
▸ 🗀 003	Balance display
▾ 🗀 004	Financial statements analysis frc
· 📇 0SAPBLNCE-01	Actual/actual comparison for ye
▾ 🗀 005	Key figures for cost of sales led
· 📇 0GB-BLNCE-01	Balance - UK
· 📇 0GB-RESUL-01	Profit and loss - UK
· 📇 0JP-BAJP-01M	Japan BSPL + product cost att
· 📇 0KR-BAKR-PL	KR: P&L Sheet
· 📇 0SAPBLNCE-01	Balance using C/S (German Tra
· 📇 0SAPPRALO-01	Annual P+L statement (Germai
· 📇 0KR-MFT-SHT	KR: Cost of goods

The drill down reporting has two components viz., Forms and Reports. The Form is a report painter form and it is created using the basic characteristics and key figures. You can define the reports on the form with drill down options. Each report is generated into an ABAP program and it will be executed when you execute the report. SAP provides a separate set of the drilldown reporting transactions for Accounting, Vendor and Customer line items.

In this section, the accounting drilldown reports are discussed. The supplier and customer drilldown reporting are discussed in the Chapter 3 and 4 respectively.

There is a separate set of drilldown reporting transactions for the accounting drilldown reports. You can create the report writer form and report using these transactions.

Transaction	Description
FSI0	Account drill down reports
FSI1, FSI2, FIS3	Create, Change and Display a new report
FSI4, FSI5, FSI6	Create, Change and Display a Form

The accounting drilldown reporting allows you to create form and report under the following types:
- Financial Statement Analysis
- Financial Statement Key Figures
- Balance Display
- Financial Statement analysis from cost of sales ledger
- Key figures for cost of sales ledger

SAP supports the drill-down reports for Profit Center Accounting. You can access the PCA drill-down reports by the following transaction codes.

Transaction	Description
KE80	PCA drill down reports
KE81, KE82, KE83	Create, Change and Display a new report
KE84, KE85, KE86	Create, Change and Display a Form

2.7.5 Financial Statement Versions

SAP uses the functionality of financial statement version (FS Version) is used to represent a legal entity's profit and loss and balance sheet. The configuration of FS version is intuitive and is done in transaction OB58. The information is stored in the table T011.

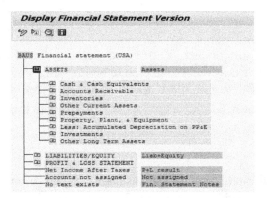

After GL accounts are assigned to financial statement item and FS version configuration is complete, you execute t-code F.01 to run the profit and loss account and balance sheet report. The main program that generates FS version is RFBILA00. This program reads totals data from GL summary table and output the report for the currency type selected. The report uses the logical database SDF.

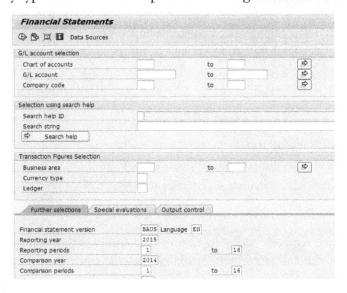

Many finance users rely on this report to view a formal profit and loss account, and balance sheet. There is also an option to run the report to output a simple trial balance list by selecting the structured balance list' checkbox.

In many companies, multiple FS versions are configured with one global FS version that is usually run with group currency and other FS versions used for foreign subsidiaries.

You can define multiple FS versions where account codes are grouped differently based on requirements. Some key aspects of FS version are as follows:

- Maintenance language to be specified

- Tied to only one chart of accounts

- Select whether group account numbers are to be used instead of the account number

- Can be run for multiple company codes so long as a common currency type is chosen

- Alternative account number can be displayed if country chart of accounts

- Output can list only financial statement items or list individual GL accounts

- Values can be shown as is or on scaled values such as in thousands or millions

- Business area level statements can be generated

- Unassigned accounts are listed separately at the end of the report

You can create financial statement version for the special purpose ledger using the report writer reports. You can generate the financial statement versions on a SAP Script form. SAP delivered two standard SAP scripts F_BILLA_ONE_L01 (for one column) and F_BILLA_TWO_L01 (for two columns) report form. You can copy these form and implement your changes.

In summary, the FS version is a simple yet powerful tool that provides several choices to the user to generate financial statements by company code, business area, by currency type.

Some important Standard reports

- RFEPOJ00 – Line item journal report (transaction code S_ALR_87009828)

- RFVBER00 – Analyze the FI update error posting and lists update termination.

2.8 Workflow

SAP delivered a multiple of FI workflow objects. The commonly used workflows are release of parked document, payment release and CO-PA planning data edit.

2.8.1 Configuration

There are few workflow configurations which are common to parked document and payment release.

Workflow Variant

The workflow variant determines whether document release is required and the amount limit after which document release is required. The workflow variant configuration is definition of release for both parking document and payment.

You can activate/deactivate the release of the parking and payment release workflow. The workflow variant defines minimum amount for release and sub-workflow to be used for the account assignment release. You can access this configuration by the transaction code OBWA and IMG menu path is Financial Accounting->Accounts Receivable and Accounts Payable->Business Transactions->Release for Payment->Create Workflow variant.

Both release workflows are handled at company code level. The defined workflow variant must be assigned to the company code. You can execute this step by transaction code OBWJ. If the workflow variant is not assigned to a company code, then there is no workflow for parking document or payment release.

Release Approval Groups

The approval group is high level definition of the approval group and it will be assigned to vendor and customers. Subsequently, when an FI document is created against the vendor / customer, the system copies the release group will be determined and release procedure based on configuration for the release group.

Release Approval Path

The release approval path is higher level definition to combine FI document types with release group and workflow variant. Based on this path allocation, you can identify approval procedures.

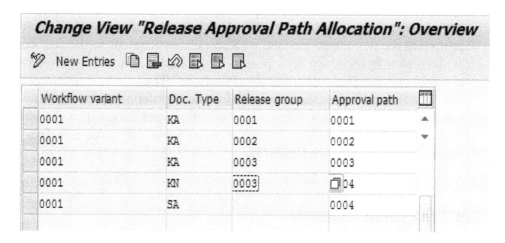

Release Approval Procedures

The release approval procedure determines the sub-workflow to be used for amount release using a combination of workflow variant, release approval path and amount. One of the three standard sub-workflows for amount release or a custom workflow could be assigned in this configuration step.

Wrkf	APth	Amount to	Crcy	Rel.levels	Swf amnt rel.	SWf pmnt rel.	
0001	0001	1,000.00	EUR	1	WS10000052		▲
0001	0001	50,000.00	EUR	2	WS10000052		▼

2.8.2 Parked Document Release

SAP provided a standard workflow for release of parked document. It supports two types of release. The main BOR object of this workflow is FIPP.

- **Amount release** – Amount release is triggered when the document is first parked. The standard system provides three different sub-workflows for amount release - WS10000052, WS10000053 and WS10000054 respectively for one, two and three levels of approval for the document. You can define your own custom sub-workflow and assign it in the configuration settings as explained below. One point to note though is that the custom sub-workflows should have the same interface as the standard interfaces.

- **Account assignment release** – Account assignment release is triggered when the document is completed. The account assignment approval is valid for all organizational objects such as position, job, and organizational unit that are assigned to the release step. You can assign persons responsible for cost centers in Organizational Management (HR) – then, the person responsible must approve all the documents created with account assignment to the cost center. If the document is approved, it is posted in the background. If it is rejected, it is sent back to the clerk to make modifications. The account assignment sub-workflow is specified in the configuration step to define the workflow variant. You can define your own custom sub workflow and assign it in the workflow variant, but the custom sub workflow must have the same interface as the standard sub workflow WS10000055.

2.8.3 Payment Release

The payment release workflow enables you to validate of individual line items and release for payment. The payment release follows the configuration explained in the configuration section. SAP delivers multiple workflow models for payment release. The main workflow framework is WS00400012 and it has three sub workflows (WS00400011, WS00400021 and WS00400022). The payment release workflow is triggered by the event CREATED of the BSEG.

2.8.4 CO-PA Planning Data

This workflow enables you to enter the planning data during sales and profit planning a planning set. It allows multiple planners can enter the planning data. The workflow uses the business object type BUS1166. SAP provides the workflow template WS020000377.

2.8.5 Enhancements

- **SAPLF051** - SAP provides a SMOD enhancement SAPLF051 for payment release and it has the following components:

  - EXIT_SAPLF051_001 – The user exit is allowed you to decide whether you can payment release WF carried out or not. The workflow can be disabled by raising NOT_RELEVANT exception. The user exit can determine this using the parameters document amount, workflow variant and document type. You can implement the same using the BTE event 2221. The user exit is triggered in the function module PR_WF_CHECK_RELEVANT.
  - EXIT_SAPLF051_002 – The user exit is check release of the parked document. User exit to raise NOT_RELEVANT exception based on document header (BKPF), Accounting line items (BSEG), Tax information (BSET) and one time account data (BSEC). You can implement same with BTE event 2213. The user exit is triggered in the function module PP_WF_CREATED.
  - EXIT_SAPLF051_003 – User exit to raise NOT_RELEVANT exception based on the document header, new and old accounting line items (XVBSEG, YVBSEG). You can decide to carry out whether CHANGED event of the parked document object type FIPP. You can implement same with BTE event 2214. The user exit is triggered in the FM PR_WF_CHECK_RELEVANT.

- **BTE 2213** – You can use this P/S BTE to decide whether a release for document parking document should b carried out or not. This is part of the function module PP_WF_CREATED.

- **BTE 2214** – The BTE is similar to the user exit EXIT_SAPLF051_003. You can decide whether the event CHANGED should be triggered for the parked document object type FIPP. This BTE is part of the function module PR_WF_CHECK_RELEVANT.

- **BTE 2216** – This BTE P/S event allows to you to decide whether you can raise DELETED event for the object type FIPP.

- **BTE 2221** – This BTE P/S event allows you to decide whether payment release should be carried or not. This is similar like the user exit EXIT_SAPLF051_001. The BTE is part of the function module PR_WF_CHECK_RELEVANT.

2.9 SAP Business Warehouse

Many companies have a data warehouse in some form. SAP's Business Warehouse product is a powerful tool that is highly integrated with other applications. A working knowledge of BW is very beneficial to both the developer and a functional analyst.

An end user would typically run several reports in SAP BW through the BEx Analyzer which is embedded in Microsoft Excel. The general practice is to create roles that align with the users's job function and create workbooks that user can launch in excel to analyze data based on flexible selection criteria

BW content is discussed in this section because it relates to reporting in general across all areas in FICO. The NetWeaver platform contains the SAP Business Warehouse (BW). SAP has delivered find pre-configured objects such as ata sources, process chains, infosources, infoproviders, roles, workbooks and queries. Collectively these are referred as BI Content. This section is restricted to listing of standard Infocubes that contain data in the FI area. SAP also delivers standard BW queries based on these infocubes.

You can easily create your own custom queries based on these Infocubes. Some of the main Infocubes are listed in the following paragraphs for your benefit.

Data Source	Description
0FIGL_C10	New GL transaction figures
0FIGL_C01	Classic GL transaction figures
0FIAR_C03	Accounts Receivable: Line items
FI_AR_C05	Accounts Receivable: Payment history
0FI_AR_C02	Accounts Receivable: Transaction figures
0FIAP_C03	Accounts Payable: Line items
0FIAP_C02 -	Accounts Payable: Transaction data
0FIAA_C02	Assets annual values
0FIAA_C03	Asset transactions
0PCA_C01	Profit center transaction data
0CCA_C11	Cost Center costs and quantities
0OPA_C11	Overhead Internal orders

0COPC_C08	Product Cost Planning cost estimates
0PC_C01	Cost object controlling transaction data
0COPA_C01	CO-PA data

2.10 Summary

In this chapter you have learnt both the functional and technical aspects of SAP components that collectively make up the 'record to report' process.

Here is a recap of topics covered in this chapter:

- Organizational units such as company code, fiscal year, business area, profit center- useful function modules and BAPIs relating to org. units.
- Useful tables, BAPIs and t-codes pertaining to cost element accounting, cost center accounting, internal order, product costing and CO-PA
- Enhancements/user exits in CO-CCA, CO-OM, CO-PA, CO-PC
- Useful tables, t-codes in FI-General ledger and FI-Special purpose ledger
- Function Modules, BAdIs and BTEs in FI-GL
- Concept of New GL
- Integration aspects – GL with logistics components
- Integration aspects – Product Costing with logistics components
- Custom development comprising RICEF objects.
- Reporting tools such as Report Painter, ABAP Query

3 Procure to Pay

The set of business processes that start from procurement of resources of an enterprise in the form of goods and services ends with payment to the suppliers is broadly referred to as Procure To Pay process. You are likely to see SAP teams organized in this manner in many companies.

In addition to covering aspects of procure to pay process, this chapter will also touch on a variety of logistics topics including material master, inventory movements, organizational units in logistics that eventually impact financial postings.

The accounts payable component of FI is tightly integrated with logistics invoice verification. The vendor payment process including sending payment files to the bank or remittance details to suppliers occurs at the end of the procurement chain. Within accounts payable, this section will cover invoice entry, down payments, taxes, GR IR process, payment program and basic reports.

In this chapter, you will be given a brief overview of the key elements of master data and transactions that are generally considered part of 'procure to pay' process. Practical examples of custom development are provided throughout the chapter relating to both master data and transactions.

In addition, we will touch on integration aspects of procure to pay process with reference to material master, costing, general ledger, production planning, banking etc.

At the end of this chapter, you will have a gained a basic understanding of key master data, transactions within the P2P process. In addition you will be able to quickly identify appropriate enhancements such as user exits, BAdIs or BTEs to fulfill non-standard requirements in your SAP environment.

The diagram below illustrates the generic procure to pay process.

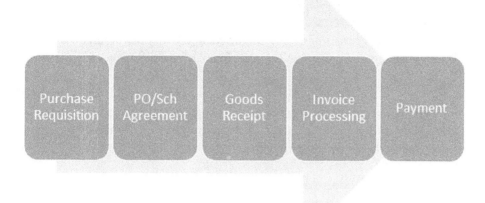

3.1 Master Data

The following are some important organizational units relevant to procure to pay process. They are repeated in this section even though it may be mentioned in elsewhere in this book.

Purchasing Organization (P.Org) drives all purchasing related actions in an enterprise. Typically the purchasing org is assigned to one or more company codes. Vendor master records need to be created for a purchasing organization. Purchasing Info Record and pricing conditions are set up for a POrg. The purchasing groups are an important sub-unit within P.Org. Most companies set up their buyers as purchasing groups. The manner in which the P.Org is defined and assigned to other organizational units determines the transaction flow.

Plant is a key organization unit in the logistics area of SAP. Production, procurement, maintenance and planning are performed at the level of the plant. The valuation of materials is also at the plant level. When purchase orders are created, the plant is at the line item.

Store location represents a physical location within a plant. In some cases the storage location may also represent an external location associated to the plant. In a storage location, stocks are managed on a quantity basis with valuation happening at the plant level. It is usual for storage locations to mirror the business process such as receiving, shipping, etc.

3.1.1 Vendor Master

The vendor master record is an important part of procure to pay process. It contains data relevant to both accounting as well as procurement groups within an organization. In many companies, the maintenance of vendor master record is centralized. Some companies also have some form of workflow to maintain vendor master.

Vendor master record is organized in separate areas such as general data, company code data and purchasing data. This allows the flexibility to maintain one record yet meet the needs of different groups.

It is critical that vendor master is updated in a timely and accurate manner as this affects both purchasing activities as well as payment to suppliers. Some key elements of vendor master data are payment terms, banking information, payment method and tax information such as tax ID or withholding tax codes.

The reconciliation account in company code view of vendor master determines how transactions are posted to the general ledger. In the purchasing view, you can influence system behavior with regard to invoice processing by setting flags for evaluated receipt settlement and GR based invoice verification.

It is also possible to implement additional checks in vendor master by controlling ability to view or edit specific fields in screens through configuration. For example the Social Security Number stored in Tax Number 1 of the Control tab of vendor master may be hidden from view for users that do not need to see that information. Similarly access to bank detail may be restricted.

It is possible to implement 'dual control' for sensitive fields such as payment method or payment terms so that another person needs to confirm a change made to those fields. In specific situations, a BAdI implementation may force the input of a tax number for certain countries.

The business object type for vendor is BUS3008, LFA1 and LFB1.

Transaction	Description
XK01	Create vendor
XK02	Change Vendor
XK03	Display Vendor

Tables

Table	Description
LFA1	General vendor master data

LFB1	Vendor master - Company code
LFAS	Vendor master – VAT
LFB5	Vendor master – Dunning info
LFBK	Vendor master – Bank details
LFBW	Vendor master – withholding tax
LFM1	Vendor master – Purch Org data
LFM2	Vendor master – purchasing data

BAPI

BAPI	Comments
BAPI_VENDOR_GETDETAIL	Get details of the vendor
VENDOR_INSERT	Insert vendor master directly.
VENDOR_UPDATE	Update vendor master directly.
BAPI_AP_ACC_GETBALANCEDITEMS	Get clearing vendor account transactions in a given period
BAPI_AP_ACC_GETOPENITEMS	Get vendor open items
BAPI_AP_ACC_GETSTATEMENT	Vendor Account Statement for a given Period
BAPI_AP_ACC_GETPERIODBALANCES	Posting Period Balances per Vendor Account in Current Fiscal Year

The following BAPIs for specific Vendor related FI accounting BAPIs.

BAPI	Comments
BAPI_AP_ACC_GETBALANCEDITEMS	Vendor Account Clearing Transactions in a given Period
BAPI_AP_ACC_GETCURRENTBALANCE	Vendor Account Closing Balance in Current Fiscal Year
BAPI_AP_ACC_GETKEYDATEBALANCE	Vendor Account Balance at Key Date
BAPI_AP_ACC_GETOPENITEMS	Vendor Account Open Items at a Key Date
BAPI_AP_ACC_GETPERIODBALANCES	Posting Period Balances per Vendor Account in Current Fiscal Year
BAPI_AP_ACC_GETSTATEMENT	Vendor Account Statement for a given Period

Direct Input: Use the direct input program RFBIKR00.

Enhancement

- EXIT_SAPMF02K_001 – User exit for checks prior to saving vendor master
- VENDOR_ADD_DATA – One of the important enhancements used for vendor master
- VENDOR_ADD_DATA_BI – Batch Input for Vendor

Technical Challenges: Add a new tab in the vendor master screen allows you to edit/display the custom fields added in the LFA1.

Solution: This involves the multiple steps. First, define the tab pages in the vendor screen group.

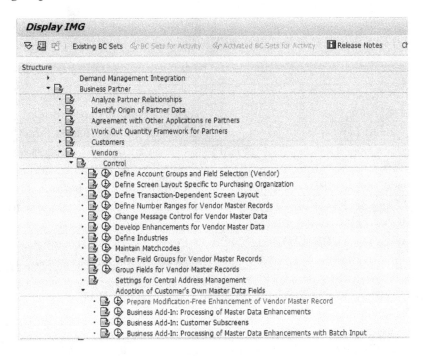

Add a new screen group Z1.

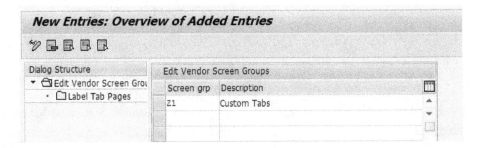

Add tab page in the screen group with function code.

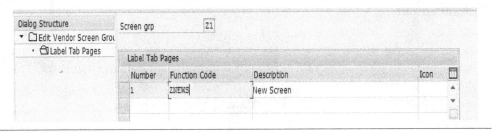

Create a new function group and add a new screen under the function group. Create two new function modules in the function group. The function group will get LFA1 and set LFA1 from BADI's methods SET_DATA and GET_DATA.

Implement a new implementation of the BADI VENDOR_ADD_DATA_CS for the screen group Z1. Activate the screen group. This method will show all pages of screen group as tabs in the vendor screen.

```
method IF_EX_VENDOR_ADD_DATA~CHECK_ADD_ON_ACTIVE.
  if I_SCREEN_GROUP = 'Z1'.
   e_add_on_active = 'X'.
  endif.
endmethod.
```

Implement BADI VENDOR_ADD_DATA_CS (GET_TAXI_SCREEN) to associate the screen to the page tab.

```
method IF_EX_VENDOR_ADD_DATA_CS~GET_TAXI_SCREEN.
 IF flt_val = 'ZP'   "<----Fliter value
   AND i_taxi_fcode = 'ZNEWS'. "<-- Tab Function code
   e_screen  = '9001'.   "<----screen number
   e_program  = 'SAPLZVZGRP'. "<--
Function Group (Main program name of the function group)
   e_headerscreen_layout = ' '.
 ENDIF.
endmethod.
```

Next step, you can pass the data between main screen to sub-screen and get the data from the sub-screen.

Implement get_data and set_data

```
method IF_EX_VENDOR_ADD_DATA_CS~SET_DATA.
 CALL FUNCTION 'ZF_SET_NEW_DATA'
  EXPORTING
   I_ACTIVITY = I_ACTIVITY
   I_LFA1   = I_LFA1
  EXCEPTIONS
   OTHERS   = 1.
endmethod.
```

```
method IF_EX_VENDOR_ADD_DATA_CS~GET_DATA.
 CALL FUNCTION 'ZF_GET_NEW_DATA'
  IMPORTING
   I_LFA1   = I_LFA1
  EXCEPTIONS
   OTHERS   = 1.
endmethod.
```

3.1.2 Info Record

The Purchasing Info Record commonly known as PIR is a form of purchasing master data which specifies the combination of vendor and material. It also contains other critical information such as price, validity dates and tax code. The info record also inherits some values from the vendor master. Examples of these are confirmation control, and GR-based IV.

Most companies maintain info records for items that are regularly sourced. The info record defaults several values in the PO. Whenever there are problems related to pricing, it would be a good idea to check the accuracy of info record.

Transaction codes

Transaction	Description
ME11	Create Purchasing Info Record
ME12	Change Purchasing Info Record
ME13	Display Purchasing Info Record
ME15	Purchase Info Record – flag for delete

Tables

Table	Description
EINA	Purchasing Info Record - General data
EINE	Purchasing Info Record – Purchase Org data
EIPA	Order Price History: Info Record

BAPIs

BAPI	Comments
ME_UPDATE_INFORECORD	Updating of Purchasing Info record Master Data
ME_MAINTAIN_INFORECORD	Maintain the info record

3.1.3 Source List

The source list lists the possible sources of supply for a vendor. Companies also flag a vendor as a fixed source for an item. In configuration it is possible to make source list mandatory for PO creation. Like the info record, the source list also allows maintenance by validity dates. You can view the sourcing list information in the transparent table EORD.

Transaction	Description
ME01	Create Source list
ME02	Change Source list
ME03	Display Source list
BAPI	Comments

ME_MAINTAIN_SOURCELIST	Maintain the source list
ME_POST_SOURCELIST	Post the source list
ME_UPDATE_SOURCES_OF_SUPPLY	Update the source of supply

3.1.4 Pricing Conditions

Pricing conditions can appear in the purchase order in multiple ways. It can be defaulted in from the info record or manually keyed in during PO creation. Some pricing conditions are maintained as accrual conditions. Examples of such conditions are accruals for freight which post to different GL accounts. The pricing procedure may also include condition types for taxes.

Pricing condition records are displayed with MEK3 transaction.

BAPI	Comments
ME_GET_CONDITIONS_TO_SEARCH	Search purchasing conditions

Tables

Table	Description
KONV	Conditions transaction data
KONP	Conditions Items
KONM	Conditions Quantity scale
KNOW	Conditions Value scale
KOMK	Pricing communication header
KOMP	Pricing communication item

3.1.5 Material Master

It could be argued that the material master is at the heart of the entire logistics process in SAP and also has a significant influence on financial postings in several ways. In many companies, there are dedicated teams or individuals that deal with material master creation and maintenance as a full time job. Through the material type it is possible to control which views of the material master are available for use. For example the company may not be using warehouse management functionality, so WM views may not show up. In another situation a service material may not be valuated.

Accounting/Costing Integration

Many of the views or tabs in material master hold critical values that influence either master data or transaction data in other modules such as sales and distribution, production planning or finance. Some of the attributes of these views are listed below.

Sales org 1 view contains taxability of the material in each country. Sales org 2 view can be used for GL Account determination through the material account assignment group. Sales General/Plant view contains the profit center that gets passed to the financial document during billing. MRP Views contain values that impact demand planning, and production planning processes.

The accounting and costing views contain values that determine how standard cost is built up for a material as well as how various transactions post to the general ledger. In costing1 view, the plant specific status can be used to control whether an item can be costed or not. Also in costing 1 view, one needs to set variance key if production orders are being used.

The quantity structure flag directs the system to look for a bill of material and routing when it is costed. Special procurement Costing field can be used to override cost calculation based on procurement type in MRP2 view. Also values in special procurement field in MRP 2 view is often used to determine from which source plant costs should be inherited in case of interplant transfers of materials.

Values defined in plant specific material status determine whether goods movements can be posted for a material. If product costing planning is active, the future and current cost estimates can be seen in Costing 2 view.

The standard cost of an item is set in accounting view. The valuation class in accounting view controls the GL account posted through account determination configuration. Price control determines the value of a material posted in financial accounting during a goods receipt.

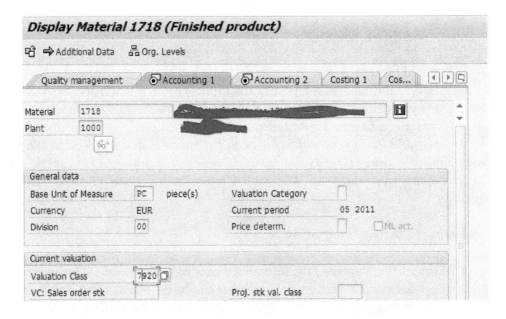

Many companies use custom programs either to create material master or change values. You will see often material master being associated with a workflow process wherein several stakeholders are responsible for sections of the material master. In some cases a comprehensive custom workflow is implemented for material master and within that workflow standard BAPIs are called. One of them is BAPI_MATERIAL_SAVEDATA.

The valuation class in accounting view controls the GL account posted through account determination configuration. Price control determines the value of a material posted in financial accounting during a goods receipt.

3.1.6 Material Movements

The configuration of material movements is a critical aspect of the logistics process. They determine how these transactions are eventually reflected in the financial statements.

The general ledger posting is a culmination of a series inter-connected configuration. It starts with the movement type and goes through account grouping, transaction key, account modifier and ends with GL account determination. You can configure the movement types using the transaction code OMJJ.

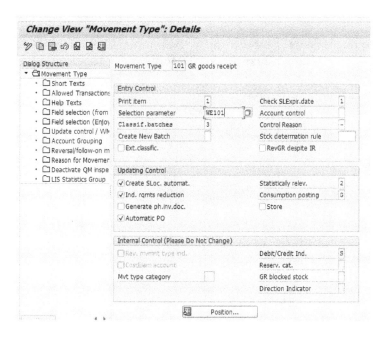

The movement type is stored in the table T156 and the assignment information is stored in T158.

There is an important step in the IMG in the section 'valuation and account assignment' where you have to establish the links between logistics movements and financial postings. This can be directly accessed from OBYC transaction.

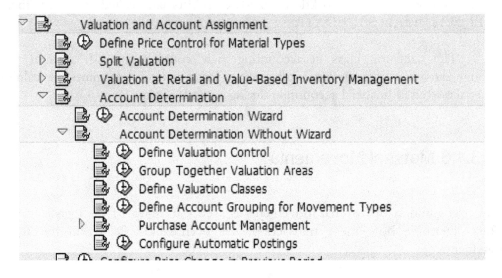

The valuation class and movement types are used for G/L determination. The movement type is used for all types of material movement. You can configure G/L accounts for the movement type. The table below lists some examples of how the material master settings eventually affect postings in the general ledger.

Moveme nt Type	Descriptio n	Trans action	Offsetting Transaction	Account Modifier	Valuation Class	GL Acct.
101	GR against Purchase Order	WRX	BSX		xx	Xx
101	GR against production order	GBB	BSX	AUF	xx	xx
201	Goods issue to cost center	GBB	BSX	VBR	xx	xx
601	Goods issue against delivery	GBB	BSX	VAX	xx	xx

The screenshot below shows how the settings in table above appear in the IMG configuration.

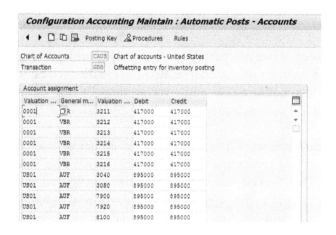

3.1.7 MM Posting Period

The opening and closing of MM period needs to be well coordinated within your organization. Often it goes hand in hand with the opening/closing of FI period. In many companies it is scheduled as a batch job for program RMMMPERI. Period close can also be performed manually with MMPV transaction.

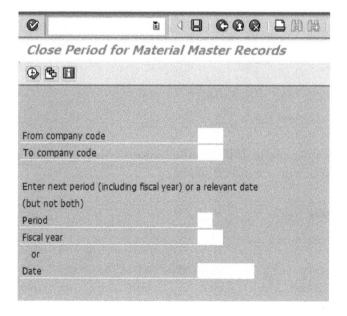

Good movements are allowed only in open periods. Stock values and stock quantities are maintained by period. In addition, logistics invoice verification and releasing of material cost estimates are allowed only in open MM period.

Generally posting to previous periods is allowed. This may be required to complete pending transactions such as production confirmations or goods issues.

Material master screen

The material master screen is one of complex screen programming. It contains a number of tabs for every different set of material related information. The material master screen has two tabs (Accounting 1 and Accounting 2) for accounting information. The accounting document is based on the plant and valuation type.

Each tab refers to a data screen. Each data screen contains a set of sub-screens and that can be arranged in a sequential order. You can group data screens to form a screen sequence. The screen sequence can be configured in IMG configuration. Also, you can assign the screen sequence to a combination of transactions, users, material types, and industry sectors. Based on the combination, SAP system displays the corresponding screen sequence.

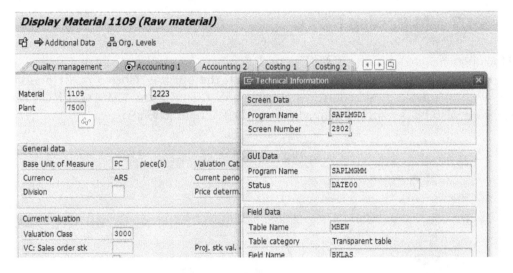

You can configure screen sequences in IMG configuration. Also, you can add new sub-screen to display custom or other standard fields.

	SSq	Scrn	Screen description	T	SCon	Maint. status	GUI status	T.	Ret.maint.status	Alt. screen desc
V1	20	Quality Management	1	4000	Q	DATE00	2		Quality Managem
V1	21	Accounting 1	1	4000	B	DATE00	2		Accounting 1
V1	22	Accounting 2	1	4000	B	DATE00	2		Accounting 2
V1	23	Classification	1	4020	C	DATE00	2		Classification
V1	24	Plant Stock	1	4000	X	DATE00	2		Plant Stock
V1	25	SLoc Stock	1	4000	Z	DATE00	2		SLoc Stock

For data screen, you can define the sub-screens and sequence.

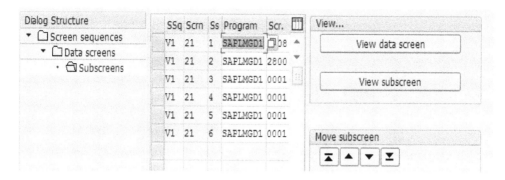

Technical Details

Tables

Table	Description
MARA	Material master data
MARC	Material maser data – company code
MARD	Material master data – plant
MBEW	Material valuation
MARM	Unit of measures
MVKE	Sales data for material

BAPI

BAPI	Comments
BAPI_MATERIAL_GETDETAIL	Get material detail
BAPI_MATERIAL_SAVEDATA	Maintain material
MATERIAL_MAINTAIN_DARK	Maintain material online
BAPI_MATERIAL_AVAILABILITY	Get material availability detail
BAPI_MATERIAL_DELETE	Delete the material
BAPI_MATERIAL_GETLIST	Get material list
BAPI_MATERIAL_EXISTENCECHEC K	Check the material existence

The BOR object type is BUS1001.

Material Enhancement

You can extend the material master at general and plant level. In this section, you are going through the material master extension at general level (MARA) table.

- You can define custom fields in the 'Append' structure of MARA table.
- In IMG configuration, create program for the customized sub-screens. The IMG activity allows you create a custom function group ZFGMGD1 (based on your programming guidelines). SAP creates the function group by copying from function group MGD1 (for retail implementation, copy from MGD2).

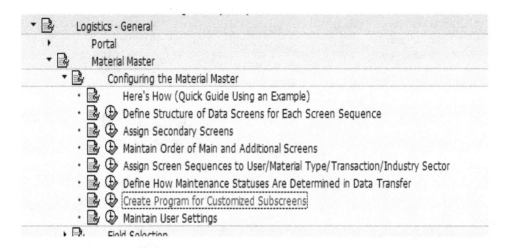

- Create a new screen in the function group. You can add the custom or standard fields in the screen. Flow Logic as follows:

```
PROCESS BEFORE OUTPUT.
    MODULE FIELD_SCREEN.   " Screen fields hide/display definition
    MODULE GET_DATA.        " Fill the data
PROCESS AFTER INPUT.
    MODULE SET_DATA.        "Pass the data
```

```
MODULE GET_DATA OUTPUT.
    CALL FUNCTION 'MARA_GET_SUB'
       IMPORTING
            WMARA = MARA
            XMARA = *MARA
            YMARA = LMARA.
ENDMODULE.

MODULE SET_DATA INPUT.
* Assign custom fields in MARA data structure
    CALL FUNCTION 'MARA_SET_SUB'
       EXPORTING
            WMARA = MARA.
ENDMODULE.
```

- Define screen sequence. You can define the sub-screen as a part of the data screen you have planned. Make sure that you pick the appropriate screen sequence number.

Note that the function module SET_MARA_SUB and GET_MARA_SUB retrieves and update the function group global variables and used in the material save execution. Also, SAP provides GET and SET function modules for the tables like MARC, MARD, MAKT, MVKE, MARM, MBEW, etc.

3.2 Purchase Order Processing

This section will cover some basic features of the most common purchasing documents viz., purchase requisitions, and purchase orders. You will be provided examples of how data contained in these documents impact FI and CO modules.

3.2.1 Purchase Requisition

Purchase requisition (PReq) is usually the first document in the Procure-to-Pay process. It is common for the PR to be created manually or by MRP process. Depending on the configuration in your company PR may also be triggered from plant maintenance, production planning and project systems.

The item detail in the PReq contains information that determines how a PReq is processed further. The account assignment category in the PReq can point financial posting to a cost center, internal order or a CO-PA segment. The item category indicates the type of business process that would follow. For example, if an item category is 'L' –sub-contracting, then the components to be issued to the vendor are defined in the material data tab in the line item

In many cases, a fixed vendor is defined as a source of supply for that product or service. System will default the address of the plant if the delivery address is not specified. The PReq also contains quantity and item value.

PReqs are subject to an approval process through configuration of release strategy which contains release groups and release codes. You are also likely to see custom workflows for PReq approvals based on amount limits and approvers for organizational units such as cost center.

It must be noted that neither the PReq nor the PO create a financial posting but contain vital information that would eventually influence the accounting posting at the time of goods receipt or invoice.

Tables:

Table Name	Description
EBAN	Purchase requisition
EBKN	PR account assignment

BAPIs:

BAPI	Comments
BAPI_PR_CREATE	Create PR
BAPI_PR_CHANGE	Change PR

BAPI_PR_GETDETAIL	Get PR detail
BAPI_ACC_PURCHASE_REQUI_POST	Accounting: Post Purchase Req.
BAPI_ACC_PURCHASE_REQUI_CHECK	Accounting: Check Purchase Req.

Enhancement

ME_PROCESS_REQ_CUST – This is one of the important BADIs used in PR maintenance. The BADI enables you enhancing the business logic on PR update. The BADI is part of the transactions ME51N, ME52N, ME53N, and ME59N, as well as the BAPIs BAPI_PR_CREATE and BAPI_PR_CHANGE. This is a single use BADI. The BADI has a number of methods and the important methods are briefly explained.

- PROCESS_HEADER – You can enhance the header data of the PR. You can raise the error messages.
- PROCESS_ITEM – Using this method, you can enhance a line item of the PR. You can raise the error messages.
- PROCESS_ACCOUNT – Using the method, you can enhance the account assignment in the PR line item. You can raise your own messages.
- CHECK – This method is used to perform an overall check on the purchase requisition. You can raise the error messages and also you can set failure flag.
- POST - You can use the POST method to prepare the requisition data for posting and database update.

The BADI methods are using the following complex interface objects.

Interface	Comments
IF_PURCHASE_REQUISITION	This is overall interface object used in open, process_header, check, post and close methods. The interface has a number of methods to fetch and set data.
IF_PURCHASE_REQUISITION_ITEM	The interface object is part of item level purchase requisition and it is used in the method process_item.
IF_ACCOUNTING_MODEL_MM	The interface is accounting interface for PR. The interface is used in the process_account.

3.2.2 Purchase Order

The purchase order (PO) is used for a various purposes. PO is issued to external suppliers of a product or service. PO is also used internally to procure inventory from another plant of your company which may or may not be assigned to the same SAP company code.

It is not necessary for a PO to have a material. Often, professional services and one off transactions are represented in a PO as a text item along with appropriate account assignment category in the PO line item. The PO inherits values from the PIR such as price. Delivery address is defaulted into the PO from the P.Req. Output types are used to generate documents that can be either faxed or emailed suppliers.

The PO document type helps distinguish the business transactions. Framework orders also frequently known as Blanket POs are used to efficiently manage frequent purchases of certain types of items. These can be set up with a value limit in by assigning 'B-Limit' in item category. These are usually account assigned POs.

Another variation of this is a Framework order with a value limit, containing an account assignment to a cost center, where the PO line item is tied to an invoicing plan. This may be used for example for rent payments, where the same amount is to be paid for a defined period of time at fixed intervals.

The item category U is used for stock transport PO. This is picked up in the delivery due list of the shipping plant. If both sending and receiving plants are assigned to same company code, at the time of post goods issue in the shipping plant, the inventory values are incremented at the receiving plant. The subsequent GR in the receiving plant is non-valuated and items in transit are shown in inventory reports separately.

In the PO line item there are some fields that need to be populated with correct values so that subsequent postings to the general ledger are accurate. For example, tax code has to be correctly determined. It may come from the info record. If the confirmation control key is set in the line item level, it means that the supplier will send an advance ship notice (ASN). In SAP the ASN is entered as an inbound delivery which is a statistical document. This is then used a reference for the actual goods receipt transaction after the goods arrive in your premises.

With account assigned PO GR may not be required. The GR flag in PO line item is turned off. The costs are expensed at the time of invoice receipt to the cost center in the account assignment of the PO line item.

Some companies may set the GR-based IV flag in PO line item thus preventing invoice entry until goods have been received. The evaluated receipt settlement (ERS) flag needs to be enabled in order for automatic posting of invoices using the designated transactions for evaluated receipt settlement or invoicing plan settlement.

It is useful to understand PO history. Depending on the nature of your business, the PO history will show goods receipts, invoice receipts, delivery in case of stock transport order, down payments, subsequent debits/credits and GR IR account maintenance transactions.

Below are some useful tables that contain details of P.Reqs and POs.

Table	Description
EKKO	PO Header
EKPO	PO Item
EKBE	PO History
EKKN	PO Account Assignment

BAPIs:

BAPI	Comments
BAPI_PO_CREATE1	Create PO
BAPI_PO_CHANGE	Change PO
BAPI_PO_GETDETAIL1	Get PO details
BAPI_ACC_PURCHASE_ORDER_POST	Accounting: Post Purchase Order
BAPI_ACC_PURCHASE_ORDER_CHEC K	Accounting: Check Purchase Order

Enhancement

ME_TAX_FROM_ADDRESS – The BADI is used to determine tax jurisdiction code from delivery address instead of plant on the P.Req.

ME_PROCESS_PO_CUST – This BADI enables you to extend the business logic of the purchase order maintenance. The BADI is applicable for ME21N, ME22N, ME23N, ME29N, the BAPIs BAPI_PO_CREATE1 and BAPI_PO_CHANGE.

- PROCESS_HEADER – You can enhance the header data of the PR. You can raise the error messages.
- PROCESS_ITEM – Using this method, you can enhance a line item of the PO. You can raise the error messages.
- PROCESS_SCHEDULE – Using this method, you can extend custom business logic on delivery schedule line item.
- PROCESS_ACCOUNT – Using the method, you can enhance the account assignment in the PR line item. You can raise your own messages.
- CHECK – This method is used to perform an overall check on the purchase requisition. You can raise the error messages and also you can set failure flag.
- POST - You can use the POST method to prepare the requisition data for posting and database update.

The BADI methods are using the following complex interface objects.

Interface	Comments
IF_PURCHASE_ORDER_MM	This is overall interface object used in open, process_header, check, post and

	close methods. The interface has a number of methods to fetch and set data.
IF_PURCHASE_ORDER_ITEM_MM	Interface used at item level
IF_PURCHASE_ORDER_ACCOUNT_MM	Account level Interface
IF_PURCHASE_ORDER_SCHEDULE_MM	Schedule level interface

3.2.3 Receiving

The next step in the P2P process is receiving of goods or services. Goods receipt (GR) can be performed against either a purchase order PO if it is from an external source. The 101 movement type is used for a GR against a PO. The same movement type is also used for a GR against a production order. In both cases the GR leads to an increase in inventory.

GR can be entered against a PO or an inbound delivery (ASN). During GR, it is possible to direct the stock update to a pre-defined storage location. GR can place the stock in unrestricted location, in blocked status for quality inspection or to a blocked stock area.

We will cover only GR against a PO and some special features relating to the GR transaction. From an accounting standpoint, the GR results in debit to inventory and credit to the offset GL Account commonly known as GR/IR clearing account.

The GR results in the creation of a material document and at the same time an accounting document if it is a valuated goods movement. Stock values are updated and both FI and CO postings are created depending on the data contained in the PO. PO history is updated, MRP data vendor evaluation data, transfer requirements in WM and inspection lots in QM are all updated.

The GR/IR clearing account is defined for the WRX transaction in the account determination process. There are some special features of the GR/IR account. It is by definition an open item managed account. It is set to maintain balances in local currency only in GL master record. In addition there is a specific sort key value 14 – Purchase order that needs to be set in GL master record for GR IR account. This automatically populates the concatenated value of PO line item in the assignment field of the FI line item. SAP has provided program SAPF124 to clear the GRIR account on a regular basis.

For account assigned POs, the recording of expense can happen either at GR or during invoice verification. Depending on how the PO was set up, some GR can be non-valuated, thereby creating only the material document without an accompanying an accounting document.

It is important to keep in mind that goods receipt is valuated on the basis of PO price or invoice price whichever happens first. This aspect is usually not considered when looks at the value of the GRIR line item in the general ledger. If your company allows for invoice to be posted without a GR then the system would set the value of the GRIR account with the invoiced value.

If the PO line item has been fully received and fully invoiced, you would have to go to GR/IR maintenance transaction MR11 to clear residual balances in the GRIR Account.

3.2.1 Material Document

The document principle is key in both logistics and financial modules of SAP. Every transaction/event that causes a change in inventory will be captured in a material document. When any goods movement is posted it is captured in a material document. An extension of that principle is that an accounting document is generated if that movement/transaction is relevant for accounting.

Similar to accounting document, the material document consists of a header and at least one line item. The material document is uniquely identified by the document number and document year. The number range is based on the document type. You can cancel material document by reversing the document. You can access the material document using the transaction code MB03. You can use transaction code MB51 to list out material documents.

At a very broad level, the material movements can be classified as Goods Receipts, Goods issues, Transfer postings and Adjustments. Each 3 digit movement type code has a specific meaning and underlying configuration explained in one of the earlier sections.

The movement type 101 can be used for both receipt against a purchase order and against a production order. But it is differentiated by the accompanying transaction type WE or WF which in turn is connected to account grouping/account modifier and finally resulting in the GL account determination.

The effect of a goods movement in the system depends on the nature of the business transaction. A receipt against production order can increment inventory, update a balance sheet inventory gl account. An issue to cost center with movement type 201 will debit a primary cost element/cost center and credit inventory. In general, a material document is associated with an inventory movement, a financial posting, and update of stock values and quantities. The AWKEY field in table BKPF represents the link between material document and accounting document. Two important tables for material documents are:

Tables:

Table	Description
MKPF	Material document
MSEG	Material document item

BAPIs

BAPI	Comments
BAPI_GOODSMVT_CREATE	Create goods movement record
BAPI_GOODSMVT_GETDETAIL	Get goods movement detail
BAPI_GOODSMVT_CANCEL	Cancel the goods movement
BAPI_GOODSMVT_GETITEMS	Get detailed list of material document

The business object types are:

- MKPF – Material document header
- MSEG – Material document item
- BUS6002 – Accounting Goods movement

Enhancements

- **MB_ACCOUNTING_DISTRIBUTE** - You can use this BADI to redefine the distribution among the individual account assignments when you entering a valuated goods receipt for an order with multiple account assignments. This BADI is called while goods receipt processing. This BADI is not applicable for services, goods issues or reversals.

- **MB_BAPI_GOODSMVT_CREATE** – You can use this BADI to populate the customer fields of the material document.

- **MB_DOCUMENT_BADI** – You can update material document data of MKPF, MSEG and VM07M. MB_DOCUMENT_BEFORE_UPDATE and MB_DOCUMENT_AFTER_UPDATE are two methods of BADI. Before update method is called up before the FI document is created.

- **MB_GOODSMOVEMENT_DCI** – You can use this BADI to implement own logic to set the delivery completed indicator for a purchase order item.

- **MB_BATCH_MASTER** – You can use this BADI to set batch data for goods movement. BADI supports MAINTAIN_INSPECTION_DATE (next inspection date) and MAINTAIN_BATCH_VENDOR (vendor data) methods.

3.3 Invoice Verification

Invoice Verification functionality is contained in the component MM-IV-LIV and occurs at the end of the supply chain. There is a lot of functionality around invoice verification such as 3-way match, automatic invoicing, EDI and invoice workflow.

The account payable component also has functionality for posting invoices without a PO. This is done with the FB60 transaction or through an EDI process of IDOC type INVOIC01. Some companies intentionally decide to use non-PO invoicing for certain business process. For example, freight invoices are often posted as non-PO invoices.

3.3.1 LIV and Accounting

The logistics invoice verification process is tightly integrated with the accounting module. Invoice document from logistics posts creates an accounts payable line item on the vendor's account. The payable is posted against the PI partner in the PO. The account assignment object such as cost center or internal order is picked up from PO line item and passed on to accounting document. Many companies set up number range configuration such that same number is passed from MM invoice to the accounting document.

During invoice entry with MIRO transaction, one needs to take care to enter correct tax code and tax amount. It is possible to allow system to calculate the tax amount by checking calculate tax flag in basic data screen. Custom line layout can configured so that you have flexibility to choose the fields and the order in which they appear in the invoice items entry portion of the MIRO screen. Unplanned delivery costs are entered in the details tab.

After an invoice is posted in the MIRO transaction, you can display the invoice from MIR4 transaction or from the PO history screen. You can bring up the associated accounting document by clicking 'follow on documents'. Depending on the account assignment objects, you are likely to see different follow on documents. Here is an example

The accounting document shows details of line items posted to the general ledger and accounts payable sub-ledger. The controlling document represents posting to an account assignment object such as cost center or internal order. The contacts tab in the invoice display shows useful information such as requisitioner, buyer and GR processor.

3.3.2 Three-Way match

The 3-way match functionality is standard in SAP. It consists of the following features:
- Received quantity is checked against ordered quantity
- Invoice price is checked against PO price
- Invoiced quantity is checked against received quantity

In the first situation, the system would issue a warning. In the second situation the invoice would be blocked for payment automatically and blocking reason flag can be seen in the invoice. In the third situation the invoice would be blocked automatically with a reason updated as quantity block updated.

It is normal for businesses to intentionally release the block the make payment to the vendor in some specific situations. If the invoice is nearing its due date and we have received confirmation of shipment from the vendor by way of an ASN, the payment block can be lifted in the MRBR transaction. Usually there exists a formal request and approval process before blocked invoices can be released for payment in this manner.

Even if one line item in the invoice is blocked for price or quantity, the entire invoice is blocked as the block is set at the vendor line item of the accounting document. Generally, invoices may remain in blocked status for a few days until they can be matched up with a goods receipt posted subsequently. The program RM08RELEASE can be scheduled as a background job to clear invoice blocks due to timing reasons.

3.3.3 Tolerances

Configuration of tolerances is an important aspect in both logistics and in accounts payable. It is also part of internal controls set up in your organization in the area of receiving and invoicing transactions. SAP has provided several tolerance keys that cover various situations that can occur during invoice verification.

You define tolerances in the IMG in the path below. It can be directly accessed via OMR6 transaction.

The most common tolerance keys you are likely to come across are PP- price variance and DQ-quantity variance. By defining upper and lower limit, you can cause the system to not block an invoice if the amount of variance calculated is less than the percentage defined.

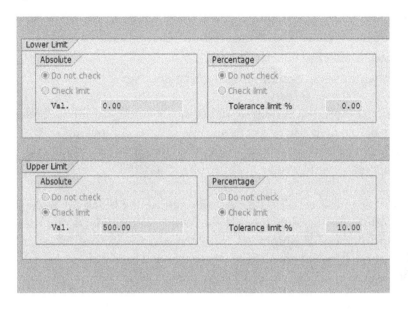

It is quite common for companies to set a fairly low amount as tolerance to avoid unnecessary handling of blocked invoices due to very small amounts of variances. Limits are set for the combination of company code and tolerance key and system will take the lower of % or absolute amount when it makes the decision to block an invoice for payment during MIRO.

3.3.4 Special Functions

In standard SAP, several special functions have been provided in the LIV component. It is possible to run evaluated receipt settlement transaction to post invoices automatically with the program RMMR1MRS (t-code MRRL). There are some pre-requisites for this functionality. Vendor master records should have AutoEval GR settlement flag set. ERS and GR Based IV flag needs to be set in the PO line item. Goods receipt must have happened prior to invoice posting. No paper or electronic invoice is received from the vendor.

Another variation of the evaluated receipt settlement is the invoicing plan settlement. This feature is used for posting invoices automatically where the amount and invoice dates are the same. The requirement is for the PO to contain an invoice plan. An example could be rent payments where the amount does not typically change for an entire year and is due on a specific date each month. A scheduled background job can be set up for program RMMR1MIS (transaction code MRIS) to post invoices.

Another method of automatic invoicing is through consignment settlement. Here the withdrawals from consignment inventory to regular inventory are evaluated and included in the invoice posting. This is carried out using t-code MRKO.

Invoice can be posted in foreign currency. Invoices are entered in the same currency as the PO. It is possible specify an exchange rate during invoice entry.

It is possible to enter both planned delivery costs and unplanned delivery costs during invoice verification. Unplanned delivery costs are entered in the details tab in the MIRO screen. They unplanned delivery costs are spread across the individual line items in proportion to the amounts. In standard SAP, they post to the price variance account. It is also possible to configure posting of unplanned delivery costs to a separate GL accounts.

In some companies there may be an internal policy that requires all invoices to be parked and posted by a different person. In some cases a workflow may be triggered to route the invoice to an approver and upon approval be posted automatically. You will see workflow covered in a separate section.

Enhancements:

- **MRM_PROPOSAL_DETERMINE** – The BADI is used to get default values of the quantity and amount. The BADI is used in MIRO, MIR7, MRBP, MRIS and ERS functions. AMNT_QUANT_PROPOSAL_DETERMINE is only one method to compute the amount and quantity.

- **LE_SHP_GOODSMOVEMENT** – You can use this BADI to change data at the interface between delivery processing and goods movement (either goods issue or goods receipt). You can change values in LIPS table such as profit center depending on your business requirement. The BADI is triggered in the post goods issue for outbound delivery and post goods receipt for inbound delivery. The BADI has one method CHANGE_INPUT_HEADER_AND_ITEMS.

- **MRM_ERS_HDAT_MODIFY** – Using this BADI, you can modify document header data in Automatic Settlement of Planned Delivery Costs (ERS). The BADI is triggered in the report RMMR1MDC. When you made change in the exporting parameter E_RBKPV_CHANGE, you must set the parameter E_CHANGE.

- **MRM_ERS_IDAT_MODIFY** – You can use this BADI to modify ERS document line item data in Automatic settlement of planned delivery cost.

3.3.5 Subsequent Debits and Credits

There may be situations where a PO has been fully invoiced but some subsequent charges may be billed by the vendor. In such situations the invoice is entered with the transaction type subsequent debit/credit. Some special features of these postings are:

- They are recorded in PO history
- The updates are on value basis only and not on quantity.
- Depending on price control the value is updated either as price variance or to inventory

At the top of the MIRO invoice entry screen, the user will have to take care to choose the correct transaction from a fixed list of 4 choices (invoice, credit memo, subsequent debit or subsequent credit). They system will default to last used transaction. Transactions such as subsequent credits/debits are entered by user and they would have to be explicitly selected in the MIRO screen. The technical field name is VORGANG and it is part of the RM0R8M. This selection determines how values are updated in PO history and also which GL accounts are posted.

3.3.6 Invoice Workflow

Many companies have implemented invoice workflow to assist with resolution of blocked invoices. This tends to be medium to complex custom development. In some cases, invoice workflow also contains functionality to retrieve archived invoice images. There are several SAP-certified third party add on packages in the area of archiving and workflow.

SAP has provided business object BUS2081 for incoming invoice which is used in workflow definition. For example, as soon as an invoice is blocked due to price or quantity, it can be routed to different processors within the organization based on their roles such as account payable clerk, buyer etc. They will get a work item in their SAP Inbox that takes them to a workflow screen that gives them multiple options to resolve that issue.

The workflow can then be linked to transactional updates in the system. For example one of the actions available to the buyer role could be to change PO quantity. From the workflow it is possible to lead them to the PO change screen. Another action is for them to provide additional information to the account payable clerk. The buyer may need to display an electronic image of the supplier's invoice copy linked to that SAP document. After corrective action is taken, the workflow itself can release the payment block on the invoice in background.

A comprehensive invoice workflow solution incorporates all of the above features. Such a solution will contain a set of technical objects such as events, function modules, BAPIs etc.

3.3.7 EDI Invoicing

A popular method of automating the entry of large volume of invoices is through the EDI method. Companies use EDI sub-systems such as GENTRAN or similar tools to convert standard EDI transactions to SAP's idoc format.

For invoices the IDOC type is INVOIC01. This IDOC is linked to a function module IDOC_INPUT_INVOIC_MRM which uses data in IDOC segments to pass values required by the MIRO transaction to post the invoice.

There is a variation of the same INVOIC01 for posting non-PO invoices. If the IDOC INVOIC01 is combined with process code INVF, then the function module IDOC_INPUT_INVOIC_FI is used to post the FI non-PO invoice.

3.3.8 Technical Structure

The BOR object for Vendor Invoice is BUS2081.

Tables

Table	Description
RBKP	Header
RSEG	Invoice Line
RBCO	Account document
RBKP_BLOCKED	Blocked invoices
RBTX	Incoming Invoice taxes
RBVD	Invoice document: Aggregation data.

The following are important BAPIs used for incoming invoice (with PO reference).

Function module	Description
BAPI_INCOMINGINVOICE_CREATE	Post invoice
BAPI_INCOMINGINVOICE_CANCEL	Reverse the invoice
BAPI_INCOMINGINVOICE_CHANGE	Change provisional invoice
BAPI_INCOMINGINVOICE_PARK	Park the invoice
BAPI_INCOMINGINVOICE_POST	Post provisional Invoice
BAPI_INCOMINGINVOICE_RELEASE	Release invoice
BAPI_INCOMINGINVOICE_GETDETAIL	Invoice Detail
BAPI_INCOMINGINVOICE_GETLIST	List incoming invoices

BAPI_INCOMINGINVOICE_DELETE	Delete the invoice
MRM_INVOICE_POST	Invoice posting
MRM_INVOICE_PARK	Park Invoice document
BAPI_ACC_INVOICE_RECEIPT_CHECK	Accounting: Check Invoice Receipt
BAPI_ACC_INVOICE_RECEIPT_POST	Accounting: Post Invoice Receipt
BAPI_ACC_INVOICE_REV_CHECK	Accounting: Check Invoice Receipt Reversal
BAPI_ACC_INVOICE_REV_POST	Accounting: Post Invoice Receipt Reversal
BAPI_ACC_PYMNTBLK_UPDATE_POST	Accounting: Post Changes to Payment Block
BAPI_ACC_PYMNTBLK_UPDATE_CHECK	Accounting: Check Changes to Payment Block

Enhancements

- **INVOICE_UPDATE** – You can use this BADI to process the data in the invoice verification. It has the following methods:
  - CHANGE_AT_SAVE – Invoice document at save
  - CHANGE_BEFORE_UPDATE – Invoice document: before update
  - CHANGE_IN_UPDATE – Invoice document during update

- **MRM_PAYMENT_TERMS** – This BAdI can be used to force a payment block in e_zlspr based on your own rules during invoice posting. The BADI has only one method PAYMENT_TERMS_SET. It allows you to change baseline date, days and percentage for Firs & Secondary Cash Discount, Deadline for Net conditions and payment block key (ZLSPR). Make sure that populate all export parameters if you do have any specific derivation logic.

- **BADI_F040_SCREEN_600** – You can use this BADI to sub-screen enhancement for FI document parking on the document header screen. The BADI is applicable to transactions FBV1, FBV2, FBV3, FBV4 and FVB0. The additional screen fields must refer to the table BKPF or VBKPF. You can save changes to BKPF fields and not VBKPF. You can display only VBKPF fields. FI_F040_600_EXAMPLE is an example implementation. The methods are:
  - PUT_DATA_TO_SCREEN
  - GET_DATA_FROM_SCREEN

- **BADI_FDCB_SUBBAS01** – You can use this BADI for sub-screen enhancement for basic data screen 010 for vendors and 510 for customers. These screens are accessed for FI document entry or MM Invoice receipt. It supports the transactions FB60, FB65, FB70, FB75, FV60, FV65, FV70, FV75 and MIRO. The implementation FI_FDCB_SUBBAS01_EX is provided for

example implementation. The screen fields must be in structure INVFO. It has the following methods:
- o PUT_DATA_TO_SCREEN_OBJECT – Transfer data to class instance attribute.
- o GET_DATA_FROM-SCREEN_OBJECT – transfer data from the class instance attribute.

- **BADI_MIRO_SPLT_ADD** – You can use this BADI to append additional fields of ACCVS to ACCIT.

Technical Challenges: Need to create FI invoice in the custom program code.
Solution: The function module BAPI_INCOMINGINVOICE_CREATE is used to create the invoice document. The invoice document is defined by the header and item data.

Step 1: Populate the header data:
```
lv_headerdata-invoice_ind = 'X'.
lv_headerdata-doc_date  = lv_doc_date.
lv_headerdata-pstng_date = lv_pstng_date.
lv_headerdata-comp_code  = lv_comp_code.
lv_headerdata-del_costs = lv_del_costs.
lv_headerdata-currency  = lv_currency.
```

Step 2: Item data Population
```
lt_itemdata-invoice_doc_item = lv_count.
lt_itemdata-po_item = poitem-PO_ITEM.
lt_itemdata-tax_code = 'I0'.
lt_itemdata-item_amount = '100'.
lt_itemdata-quantity = '1'.
lt_itemdata-po_unit = poitem-po_unit.
append lt_itemdata.
```

Step 3: Accounting data Population
```
loop at lt_ekkn INTO lv_ekkn.
  lt_accountdata-gl_account = lv_ekkn-sakto.
  lt_accountdata-cost_center = lv_ekkn-kostl.
  lt_accountdata-quantity    = lv_ekkn-menge.
  append lt_accountdata.
endloop.
```

Step 4: Creating Invoice
```
call function 'BAPI_INCOMINGINVOICE_CREATE'
  exporting
  headerdata     = lv_header
  importing
```

```
invoicedocnumber = lv_belnr
fiscalyear       = lv_gjahr
tables
itemdata         = lt_item
accountingdata   = lt_accountingdata
taxdata          = lt_tax
return           = lt_return.
```

Step 5: Commit the changes.

```
call function 'BAPI_TRANSACTION_COMMIT'
* EXPORTING
*   WAIT       =
* IMPORTING
*   RETURN     =        .
```

3.4 Payment

The accounts payable module provides robust functionality out of the box for making payments. There are multiple options including transactions to post manual payments to individual vendors and a comprehensive automatic payment program. This section will highlight some prominent aspects of the payment process.

3.4.1 Process Flow

In addition to recording the payment in the sub-ledger and general ledger and clearing the open items, the payment program also has functionality to generate output files in the form of remittance advice or payment medium files in various formats that can be transmitted to the bank. Check printing feature is also available. The payment program has functionality to receive incoming payments in which a draft file is sent to the bank to pull funds from customers account.

The payment process brings together the configuration settings, relevant data from vendor master, transaction data from vendor open items and creates accounting postings as well as generate payment medium in the form of a file or a check.

The payment process also has the ability to process payments to customer. This may be necessary in some special situations such as a requirement to issue a refund to a customer. Some companies may define commission agents as customers in SAP and post credits to their account through the rebate settlement process. Those credits are then picked up in payment program to be paid.

Listed below are some useful transactions relating to payment process:

- F-53 – Manual outgoing payment – no forms are output- single vendor
- F-58 – Post+ print forms –generates both check and payment advice – single vendor
- F110 - Automatic payment program

This section will cover only the automatic payment program in detail.

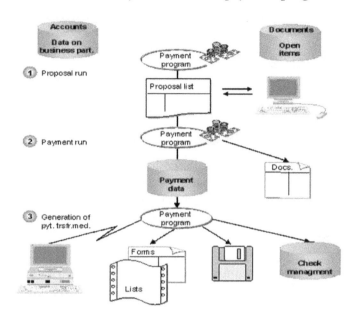

3.4.2 Configuration

It is beneficial to have a basic understanding of the configuration that supports the payment program. The basic configuration steps for payment program can be accessed with t-code FBZP.

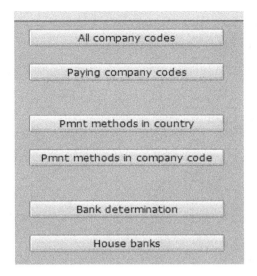

In all company codes step, you define the sending and paying company code, grace days and which type of special GL transactions are to be paid. It is a popular practice to centralize payment operations in a shared service set up and actual cash outlay may be effected from a company code different from the company code where the vendor open items reside.

In paying company codes, minimum amounts and form for payment advice is defined. In the step 'payment methods in country', you define whether it is an incoming or outgoing payment and the currency allowed for that payment method. Leaving currency it blank is preferred as this will allow open items in multiple currencies to be paid using that payment method. In addition, you specify the details that need to be maintained in the vendor master record for this payment method. This validation is useful as a check payment requires street address information and electronic funds transfer needs correct bank information in the vendor master. The selection of payment medium program is made here. You chose whether it will be classic payment medium programs that begin with program names RFFOxx or payment medium workbench using the DME engine for generating custom file layouts. This is covered in a separate section.

The step 'payment methods in company code' contain specifications of minimum and maximum amounts that can be paid. You can specify whether a foreign business partner can be paid, foreign currency is allowed for that payment method. The form for payment medium is defined in this step. This is usually a SAP Script.

You need to define house banks at a company code level and account IDs within the house bank. If payment files in EDI format are required, the house bank needs to be defined as an EDI partner and those payment methods need to be flagged as EDI-compatible in this step.

After this the account ID is set up for the house bank. Account ID usually represents an actual bank account where the funds are processed. It is common for several account IDs to be set up within a house bank. The GL Account posted at the end of the payment process is tied to the account ID.

The step 'bank determination' contains several tasks that determine how an open item is included in the payment proposal. Ranking order definition specifies which house bank is to be selected for the combination of payment method and currency. In 'bank sub-account' you define the GL account to which transactions are posted. The amounts available for payment for each currency/account/payment method combination are defined 'available amount' option. This may be required because there may be restrictions on daily withdrawal of funds on those bank accounts.

The above steps cover just the configuration of payment program. In the next section, you will be given an overview of payment medium workbench and the usage of DME engine.

3.4.3 Payment Processing

The payment program can be executed with F110 transaction. Some companies also set up the payment program RFF110S to run as a scheduled batch job pre-defined parameters.

As mentioned earlier, it is possible to generate payments for both vendors and customers through the payment program. The F110 payment program requires the below steps to be defined.
- o Selection parameters – here the company code, vendors and payment methods to be included are specified
- o Free selection – this is an optional step and used to restrict line items by document number, currency, document date etc.
- o Additional log- this is selected and helps in trouble shooting should any line items not get picked up payment proposal
- o Print out/Data medium – this is a critical step that generates the payment medium in the form of a check or a payment file or an IDOC. The underlying configuration for payment method determines which payment medium program will be triggered and also which list output will be created for the payment list.

Some companies may have an internal policy wherein the payment proposal is first presented to either to a manager or treasury person who signs off on it before the payment run is completed.

At the end of the payment program, a financial posting is generated and payment medium in the form of a check or file is created. If payment medium program is RFFOUS_C or a variation thereof, then a check is created. There are several classic payment medium programs in RFFOUSxx that generate country specific formats.

Note that the payment medium program is based on the payment terms and country in the configuration table T042Z. The custom payment program can be configured in this program.

The RFFOEDI1 program generates idocs of type PEXR2001 or PEXR2002 which is then mapped in an external EDI sub-system into an EDI 820 file before being sent to the bank. We already covered the file generation with payment medium workbench in an earlier section.

3.4.4 Data Medium Exchange

The payment medium workbench (PMW) offers a generic payment medium program. The generic program for PMW is SAPFPAYM. Payment medium format is to be defined for each payment method separately. This format usually is determined by the requirements of the bank where the payment file is to be sent.

Often in Europe and Asia, banks do not have standard file formats or EDI interfaces. In those situations the payment medium file in the custom format required by the banks can be created utilizing the payment medium workbench and DME engine.

In the payment medium format, you specify whether accompanying documents are required with the payment medium file, and file type such as idoc, XML or flat file. The payment medium format must have the same name as the DMEE mapping tree.

The DMEE Mapping Engine can be accessed in t-code DMEE. Here is an example of DMEE format tree which is linked to the payment medium format.

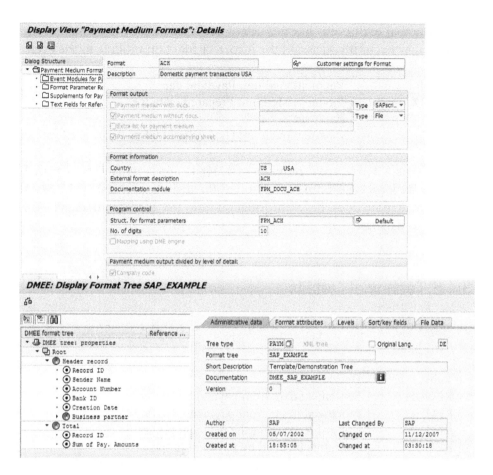

This generates a file in the desired bank format. This file is generated as part of payment media creation step of the F110 payment program and can be downloaded from the file path F110-Environment-Payment medium-DME Administration.

Two sample formats are available that highlight the features you can use when you create a format tree. They are both called SAP_EXAMPLE, and are delivered for tree types PAYM and MCSH.

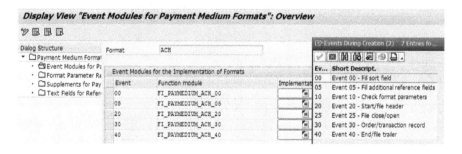

You can define the function module for each event. You can use function module FI_PAYMEDIUM_SAMPLE_nn with "nn" representing the event as a template for requirement. Using these function modules, you can enhance your DME format. Note that each event has different interfaces used by the function module. A short dump may occur if you assign the incorrect function module in the event.

FPAYH	Payment medium: Payment data
FPAYHX	Payment Medium: Prepared Data for Payment
FPAYP	Payment medium: Data on paid items

Technical Tips - There are a number of DMEE tables which starts with DMEE_. You can see the local class implementation in the include LDMEE1_ABACDH. The class implementation does have information how to load from database and save DMEE tree to database.

3.4.5 Technical Details

The business object type for payment request is BUS2021.

Tables:

Table	Description
REGUH	Settlement data from payment program
REGUP	Processed items from payment program
REGUV	Control records for the payment program
REGUS	Accounts blocked by payment proposal
T042X	Company codes blocked by payment program
PAYRQ	Payment request

Transaction codes:

Transaction	Description
FBZ0	Display/Edit payment proposal
FBZ8	Display payment run
F110	Parameters for Automatic payments
FBZP	Maintain payment program configuration
FBZA	Display Payment program configuration

ABAP programs:

Report	Description
RFZALI20	Payment List report
SAPF110S	Payment program
SAPFPAYM_SCHEDULE	Payment medium – Schedule creation

BAPIs:

Function Module	Description
BAPI_PAYMENTREQUEST_CREATE	Create the payment request
BAPI_PAYMENTREQUEST_GETLIST	Get list of payment requests

BAPI_PAYMENTREQUEST_GETSTATUS	Get current status of payment request
BAPI_PAYMENTREQUEST_POST	Post the payment request
BAPI_PAYMENTREQUEST_RELEASE	Release payment request.
BAPI_PAYMENTREQUEST_CANCEL	Cancel the payment request
DELETE_PAYMENT_PROPOSAL	Delete the payment proposal
SCHEDULE_PAYMENT_PROPOSAL	Schedule the payment proposal
COPY_PAYMENT_PARAMETERS	Copy the payment parameters
DELETE_PAYMENT_PARAMETERS	Delete the payment parameters
FI_PAYMENT_METHOD_PROPERTIES	Fetch the payment method properties

3.4.6 Enhancements

- **FI_F110_SCHEDULE_JOB** – You can use this BADI to implement to do additional checks when you schedule a payment proposal or run. The method CHECK_PARAMETERS is used to do custom validation and the parameter E_PARAM_OK is used to determine whether parameters are valid or not. If the E_PARAM_OK is space then hard error is raised.

- BTE 1810 – This process BTE event allows you to determine bank detail and partner bank details used for the payment. The authorized bank details are transferred in table form. It has two table parameters T_HBANK (for housing banks) and T_PBANK (for partner bank details). For example, if you want to prevent the bank details from the payment program then set the indicator XCUSF on the relevant line item.

- BTE 1819 – You can use this process BTE event once the payment run is scheduled. (Payment Release list) is active. You can implement this event to trigger a workflow at the end of the payment process. Note that by default, the event 1819 is not activated. You can activate manually by maintaining 1819 entries in the TPS01 and TPS02 configuration table.

- BTE 1820 – You can use this process BTE event to change payment block or payment method in an open customer or vendor item directly after the line item selection. The account type parameter I_KOART determines the customer (D) or vendor (K) and the function module receives the index data table BSID or BSIK. The parameter C_ZLSPR is used to change payment block and C_ZLSCH to change the payment of the line item selected.

- BTE 1830 – This process BTE event is used to exclude individual items or entire line items from a group for payment after the items are grouped. If you set the XIGNO of the parameter C_REGUH then all items in the group appear on the exception list. If the value XIGNO in a line of table parameter T_REGUH, then the corresponding line item is excluded from the payment and appears on the exception list.

- BTE 2105 – This P/S BTE event is triggered before the payment schedule or proposal schedule is run.

- BTE 2110 – This P/S BTE event is triggered in REGH LATE event of the payment list program RFZALI20. The program uses the logical database PYF. The event allows you to modify the processed items in the payment list report.

  Note that all BTE events (except 2110) are executed only when the application FI-PRL is active

- **DMEE_EXIT_TEMPLATE_EXTEND_ABA** - This is user exit triggered in the DMEE mapping configuration   This template can be add your own custom code if mapping cannot be accomplished with just configuration. Sample code is given below for getting foreign bank key information from vendor master.

```
DATA: ls_lfb1 TYPE lfb1.
DATA ls_item TYPE dmee_paym_if_type.

CLEAR: ls_item, ls_lfb1.
MOVE i_item TO ls_item.

SELECT SINGLE * FROM lfb1 INTO ls_lfb1
   WHERE lifnr = ls_item-fpayh-gpa1r
   AND   bukrs = ls_item-fpayh-zbukr.

MOVE ls_lfb1-kverm(1) TO c_value.
```

Make sure that exit module is not bottlenecking your performance. The parameter i_item does have item information with payment detail.

3.5 Reporting

Reporting in Procure to Pay process can cover a variety of topics. In this section we will only cover reporting as it relates to accounts payable functions

Reports can be broadly classified into two categories:
- Standard SAP reports – summary and line item level reports
- Custom Reports - to address specific reporting needs of your business

Even though SAP has provided a number of standard reports, companies have over the years tended to develop custom reports because the elements of information may not be available in a particular format in a single standard report.

3.5.1 Standard Reports

Several standard reports are available in the information system area of accounts payable component.

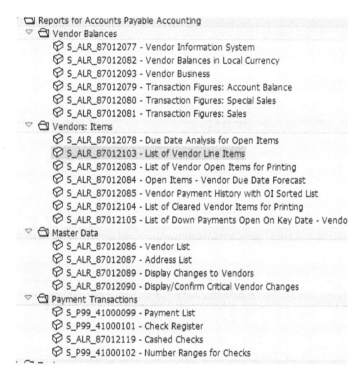

Standard reports are based on line item tables BSIK, BSAK that contain open and cleared vendor line items respectively.

The concept of "key date/ as of date" is important especially in sub-ledger reporting. For example, an invoice may have been in unpaid status on December 31st and was paid on January 5th. If you run a report as of December 31st, you want it to show in open items list. It is because of this reason that most standard reports in accounts payable read both BSIK and BSAK table. For payment and check information, data can be selected from REGUH, REGUP and PAYR tables.

In addition some reports may also use logical database KDF which makes data from several tables available for selection in the report.

3.5.2 Drill-Down Reports

The drilldown reporting overview is discussed in the chapter 2.7.4. In this section, the vendor accounting drilldown reporting are discussed. You can execute the vendor related drill-down reports using the transaction FKI0. It has two types Balance display and Line item analysis.

Execute Drill-Down Report: Initial Screen

New selection

Report	Description
▼ 🗀 Report type	
▼ 🗀 001	Display balances
• 🔲 0SAPFD10-01	Transaction Figures: Account B
• 🔲 0SAPFD10-02	Transaction Figures: Special Sal
• 🔲 0SAPFD10-03	Transaction Figures: Sales
▼ 🗀 002	Line item analysis
• 🔲 0SAPDUEAN-01	Due Date Analysis for Open Ite

You can create custom form and report under the report type. The drill down report uses the logical database KDF. Each report type uses different selection screen.

Transaction	Description
FKI0	Vendor drill down reports
FKI1, FKI2, FKI3	Create, Change and Display a new report
FKI4, FKI5, FKI6	Create, Change and Display a Form
FKIX	Delete Reports
FKIY	Translate Reports
FKIZ	Delete Forms

3.5.3 Custom Reports

As mentioned earlier, custom reports are sometimes determined by specific needs of the business. It could also a matter of preference to have a custom report that combines the data in one place instead of having to gather the information from several standard reports.

Two common topics for which custom reports are developed in accounts payable are for AP Aging and GR IR Aging. Sometimes there may be a requirement to sort/group/sub-total based on some vendor master fields such as Group Key which may not be available in standard reports.

Coding snippet for Vendor ageing report:

```
FORM FETCH_DATA.
SELECT *
 INTO TABLE lt_bsik
 FROM bsik
 WHERE bukrs IN so_bukrs
 AND   gjahr IN so_gjahr
 AND   lifnr IN so_lifnr
 AND   umskz IN so_umskz
 AND   umskz NOT IN ('F','P','L','G').

 SELECT *
  INTO TABLE lt_bsak
  FROM bsak
  WHERE bukrs IN so_bukrs
  AND   gjahr IN so_gjahr
  AND   lifnr IN so_lifnr
  AND   umskz IN so_umskz
  AND   umskz NOT IN ('F','P','L','G')
  AND   AUGDT > p_augdt.

  LOOP at lt_bsak INTO lv_bsak.
   move-corresponding lv_bsak to lv_bsik.
   append lv_bsik TO lt_bsik.
  ENDLOOP.
ENDFORM.
```

Get the vendor information for the selected open and cleared vendor line items.

```
FORM PROCESS_DATA.
 IF lt_bsik[] IS NOT INITIAL.
  select lifnr
        name1
        adrnr
   into table lt_lfa1
   from lfa1
   for all entries in lt_bsik
   where lifnr = lt_bsik-lifnr.
ENDIF.
* GET address from the table ADRC from lifnr-adrnr
* Populate the internal table lt_output based on your logic
 LOOP at lt_bsik INTO lv_bsik.
  MOVE-CORRESPONDING lv_bsik TO lv_output.

Vendor Ageing Report to Calculate the Outstanding Days
Sample report is developed for FI for vendor ageing
```

```
*&------------------------------------------------------------*
*& Report  ZFI_VENDOR_AGEING                        *
*&                                    *
*&------------------------------------------------------------*
*& Title - Vendor Ageing report to calculate the outstanding days    *
*& Name- Pavan Praveen valluri
*&      ABAP/4 Consultant                     *
*& Module - FI                          *
*&------------------------------------------------------------*
 REPORT  zfi_vendor_ageing.

TABLES : bsik, BAPIFVDEXP_VZZBEPP.

DATA : t_bsik LIKE bsik OCCURS 0 WITH HEADER LINE,
     t_bsak LIKE bsak OCCURS 0 WITH HEADER LINE,
     days like BAPIFVDEXP_VZZBEPP-NUM4.

DATA : BEGIN OF t_lfa1 OCCURS 0,
      lifnr LIKE lfa1-lifnr,
      name1 LIKE lfa1-name1,
      adrnr LIKE lfa1-adrnr,
      END OF t_lfa1.

DATA : BEGIN OF t_adrc OCCURS 0,
      adrnr LIKE lfa1-adrnr,
      street LIKE adrc-street,
      city1 LIKE adrc-city1,
      END OF t_adrc.

DATA : BEGIN OF t_BSEG OCCURS 0,
      zfbdt LIKE BSEG-zfbdt,
      KOART LIKE BSEG-KOART,
      KOSTL LIKE BSEG-KOSTL,
      PROJK LIKE BSEG-PROJK,
      END OF t_BSEG.

DATA : BEGIN OF t_prps OCCURS 0,
      POSID like prps-posid,
      OBJNR like prps-objnr,
      END OF t_prps.

DATA : T_KOSTL LIKE BSEG-KOSTL,
     T_PROJK LIKE BSEG-PROJK,
     TEXT(15).

DATA : BEGIN OF t_output OCCURS 0,
      lifnr LIKE lfa1-lifnr,
      name1 LIKE lfa1-name1,
      street LIKE adrc-street,
```

```abap
        city1 LIKE adrc-city1,
        OBJNR LIKE prps-OBJNR,
        posid LIKE prps-posid,
        KOSTL LIKE BSIK-KOSTL, " COST CENTER
        UMSKZ like bsik-UMSKZ,
        belnr like bsik-belnr,
        bukrs like bsik-bukrs,
        gjahr like bsik-gjahr,
        wrbtr like bsik-wrbtr,
        hkont like bsik-hkont,
        dif1  like bsik-wrbtr,
        dif2  like bsik-wrbtr,
        dif3  like bsik-wrbtr,
        dif4  like bsik-wrbtr,
        dif5  like bsik-wrbtr,
        days like BAPIFVDEXP_VZZBEPP-NUM4,
      END OF t_output.


* Alv data declaration
TYPE-POOLS : slis.
DATA :alv_fieldcat        TYPE slis_t_fieldcat_alv,
     alv_fieldcat_line    LIKE LINE OF alv_fieldcat,
     alv_sort             TYPE slis_t_sortinfo_alv,
     alv_sort_line        LIKE LINE OF alv_sort,
     alv_layout           TYPE slis_layout_alv,
     g_repid              LIKE sy-repid VALUE sy-repid,
     alv_status_set       TYPE slis_formname VALUE 'ALV_STATUS_SET',
     alv_user_comm        TYPE slis_formname VALUE 'ALV_USER_COMM',
     grid_title           TYPE lvc_title,
     alv_fieldcat_acty    TYPE slis_t_fieldcat_alv,
     g_save,
     gs_variant           LIKE disvariant,
     g_exit_caused_by_caller  TYPE c,
     gs_exit_caused_by_user   TYPE slis_exit_by_user.


DATA: alv_fieldcat_line_acty  LIKE LINE OF alv_fieldcat_acty,
     alv_layout_acty      TYPE slis_layout_alv,
     gt_list_top_of_page  TYPE slis_t_listheader,
     gt_events            TYPE slis_t_event,
     message              TYPE string,
     r_ucomm     LIKE sy-ucomm,
     rs_selfield TYPE slis_selfield.

CONSTANTS:
   gc_formname_top_of_page TYPE slis_formname VALUE 'TOP_OF_PAGE'.

SELECTION-SCREEN BEGIN OF BLOCK b1 WITH FRAME TITLE text-001.
SELECT-OPTIONS : s_bukrs FOR bsik-bukrs,
```

```
          s_gjahr FOR bsik-gjahr,
          s_lifnr FOR bsik-lifnr,
          s_umskz FOR bsik-umskz.
parameters    : p_augdt like bsik-augdt OBLIGATORY.
SELECTION-SCREEN END OF BLOCK b1.
SELECTION-SCREEN BEGIN OF BLOCK b2 WITH FRAME TITLE text-002.
SELECT-OPTIONS : s_date1 FOR BAPIFVDEXP_VZZBEPP-NUM4 NO-
EXTENSION OBLIGATORY
          DEFAULT 1 TO 30,
      s_date2 FOR BAPIFVDEXP_VZZBEPP-NUM4 NO-EXTENSION
OBLIGATORY
          DEFAULT 30 TO 60,
      s_date3 FOR BAPIFVDEXP_VZZBEPP-NUM4 NO-EXTENSION
OBLIGATORY
          DEFAULT 60 TO 90,
      s_date4 FOR BAPIFVDEXP_VZZBEPP-NUM4 NO-EXTENSION
OBLIGATORY
          DEFAULT 90 TO 120,
      s_date5 FOR BAPIFVDEXP_VZZBEPP-NUM4 NO-EXTENSION
OBLIGATORY
          DEFAULT 120 TO 150.
SELECTION-SCREEN END OF BLOCK b2.

INITIALIZATION.

START-OF-SELECTION.
  PERFORM fetch_data.
  PERFORM display.

*&---------------------------------------------------------------------*
*&      Form  fetch_data
*&---------------------------------------------------------------------*
*       text
*----------------------------------------------------------------------*
*  --> p1        text
*  <-- p2        text
*----------------------------------------------------------------------*
FORM fetch_data .

 SELECT *
 INTO TABLE t_bsik
 FROM bsik
 WHERE bukrs IN s_bukrs
 AND   gjahr IN s_gjahr
 AND   lifnr IN s_lifnr
 AND   umskz IN s_umskz
 AND   umskz NOT IN ('F','P','L','G').
*  AND   zfbdt <= P_augdt.
```

```abap
   if sy-subrc = 0.
    SELECT *
    INTO TABLE t_bsak
    FROM bsak
    WHERE bukrs IN s_bukrs
    AND   gjahr IN s_gjahr
    AND   lifnr IN s_lifnr
    AND   umskz IN s_umskz
    AND   umskz NOT IN ('F','P','L','G')
    AND   AUGDT > P_augdt.

    loop at t_bsak.
      move-corresponding t_bsak to t_bsik.
      append t_bsik.
    endloop.

    loop at t_bsik.
      if t_bsik-zfbdt is initial.
        t_bsik-zfbdt = t_bsik-bldat.
        modify t_bsik transporting zfbdt.
      endif.
      if t_bsik-zfbdt > P_augdt.
        delete t_bsik.
      endif.
*      if t_bsik-umskz > P_augdt.

    endloop.

    select lifnr
         name1
         adrnr
    into table lt_lfa1
    from lfa1
    for all entries in lt_bsik
    where lifnr = lt_bsik-lifnr.
    if sy-subrc = 0.
      select ADDRNUMBER as adrnr
           street
           city1
      into table lt_adrc
      from adrc
      for all entries in lt_lfa1
      where ADDRNUMBER = lt_lfa1-adrnr.
    endif.
   endif.
  LOOP AT t_bsik.
    if lv_bsik-shkzg = 'S'.
      lv_output-WRBTR = lv_bsik-WRBTR * -1.
    endif.
```

```
READ TABLE lt_lfa1 INTO lv_lfa1 WITH KEY lifnr = t_output-LIFNR.
IF sy-subrc EQ 0.
    move-corresponding lv_lfa1 to lv_output.
    READ table lt_adrc INTO lv_adrc WITH KEY adrnr = lv_lfa1-adrnr.
    MOVE-CORRESPONDING lv_adrc TO lv_output.
ENDIF.
lv_output-days = p_augdt – lv_bsik-zfbdt.
* Add your logic to populate fields for lv_output
    APPEND lv_output TO lt_output.
ENDLOOP.
ENDFORM.
```

Output the result.

```
FORM display_data.
  CALL FUNCTION 'REUSE_ALV_GRID_DISPLAY'
   EXPORTING
    i_callback_program      = lv_repid
    i_callback_pf_status_set = lv_status_set
    i_callback_user_command  = lv_user_comm
    i_grid_title         = lv_title
    i_save             = lv_save
    is_variant           = lv_variant
    is_layout           = lv_layout
    it_fieldcat          = lt_fieldcat[]
    it_events           = lt_events[]
    it_sort            = lt_sort[]
   IMPORTING
    e_exit_caused_by_caller  = lv_exit_caused_by_caller
    es_exit_caused_by_user  = lv_exit_caused_by_user
   TABLES
    t_outtab            = lt_output.
ENDFORM.
```

Another situation is a requirement to show data from GL, AP and MM modules such as PO line item detail and bring them together in a detailed aging report where a custom report will be required. Such a report will select and process data from BSIS, BSAS, EKPO, LFA1, EKKO etc. to show the desired output. The function module REUSE_ALV_GRID_DISPLAY is highly used in the custom programs for report output.

3.6 Summary

In this chapter we covered organizational units relevant to procure to pay process such as purchase organization, plant and storage location. Then key master data such as vendor, PIR, pricing conditions, material master were covered.

You were given an overview of the integration aspects of material master with reference to accounting and costing. Invoice verification and payment process were covered including examples of custom enhancements. Finally, standard reports and examples of custom reports were mentioned in this section.

4 Order-To-Cash

Order to Cash Process encompasses a series of business events starting from initial customer contact, progressing to sales order processing, shipping of product to customer, invoicing, customer payment and reporting. On the front end, it can be extended to include customer quote through creation of sales order but that would logically belong in SAP CRM and hence not covered in this chapter. The scope of this section will be restricted to 4 broad topics within the order to cash process and particularly how these interact with the FI module. In addition reporting aspects will be covered briefly at the end of this chapter.

Two related topics credit management and dispute management will be covered briefly. They have not been taken up in detail as in recent years they have been bundled as part of FSCM component along with biller direct and treasury management.

The four key topics covered in this chapter are:

➤ Sales order and its implications for FI and CO
➤ Delivery processing and goods movement
➤ Invoicing
➤ Payments including lockbox process

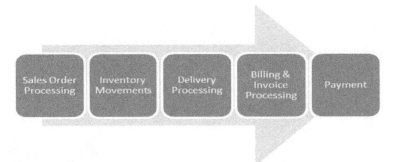

From this chapter, you will understand key master data elements, critical configuration impacting the order to cash process. In addition, you will be given several examples of enhancement opportunities in the form of BTE, BAdI, user exit which will prove to be valuable in designing solutions. Sample custom ABAP code will be given wherever appropriate within these topics.

4.1 Organizational Units

The order to cash process depends on proper definition and assignment of several organizational units such as sales org, plant, distribution channel, shipping point and credit control area. Many of these also influence the way transactions are processed in FI and CO modules. Hence it is important that organizational structure is well thought out and properly configured taking into consideration the integration with materials management and FICO

For example, the assignment of a plant to a sales organization tied to another company code will result in an intercompany billing transaction. If these company codes have different local currencies, it will involve a currency conversion at a transactional level. Similarly, internal customer can be assigned to a plant to facilitate intercompany transactions based on stock transport orders.

In this section we will cover some of the key organizational units in sales and distribution. These org units also have a bearing on financial transactions as they may be used in account determination in billing documents.

4.1.1 Sales Organization

The sales organization (sales org) is the highest organizational unit in sales and distribution module. Generally it closely resembles the organizational structure for sales in your company. The sales organization is assigned to only one company code. It is common practice for sales org to be assigned a four character alpha numeric code. The field name for sales org is VKORG.

All transaction data such as sales order, delivery and billing document belong to the sales organization. You can use t-code OVX8 (Report RVOCHECK) to check whether the org structure for sales and distribution has been configured properly.

Check Report for Customizing - Organization - SD

Details ⊕ Execute   Select line

☑ Sales organizations...

☑ Distribution channels...

☑ Divisions...

☑ Sales offices...

☑ Sales groups...

☑ Shipping points...

☑ Plants...

4.1.2 Plant

Even though plant has been covered multiple times in other chapters, it merits a mention her too as it plays an important part in the order to cash process. A plant can be assigned to multiple sales organizations. In such situations, an intercompany billing is triggered provided the required configuration steps have been set up properly.

4.1.3 Shipping Point

A deliver is uniquely attached to a shipping point. Often the shipping is one of the factors that determine shipping point. It is common for companies to have dedicated shipping points that align with the nature of materials being handled, packaged and shipped in designated areas within their manufacturing or distribution facility. Field name for shipping point is VSTEL.

4.1.4 Storage Location

A storage location organizes the inventory in your facility in logical categories. This is also referred to as the IM-inventory management level. In a typical set up, separate storage locations are set up for receiving, shipping and returns. Materials requiring special handling can be managed in a dedicated storage location. The definition of storage locations is dependent on the size and complexity of the business. We are not going to cover warehouse management in this section.

4.1.5 Distribution Channel

Distribution channel represents how products or services are sold to customers. A distribution channel can be as assigned to several sales organizations. For practical reason including reduced master data maintenance, companies configure only one or two distribution channels and achieve the desired granularity for reporting purposes by defining other units such as sales office, and sales district.

4.1.6 Division

The division is generally used for determination of business area via the plant/division combination. SAP recommends that to use the generic '01' division unless there is good reason to distinguish by division. Because a material is assigned to only one division, many companies prefer to maintain only one division and distribution channel to simplify master data maintenance.

4.1.7 Sales Area

The sales area is defined as a combination of sales org, division and division. The sales related views of the customer master are at sales area level. Master data elements such as sales district, ordering currency, sales group, pricelist, shipping and billing requirements are defined at the sales area level.

4.1.8 Sales Office

Sales office generally represents a unit within the sales organization for which sales performance needs to be measured and reported. For example, it may represent a sales territory or a key account or a sales team.

4.1.9 Sales Group

The sales group is at a lower level than a sales office. It may represent a sales representative or a particular group of customers. You can assign employees to a sales group. The sales group is used for reporting purpose.

4.1.10   Credit Control Area

Credit limit for customers and specified and monitored for a credit control area. The company code and sales are both assigned to a credit control area. Automatic credit checks are performed during both order entry and delivery creation based on credit limits defined. Several custom enhancements are possible around credit control area and credit checking and those will be covered later on in this chapter. The technical name for credit control area is KKBER. The credit control area plays a role both in FI and SD modules. Credit limits are set in the credit management view of the customer master and dynamically checked during sales order and delivery processing.

The credit update group defined in credit check configuration in transaction OVA8 controls how values are updated from open sales orders, deliveries and billing documents.

Tables

Table	Comments
TVKO	Sales organization
TVKOV	Distribution Channel
TVKOS	Divisions by Sales org
TSPA	Sales Division
T001	Plant
T001L	Storage location
T014	Credit Control Area

4.2 Master Data

The attributes or values from master data work with organization units to control the way transactions are posted in SD. They also have a huge influence on how these transactions are reflected in FI and CO.

As an example, you may have set up USD as default currency in sales tab of sales area of customer master. If required, you can also define an alternate exchange rate type so that transactions are converted at that rate instead of the default M rate. Similarly the customer account assignment group (CAAG) may be used to direct postings to a specific general ledger account in account determination.

Partner functions such as Payer and Bill To party are important because your customer may asked to be invoiced in one location but the receivables may be posted against a different customer number. In this section we will touch on some key features of master data.

4.2.1 Business Partners & Customer

The concept of Business Partner came into the picture with the introduction of SAP components such as CRM, FSCM and is also in heavy use in several industry specific add-on solutions. The business partner can be a natural person or a legal entity that has dealings with your company. By assigning a business partner role, you can perform a logical classification of that partner.

It is important to distinguish between business partner and the partner functions of the customer master. Through configuration settings, you can automatically create a customer when a business partner is created. The customer master record and business partner are different objects and it would be erroneous to use them interchangeably.

The discussion in this sub-section will be restricted to customer master and its attributes. In the IMG you define account groups for customers or create customer master records under any of the SAP-delivered account groups. Account groups determine number interval, internal or external assignment and field status.

It helps to have a working knowledge of various attributes of the customer master as they influence both transaction flow and reporting. The customer master is divided into general data, company code data and sales area data.

The general data contains name, address and communication details. Control tab has the tax related information. It also has the business type and industry type required for reporting in South Korea and VAT number required for transactions within the European Union. The bank details tab of general data contains important information that is used during processing of customer receipts from your bank in electronic format. This is often referred to as the lockbox or auto-cash process and one of the key steps in this process is the

The company code area contains the reconciliation account to which receivable is posted in the general ledger. This also contains payment method, payment term, alternate payer and dunning information.

The sales area data in customer master contains critical information that determines how a sales order, deliveries and billing documents are processed. Sales tab contains information that determines the pricing procedure to be applied, and the ordering currency. The shipping tab contains information regarding how a particular order has to be processed from an operational perspective. Values for shipping conditions govern order priority, and the delivering plant can be specified in this tab. The billing documents tab has inco terms, payment terms, customer account assignment group, and tax classification by country. The customer account assignment group is often used in GL account determination.

The next tab in customer master record is the partner functions tab. Each of these partner functions has a specific meaning. In FI-AR the receivable is posted against the payer partner. The pricing is picked up for the sold to partner. The tax determination happens for the address of the ship to partner. The invoice is sent to the Bill to partner by print, fax, email or EDI. In addition to these core partner functions it is possible to maintain additional partner functions to represent an employee or sales person that manages the customer account.

Table BUT000 is the base table for a Business partner. The table represents the business partner's general data. You can list out all business partner tables by prefix BUT0*.

The following partner roles of business partners are used highly in the order-to-cash process.

- Sold-to Party
- Ship-to Party
- Bill-to Party
- Payer

Customer

You can create a customer master record without a business partner also. You can access customer master data using the transaction code FD01/FD02/FD03. You can assign a customer master record to the business partner using Customer business partner role.

When you create a business partner and customer business partner role will create a customer master record automatically. There are customer business partner roles which creates the customer master record. These business partner roles can be configured in the IMG configuration.

Role Cat.	Description
FLCU00	Business Partner FI Customer (FS: BP)
FLCU01	Business Partner Customer (FS: BP)
MKK	Contract Partner
PSSP01	Sponsor
TR0100	Main Loan Partner (FS: CML)
TR0120	Authorized Drawer (FS: CML)
TR0121	Other Loan Partner with Customer Account (FS: CML)
TR0150	Issuer (FS: CFM / CML)

Change View "Set BP Role Category for Customer Integration": Overview
New Entries — BC Set: Change Field Values
Set BP Role Category for Customer Integration

Technical Structure

Table	Description
KNA1	Customer master
KNB1	Customer with company code
KNVV	Customer master Sales org
KNVK	Customer master Contact Partner
KNEX	Customer master sanctioned party list
KNVA	Customer master uploading point
KNVP	Customer master partner functions
KNVD	Customer master record sales request form
KNVI	Customer master tax indicator
KNVL	Customer master licenses
KNBK	Customer master – bank details
KNAT	Customer master – Tax groupings

KNAS	Customer master – VAT

Reports:

- RFDKLI10 – You can use this report to list out customers with missing credit data. The report checks central data, and control area-related data per customer.
- RFDKLI30 – This report provides you a short overview of all credit limit-related data per customer. This is an ALV report.
- RFDKLI40 – You can generate a credit data list for credit management for a customer. You can restrict the selection of customers by credit account, credit control area and credit representative group. This is an ALV report.
- RFCMCRCV – Credit Management – Create A/R summary
- RFCMDECV – Credit Management Delete A/R Summary data
- RFDKLI41 – Credit master sheet
- RFDKLI50 – Credit limit data mass change
- RFDUZI00 – This program debits interest on arears per customer account and currency.

Search Help	Description
DEBIA	General customer search help
DEBID	Customer search help by company code
DEBIE	Customer search help by country/company code
DEBIT	Customer search help by tax information

Enhancements

The following enhancements are a part of customer master data processing. There is one SMOD enhancement and three BADIs.

- **SAPMF02D** – This is a SMOD enhancement that allows you to check the entered data before saving customer master record. The function module EXIT_SAPMF02D_001 is part of the enhancement and passes all customer related data. You can raise any error message for inconsistent data based on your requirements.

- **CUSTOM_ADD_DATA_CS** – This filter-dependent BAdI serves for the inclusion of your sub-screens into the customer master record dialog. On the sub-screens, you can implement the maintenance of your own fields. The filter is the screen group created by you in the customizing. With the filter dependency it is achieved that only the active implementation of the respective screen group will run in the flow control of the sub-screen container from the standard in which your sub-screen for the runtime is included.

- **CUSTOM_ADD_DATA** - The BAdI contains methods which occur in the interactive environment but which are independent of the sub-screen container in which your sub-screens are included for the runtime. For example these are methods for the defaulting of data or for the saving of the data.

- **CUSTOM_ADD_DATA_BI** – The BAdI is used in the area of ALE-distribution and standard batch input. There are available methods with which you can fill own ALE-segments in the ALE-outbound or make an evaluation of own change pointers. The ALE-inbound and the standard batch input of the customer master provide methods with which you can integrate own data into the batch input data that were calculated by the standard-program.

Technical Challenge: Custom fields are added in KNA1 and require updating using a separate screen.
Solution:
- Create the screen group (ZG) and define the tab pages with function code.
- Activate the screen group by implementing the BADI CUSTOMER_ADD_DATA. You can implement a separate implementation for each screen group or you can implement one implementation for all your custom screen groups.

Name: CUSTOMER_ADD_DATA		Multiple Use: Yes	Filter: No
Description: Additional data at customer master data			
Method: CHECK_ADD_ON_ACTIVE			
Description: Activate the screen group			
Name	Type	Data Type	Description
I_SCREEN_GROUP	Importing	CUST_SCGR	Screen Group
E_ADD_ON_ACTIVE	Changing	FLAG	Enhancement flag
Sample code: You must activate the screen group			
CHECK i_screen_group = 'ZG'.			
e_add_on_active = 'X'.			

- Create screen for your requirements under function group (ZCUST_SCREENEXT). Note that you need a separate screen for each tab page of the screen group.
- Implement the BADI CUSTOMER_ADD_DATA_CS for the screen group.

Name: CUSTOMER_ADD_DATA_CS	Multiple Use: Yes	Filter: Yes
Description: Additional data screen at customer master data. The filter is based on the screen group. This BADI is used only when ADD_ON_ACTIVE is set for the screen group.		
Method: CHECK_ADD_ON_ACTIVE		
Description: Activate the screen group		

Name	Type	Data Type	Description
FLT_VAL	Importing	CUST_SCGR	Screen Group
I_TAX_FCODE	Importing	TAXITABS-FCODE	FCODE of tab page
E_SCREEN	Changing	DYNNR	Subscreen
E_PROGRAM	Changing	REPID	Subscreen program
E_HEADERSCREEN_LAYOUT	Changing	CHAR1	B – Company code, V – Sales Area; space-General data.

Sample code: You must set the screen, program and area of definition
```
case i_taxi_fcode.
  when 'ZTB1'.
    e_screen  = '9000'.
    e_program = 'SAPLZCUST_SCREENEXT'.
    e_headerscreen_layout = ' '.
endcase.
```

You can create function modules ZFM_SET_DATA and ZFM_GET_DATA in the function group to interface the variables between BADI implementation and screens. The function module will update the global variables which are used by the screen layout. If you have any derivation field and execute the logic in these function modules. You can define the parameter interfaces of the function modules based on the requirement.

The sample code:

```
FUNCTION ZFM_SET_DATA .
*"----------------------------------------------------------------
*"*"Local Interface:
*"  IMPORTING
*"     REFERENCE(I_ACTIVITY) TYPE  AKTYP
*"     REFERENCE(I_KUNNR) TYPE  KUNNR
*"     REFERENCE(I_ZKNA1) TYPE  ZSKNA1
*"     REFERENCE(I_ZKNB1) TYPE  ZSKNB1
*"----------------------------------------------------------------
g_activity  = i_activity.
g_kunnr     = i_kunnr.
g_zkna1     = i_zkna1.
g_zknb1     = i_zknb1.

ENDFUNCTION.
```

```
FUNCTION ZFM_GET_DATA .
*"----------------------------------------------------------------
*"*"Local Interface:
```

```
*"  EXPORTING
*"     REFERENCE(E_CHANGED) TYPE  FLAG
*"     REFERENCE(E_ZKNA1) TYPE  ZKNA1
*"     REFERENCE(E_ZKNB1) TYPE  ZKNB1
*"-----------------------------------------------------------------
e_changed = g_is_changed.
e_zkna1   = g_zkna1.
e_zknb1   = g_zknb1.


ENDFUNCTION.
```

Implement the SET_DATA method to transfer data to the screen and GET_DATA method to get the data from the screen. Both methods interface most of customer data structures like general data (KNA1), company code, sales, VAT, Dunning data, Bank details, etc.

Method: SET_DATA
Description: Transfer data to the screen

Name	Type	Data Type	Description
FLT_VAL	Importing	CUST_SCGR	Screen Group
I_ACTIVITY	Importing	AKTYP	Activity category
S_KNA1	Importing	KNA1	Customer general data
S_KNB1	Importing	KNB1	Cust. Company data
..	…	…	…
…..	…..	…..	…..

Sample code: You must set the screen, program and area of definition
```
DATA: l_changed  TYPE flag,
     lv_zkna1   TYPE zkna1,
     lv_zknb1   TYPE zknb1.
* Move data to KNA1 table
  MOVE-CORRESPONDING s_kna1 TO lv_zkna1.
  MOVE-CORRESPONDING s_knb1 TO lv_zknb1.

* set data for changed flag and append structure
  CALL FUNCTION 'ZFM_SET_DATA'
    EXPORTING
      i_activity = i_activity
      e_zkna1    = lv_zkna1
      e_zknb1    = lv_zknb1
    EXCEPTIONS
      OTHERS    = 1.
```

Method: GET_DATA
Description: Get data from the screen

Name	Type	Data Type	Description
FLT_VAL	Importing	CUST_SCGR	Screen Group
S_KNA1	Changing	KNA1	Customer general data
S_KNB1	Changing	KNB1	Cust. Company data

..	...	...	...

```
Sample code:  You must set the screen, program and area of definition
DATA: lv_changed TYPE flag,
    lv_zkna1   TYPE zkna1,
    lv_zknb1   TYPE zknb1.

* Get data for changed flag and append structure
  CALL FUNCTION 'ZFM_GET_DATA'
   IMPORTING
    e_changed = lv_changed
    e_zkna1  = lv_zkna1
    e_zknb1  = lv_zknb1
   EXCEPTIONS
    OTHERS   = 1.

  CHECK lv_changed = 'X'.

* Move data to KNA1 table
  MOVE-CORRESPONDING lv_zkna1 TO s_kna1.
  MOVE-CORRESPONDING lv_zknb1 TO s_knb1.
```

The BADI CUSTOMER_ADD_DATA_CS has a number of methods and explained in brief.

- **SET_FCODE** – This method provides you set the function code when your tab page is displayed. However, the method is not called if the user wants to change to one of your other tab pages.

- **GET_FIELDNAME_FOR_CHANGEDOC** – The method is used to inform the standard program about the name of the field, for which the change documents are to be determined. If this is a field from one of your own tables you must then define an own change document object for this table and ensure that change documents for this change document object are written in your update routines.

- **GET_CHANGEDOC_FOR_OWN_TABLES** – The method is to inform the standard about your change document object. In this process, it is important that change documents for your change document object are stored in the system with the customer number as object ID.

- **SUPPRESS_TAXI_TABSTRIPS** – You can hide tab pages depending on the activity and the organizational data. For example, you can hide a tab page which contains company code data if no company code was entered.

- **INITIALIZE_ADD_ON_DATA** – You can initialize your work structures. It is called when you access the dialog and when the user changes the customer during the processing of a customer without exiting the transaction.

- **READ_ADD_ON_DATA** – This method is executed when you display or change existing customer and you can read your own tables.
- **CHECK_DATA_CHANGED** – You can use this method to inform the standard program whether the user made changes to your own tables. This method is not applicable when custom fields are part of append structure of standard tables.
- **SAVE_DATA** – You can use this method to save your own tables. Make sure that commit statement is not used in this implementation. The commit and update tasks are part of the standard SAP process.
- **CHECK_ALL_DATA** – This method will be executed when the user pressed the save button. You can check whole data for consistency again.
- **MODIFY_ACCOUT_NUMBER** – If you work with internal number assignment during the setup of a customer, you can use this method to change the customer number that was determined from the system-side. The method is not called if the creation of the customer occurs via the ALE interface. **CHECK_ACCOUT_NUMBER** – You can carry out additional checks that are not covered by the number range when you work with external number assignment during the setup of a customer. The method is not called if the creation of the customer occurs via the ALE interface.

4.2.2 Customer Hierarchies

Customer hierarchies are created to resemble the structure of your customer's business. If you have a customer with operations in multiple countries or regions, the individual sold to customer numbers relating to that group can be tied together using a customer hierarchy. They are used with great effect in pricing to simplifying master data maintenance. Customer hierarchies also come in handy during reporting. The customer hierarchies are stored in the table KNVH.

4.2.3 Material Master

The material master is covered here again as it has relevance to how transactions are processed in SD module. The sales-related data are in sales1, sales 2 and sales general/plant views of material master. SalesOrg 1 view contains the default delivering plant, sales unit if different from base unit and cash discount relevancy flag. Sales Org 2 view contains material account assignment group (MAAG) used in GL account determination and item category group. The item category group determines the item category which in turn controls many aspects of sales documents such as pricing, billing and delivery processing.

4.2.4 Condition Records

SAP delivers several condition types that represent basic elements of pricing such as material prices, discounts, and surcharges. In the IMG, condition tables, condition types, and access sequences are defined. The condition types are included in the pricing procedure and eventually get picked up in sales documents such as sales order and billing document.

Useful transaction codes are VK11/VK13(Create), VK12/VK32(Change), VK13/VK33 (Display). Some pricing related tables are provided below.

Table	Description
KONV	Conditions transaction data
KONP	Conditions Items
KONM	Conditions Quantity scale
KNOW	Conditions Value scale
KOMK	Pricing communication header
KOMP	Pricing communication item
VEDA	Contract data

You can run a report of conditions with transaction V/LD. You can create a pricing report using the transaction V/LA. The logical database for the condition reports is V12L.

4.3 Sales Order Processing

The order to cash process has often been extended further upstream to include customer inquiries, quote and contracts. But these transactions by themselves do not directly influence the values posted in an accounting or CO document. Hence the following two sections will cover only sales order and delivery processing.

Before sales order, there are pre-sales activities like Contact, Inquiry, Quotation and Scheduling agreements. Pre-sales activities involve low or no financial integration. So in this chapter, you are going through sales order processing and delivery processing only.

4.3.1 Sales Order

Sales order is often the starting point in the order to cash process. Like other documents in SAP, sales order is also organized as header and line item. The financial document or CO document is impacted indirectly by the values updated in the sales order header and line item. You will learn some examples of that in the following paragraphs.

Order Header information is organized in different tabs. The sales tab contains information such as order type, sales area data, order reason, currency, pricing procedure, sales district, customer group and pricing date. Shipping tab contains shipping condition which influences the delivery creation and weight information. Billing tab has inco terms, payment terms, billing block and billing date.

Accounting tab has details of customer account assignment group, exchange rate, dunning key and dunning block. The conditions tab presents a header level view of the pricing conditions contained in the sales order as determined by the pricing procedure. They may be conditions that were input by user or determined automatically through condition records.

Header partners tab generally contains at a minimum Sold to, Ship to and Payer partners. It is common for companies to have other partner functions defined as well to facilitate internal reporting. Order data contains customer PO information. The status tab provides information on overall status of the order, credit check status, invoicing status as well as order complete status. Additional data A and additional data B status tab provides some fields where information specific to your company is captured. We have seen custom fields added to sales order such that it appears in additional data B tab.

The document flow provides the preceding and follow-in documents associated with the sales order.

Document Flow

Status overview   Display document   Service documents

Business partner 0000099999 Gourmet Market
Material B-7000 Brochure: New high tech range

Document	Quantity	Unit	Ref. value	Currency	On	Status
Sales activities (CAS) 0100000069					05.06.1998	Completed
Deliv.Free of Charge 0000005455 / 10	19	PC	0,00	DEM	05.06.1998	Completed
Delivery 0080003844 / 10	19	PC			05.06.1998	Completed
WMS transfer order 0000000031 / 1	19	PC			05.06.1998	Completed
GD goods issue:delvy 0049007385 / 1	19	PC	285,00	DEM	05.06.1998	complete

Let us look how many values in the order header eventually influence accounting postings. A pricing condition record may be maintained such that the combination of Sold to Party/Product Hierarchy has a certain percentage defined. Through the account key in pricing procedure, the system determines the GL account that should be posted when this pricing condition appear in the billing document. The order reason in sales order header can be linked in configuration to a cost center. In such cases the account assignment tab is automatically filled with that cost center which then carries over into delivery and to billing/accounting document. In this example the order reason has impacted the FI line item and CO document.

The pricing date controls which pricing conditions are picked up based on their validity for that date and that can impact what amounts and which GL accounts are posted in a given accounting document originating in SD. From the accounting tab, customer account assignment group is used for account determination and can be seen in C<nnn> tables. It is possible to enter an alternate exchange rate in the header. This will ignore the usual exchange rate (M rate is the most commonly used transactional rate) and apply the override rate all the way through billing.

The billing date is passed as FI document posting date and that has to be in an open FI posting period if not we will be faced with a situation of an invoice that failed to post accounting. The document currency is usually inherited from the customer master and it becomes the currency of the accounting document header. Sales district is used in management reporting along territory, business units or key accounts based on the company's needs.

The information contained in conditions tab is important for accounting. The various pricing conditions relating to selling price, surcharges, discounts, allowances and accrual conditions eventually flow through to accounting by way of the billing document. The tax procedure determines the various levels of taxes. If an external tax tool such as Vertex is used, SAP makes a real-time RFC call to that system to get back tax amounts for each level. In addition, the pricing conditions are mapped to CO-Profitability analysis and it creates a CO-PA transaction with record type A thus differentiating it with the CO-PA transaction generated by billing document with record type F.

If your company accepts credit cards during order entry, payment cards would have been configured. Card authorization happens during sales order creation. Often companies use add-on ABAP tools for credit card processing provided by companies such as Paymetric, Delego etc. to manage credit card processing in both order entry and invoicing. They provide a mechanism to connect to the payment processor such as First Data Corporation or Paymentech thus completing the loop between your company, your bank, the card issuing bank and the customer.

The partner tab usually contains 4 partner functions viz., Sold-To partner, Ship-To partner, Bill-To and the Payer partner. Every one of them serves a specific purpose. Pricing records are maintained for the sold-to partner. Most master data information such as order currency etc. is inherited from sold to partner. CO-PA is updated with sold-to partner.

Ship to partner is used for tax determination. SAP allows the use of a generic Ship to party and then dynamically change the address details in the sales order. This flexibility is handy if you have to ship to thousands of individual addresses in a business to consumer scenario.

Bill to partner is where invoices are sent. This becomes relevant if the Payer and Bill to have different addresses. In an EDI scenario the invoice IDOC is generated to the Bill to Party. The Payer partner is where the accounts receivable line item is posted. The bank information of your customer is maintained in the payer and is used during cash application to find a customer match. We will cover this in greater detail in the cash application section.

The sales order line item also has several important fields relevant to accounting. The account assignment tab contains the profit center determined from material master. If it is a cross company code transaction, an additional field 'profit center for billing' is also populated. It is possible to programmatically override the profit center from material master with a different profit center value that represents a business unit. The CO-PA profitability segment is also set in the order line item. Generally, it contains customer, product, product hierarchy, and profit center. This information is later on used for internal reporting.

Automatic credit checks are carried out based on the delivery date in schedule lines tab. Order items with delivery dates beyond the credit horizon are ignored. When back order rescheduling is carried out, system will perform credit check again. Also if order quantities or order values are changed for any reason, credit check will be carried out automatically even though it may have passed credit check earlier.

Companies may have a need to implement a drop ship process also known as external fulfilment. This can be set up in such a way that, there is no physical handling of inventory in any of the company's facilities. There is no delivery or post goods issue transaction. The item category TAS in sales order line marks it as a third party item and it triggers a purchase requisition which can be seen in the schedule lines tab. The account assignment on this purchase requisition (PR) is usually mapped to the cost of goods sold account. This will be an order-related billing on the customer's account. Customer Invoice with VF01 can be created only after the vendor's invoice is entered against the PO with the MIRO transaction.

Some companies may have a configure-to-order process implemented. In the order line item, when a configurable material is entered, the configuration editor is presented where you enter the characteristics of the configurable material. Availability check is carried out and sales order is saved with the configuration details of that material.

Sales orders can also be created with make to order items. In such cases, the sales order line item creates individual requirements that result in creation of a production order. In this case the stock is exclusively assigned to that order.

Several user exits have been provided in sales order processing to meet non-standard business requirements. Some of these are discussed in the following section on enhancements.

4.3.2 Technical Details

Important Tables used in the sales processing:

Table	Description
VBAK	Sales Order header
VBAP	Sales Order Item
VBKD	Sales Order business data
VBFA	Sales order flow
VBPA	Sales order partner
VBEP	Sales order schedule line
VBUP	Sales document Item status
VBUV	Sales document incompletion log
VBKA	Sales activities
VBUK	Sales document: header status and administrative data
VBUP	Sales Document: Item status

The function module RV_CALL_DISPLAY_TRANACTION allows you to display the document (in the document flow). The function module covers all of the document types and transaction codes used in the document flow.

Function Module	Description
BAPI_ACC_SALES_QUOTA_POST	Accounting: post customer quotation
BAPI_ACC_SALES_QUOTA_CHECK	Accounting: Check Customer Quotation
BAPI_ACC_SALES_ORDER_POST	Accounting: Post sales order
BAPI_ACC_SALES_ORDER_CHECK	Accounting: Check sales order
ACC_INPUT_SALES_DOCUMENT	Accounting: Inbound sales documnet

4.3.3 Enhancements

FV45K001 – You can use this SMOD enhancement to change the credit control area while sales order processing. It has a user exit component EXIT_SAPFV45K_001 that is used to determine the credit control. The function module has import parameters VBAK and VBKD entries and it returns credit control area. The returned credit control area should be valid for the company code. Otherwise, it raises the error message 'Credit Control area for company code is not permitted'.

In configuration for profit center accounting, there is a provision to create a substitution rule tied to a user exit which will allow you to override the profit center determined from material/plant natively, with a new value calculated based on your own business rules. This substitution exit is part of the routines coded in module pool program for FI substitutions. You need to regenerate the substitution rules using the report RGGBS000 as explained in the chapter 1.

4.4 Delivery Processing

The delivery document is a key object within logistics processes. It functions as a starting point and driver for all subsequent logistics processes including picking, packing, transportation and goods issue. Only the outbound delivery is discussed in this section. It is also frequently referred to as the delivery order (D).

Delivery plays a role not only in external customer transaction but also in inter-plant and inter-company transactions. Deliveries are created individually in the VL01N transaction or directly from the sales order. It is a common practice in most companies to schedule delivery creation as a background job at pre-defined intervals. The delivery due list program is RVV50R10C and variants are maintained specifying values for shipping point, order type etc.

After delivery, the subsequent processes are shipment creation which may be configured to be optional, picking, packing and post goods issue (PGI). Of these, only the PGI is relevant to accounting and is covered in the next section.

The delivery document has the standard SAP structure of header and line item. LIKP and LIPS are the delivery header and line item tables respectively. SAP has provided several standard delivery types that represent different types of business transactions. The item category in the delivery line item controls several aspects such as allowing zero quantity, text item, minimum delivery quantity, picking relevancy and automatic determination of storage location.

Even though delivery is primarily a logistics document, it influences FI and CO postings with respect to the following:
- ➤ Cost center in line item
- ➤ Profit center in line item
- ➤ Automatic credit check
- ➤ Tax calculation

The cost center or profit center value in financial processing tab is passed on to FI and CO document during post goods issue transaction.

4.4.1 Technical Details

The list of the tables used in delivery processing.

LIKP	Delivery document – Header data
LIPS	Delivery document – Item data
VTTK	Shipment Header
VTTP	Shipment Item
VTPA	Shipment partners
VEKP	Handling Unit – Header
VEPO	Handling Unit - Item

Enhancements

One of the enhancements possible is a user exit to change the profit center determined by the system at the line item level. The user exit is MV50AFZ1.

4.5 Inventory Movements

The goods issue posting is the first instance where an accounting document is created. The system inherits values from the delivery during creation of material document and corresponding accounting document. The goods issue transaction is often referred as PGI. This happens at the end of shipping activity.

4.5.1 Post Goods Issue - PGI

Some common goods issue postings are for movement types such as 601 – Goods issue against delivery, 641 – Transfer to stock in transit etc. The MM account determination configuration takes effect during PGI. Let us analyze the most common movement type during a PGI transaction. In account grouping for movement types, the 601 movement type is flagged for value update. The movement indicator is L- movement for delivery note. The transaction will be GBB – the offsetting entry to inventory posting. The account modifier in standard system for this combination if VAX.

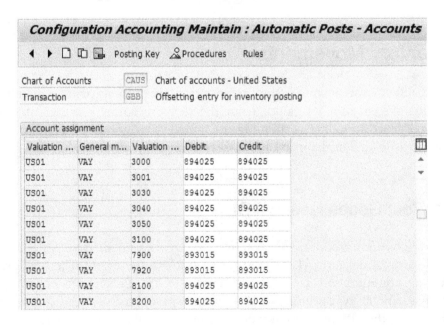

Display View "Account Grouping": Details

Movement Type 601 GD goods issue:delvy   Special Stock
☑ Value Update   Movement ind. L
☐ Quantity updating   Consumption
Value String   WA01

Current Entry

2	GBB	Offsetting entry for inventory posting	VAX	☑ Check

Trans./Event Key for String

TEKey	Description	Acct modif	Check
BSX	Inventory posting		☐
GBB	Offsetting entry for inventory posting	VAX	☑

You will then set up account determination for VAX account modifier based on valuation class if applicable. The configuration looks like this example below.

Configuration Accounting Maintain : Automatic Posts - Accounts

◀ ▶ ☐ ☐ ☐ Posting Key &Procedures Rules

Chart of Accounts   CAUS   Chart of accounts - United States
Transaction   GBB   Offsetting entry for inventory posting

Account assignment

Valuation ...	General m...	Valuation ...	Debit	Credit
US01	VAY	3000	894025	894025
US01	VAY	3001	894025	894025
US01	VAY	3030	894025	894025
US01	VAY	3040	894025	894025
US01	VAY	3050	894025	894025
US01	VAY	3100	894025	894025
US01	VAY	7900	893015	893015
US01	VAY	7920	893015	893015
US01	VAY	8100	894025	894025
US01	VAY	8200	894025	894025

This is often known as OBYC configuration and is stored in table T030. You want to be careful when creating a transport request for changes to entries through OBYC. All entries that have the same account modifier will be included in the transport even though you may have changed only one record.

The successful completion of PGI creates both an accounting and material document. Here is an example of a material document for 601 movement type- goods issue against delivery note.

Display Material Document 4900034675 : Overview

🖨 🔍 🔍 Details from Item   Material   Accounting Documents...

Posting Date	16.11.2005	Mat. Slip	0080014871	Name	MAASSBERG

Items

Item	Quantity	EUn	Material	Plnt	SLoc	Batch	Re	MvI	S	S
		BUn	Material Description			Reserv.No.		Itm		FIs
1	263	PC	1400-400	1000	0001			601	-	
			Motorcycle Helmet - Standard							
2	576	PC	1400-100	1000	0001			601	-	
			Deluxe Headlight							

The following information can be handy if you are developing reports based on data from inventory movements. The header of material document you can see the event type WL, the reference to delivery document is available as well.

In the document line item, quantity, material number, plant and storage location information are available. The concatenation of material document number and fiscal year is stored in reference key field in header of accounting document.

Non-standard requirements during PGI posting can be met with some custom enhancements. It is usually a technical challenge to populate the accounting document with certain values from the sales document. You may have a need to capture the order reason from sales order header in the line item of the accounting document created during PGI. This can be accomplished with a custom implementation of BAdI – AC_DOCUMENT.

The import parameter im_document is available in this BAdI. This contains values from sales documents. This can be then be used to populate one of the substitutable fields in ACC_DOCUMENT_SUBST structure

Technical Tips - The field needs to be enabled as a substitutable field in table GB01 where the Exclusion indicator will be blank.

Table GB01 Display

Check Table...	
Bool. class	9
Class type	S
Table	BSEG
Field	PRCTR
Exclude	

It is worth remembering some unique aspects of the PGI transaction. The PGI transaction results in recognition of cost of goods sold (COGS) where the COGS account is debited and inventory account is credited. The recognition of revenue happens at a different point in time in the billing document.

In delivery-related billing the billing date is set based on actual goods issue date. Thus the system automatically ensures costs and revenue go together. In addition, CO-PA ledger posts the costs and revenue together based on condition types in billing document which are mapped to value fields. Sales-related pricing conditions are usually mapped to VV01 value field and standard cost is defined in standard system by the VPRS pricing condition. This is mapped to VV10 value field. They are posted together in the same CO-PA document thus ensuring data integrity.

Besides posting to the general ledger, the PGI transaction also creates a document in CO and in profit center accounting.

You can use the function module WS_DELVIERY_UPDATE instead of BAPI_GOODSMVT_CREATE to post PGI and provide delivery number in VBKOK_WA-VBELN_VL and WABUC as 'X'.

4.5.2 Customer Returns

The returns process may vary depending on the complexity of the business. Companies tend to create separate sales order types for customer returns. A returns delivery is created with reference to this sales order and this serves as the basis for all related goods movements for that customer return. LR is the standard delivery type for returns. From this point though, the treatment of returns in accounting varies from one company to another.

The practice of insisting on a pre-issued return authorization (RA) or return material authorization (RMA) is widely followed. You may see instances where the return sales order is mentioned itself as the RA document.

The return PGI transaction is posted. The item category in delivery line item may make this transaction not relevant for billing. The actual issue of credit memo to the customer may happen through a separate set of transactions which may follow a different internal procedure in your company.

The return authorization function is integrated with Post-Processing Framework (PPF) in CRM. The PPF is a basic SAP technology that is used in CRM/SRM for scheduling and processing actions and outputs with an application document. The PPF uses a number of BADIs so you can implement the custom requirements.

The RMA sales order is identified by the document type RE. The RMA sales order should have sales order to reference to.

4.5.3 Miscellaneous

There are other movement types that affect accounting. Other movement types relevant to customers are samples, warranty and replacements. Besides movement types relating to customer-facing processes, there are also several other movement types such as 201- issue to a cost center where costs are debited to an cost center/primary cost element combination, 241-issue to an asset etc. They follow the general principles outlined in earlier paragraphs.

4.5.4 Technical Details

Information from goods movements can be accesses primarily from MKPF and MSEG tables. It helps to know the transaction/event type, movement types so you select the correct records. User exits and BAdIs relating to goods movements are available. One of them is BAdI LE_SHP_GOODSMOVEMENT in which changing parameter ct_ximseg and cs_imkpf have been provided where you can modify certain values in the material document header and line item.

4.6 Invoicing and Accounting Documents

Invoicing is a crucial part of order to cash process. Invoicing is part of application area SD-BIL and covers a range of functions including account determination, output control, invoice list, payment cards and rebate processing.

The data for billing is passed from both sales order and delivery. Values for various pricing conditions are determined during billing document creation. The billing document is then passed on to accounting. It is common for companies to have the same number for billing document in SD its corresponding accounting document in FI.

In addition to posting revenue and receivable in FI, the billing document is also the source of data for the profit center ledger and CO-PA. Customer and material information is passed to profit center ledger at a line item level. Pricing conditions in billing document are mapped to value fields in CO-PA.

Important tables in billing documents:

Table	Description
VBRK	Billing – Header data
VBRP	Billing – Item data
VBRL	Sales document: Invoice List
VRKPA	Sales Index: Bills by partner functions
VRPMA	SD Index: Billing items per material
TVCPF	Billing: Copying control
TVFS	Billing: Blocking reasons
TVKT	Customers: Account assignment groups

4.6.1 Accounting Integration

The information from billing document is automatically passed on to financial accounting (FI), profit center ledger and controlling modules. The integration occurs in several ways. Through the process of account determination, revenues and deductions are posted to the correct GL accounts. Allowances and accruals are posted to the general ledger in the same manner. The definition of the pricing condition influences the way it posts in the FI document. The following diagram explains the flow of data from billing document to FI document.

You can assign an FI document type when configuring the billing types. If the FI document type is not defined then the system automatically assigns document type RV.

In following paragraphs, the various aspects of billing document in relation to FI and CO postings will be covered in detail.

4.6.2 Account Determination

You can branch to the account determination analysis from the display of billing document in VF03 transaction. Once there select –revenue accounts- and you will be taken to the analysis screen. Here the GL account determination for each pricing condition within each line item of the billing document can be seen. GL Account determination happens in a sequential manner. Generally, the most specific combination is at the top and it kicks in only for those specific combinations. Often the default value of account key is picked up by the system during GL account determination

Some common elements used in account determination are sales org, customer account assignment group (CAAG), material account assignment group (MAAG) and material group. When combined with the account key, a unique GL account is determined for that pricing condition. You can configure the account determination in IMG configuration.

Change View "Acct Determination for Val. Areas": Overview

Val. Area	CoCode	Company Name	Chrt/Accts	Val.Grpg Code
0001	0001	P A.G.	INT	0001
0005	0005	IDES AG NEW GL	INT	0001
0006	0006	IDES US INC New GL	CAUS	US01
0007	0007	IDES AG NEW GL 7	INT	0001
0008	0008	IDES US INC New GL 8	CAUS	US01
0099	1000	IDES AG	INT	0001

Account Assignment Analysis

Analysis Accnt Determination

Procedure	Description
▾ KOFI00	Account Determina...
▾ PPSV	Service Price Item
• 10(KOFI)	Cust.Grp/MaterialGr...
▸ VA00	Variants

View

Access details 10 (KOFK)

Access	Message	Description
10	120	G/L account 0000800000 determined from Account determination type KOFK

Access	(complete)	
Field in condition table	Field in document	Value in doc.
Chart of Accounts	Chart of Accounts	INT
Sales Organization	Sales Organization	1000
AcctAssgGr	AcctAssgGr	01
Acct assignment grp	Acct assignment grp	02
Account key	Account key	ERL

When account determination fails, the invoice does not post to accounting. This is a common problem caused by configuration not being in alignment with master data or transaction data. For example, the material account assignment for an invoice line item may not be configured in account determination.

Once the account determination error is resolved, the invoice can be released to accounting with transaction VFX3. Just saving the invoice with the VF02 – Change document would have the same effect. It is possible that the posting period is closed so one would have to change the billing date before it can be posted in accounting.

You can also release the billing document to FI accounting in the transaction code VF02 in the menu Billing Document->Release ToAccounting. You can identify the status of the accounting interface in the field VBRK-RFBSK. If the status is C then the posting document has been created. The possible values of the status are:

Status	Description
Blank	Error in Accounting interface
A	Billing document blocked for forwarding to FI
B	Posting document not created (Acct. determ. Error)
C	Posting document has been created
D	Billing document is not relevant for accounting
E	Billing document canceled
F	Posting document not created (pricing error)
G	Posting document not created (export data missing)
H	Posted via invoice list
I	Posted via invoice list (account determination error)
K	Accounting document not created (no authorization)

While releasing the billing and invoice list, the accounting document will be created in the FI components. The relevant fields of the SD documents (VRBK, VBRP, VBPA, and KONV) are transferred to the interface tables XACCHD, XACCIT and XACCCR. The interfacing is done by the following function modules.

While releasing the billing and invoice list, the accounting document will be created in the FI components. The relevant fields of the SD documents (VRBK, VBRP, VBPA, and KONV) are transferred to the interface tables XACCHD, XACCIT and XACCCR. The interfacing is done by the following function modules.

Function Module	Description
RV_ACCOUNTING_DOCUMENT_CREATE	Creating account document for billing document
RV_ACCOUNTING_DOCULIST_CREATE	Creating account document for Invoice list.
SD_ACCOUNT_DETERMINATION_SHOW	Displaying account determination analyss

4.6.3 Document Summarization

This feature is used effectively by many companies to combine invoice line items with similar characteristics in accounting document. This will be necessary as each invoice line item can explode into dozens of line items in the accounting document depending on the number of pricing conditions within each SD invoice line item. It is possible that you may hit the 999 line item limit in the FI document. To get around this issue, 'summarization' can be configured in table TTYPV with transaction code OBCY.

SAP has further extended this functionality as of ECC 6.0. Extended summarization at company code or document type level has now been enabled. This can be done with t-code OBCYX and the table name is TTYPVX. If the transaction code OBCYX does not exist in your system, implement OSS note 1779136.

Note that the classic summarization in transaction OBCY and the extended summarization in transaction OBCYX cannot be maintained in parallel for the same object types.

Ref. Transactn VBRK
Name   Billing document

Table Name	Field Name
BSEG	AUFNR
BSEG	BPMNG
BSEG	BPRME
BSEG	BWTAR
BSEG	ERFME
BSEG	FKBER
BSEG	KSTRG
BSEG	LSTAR
BSEG	MATNR
BSEG	MEINS
BSEG	MENGE
BSEG	NPLNR
BSEG	PAOBJNR
BSEG	POSN2
BSEG	PPRCT
BSEG	PROJK
BSEG	VBEL2
BSEG	WERKS
BSEG	ZEKKN

One of the issues in document summarization is that you cannot post invoices with more than 999 line items. The system issues message 'Maximum number of items in FI reached'. The issue is not at invoice document but FI module. The main reason for the issue is that BSEG-BUZEI length of 3 characters. It does not support more than 999. You can resolve this by implementing the OSS notes 36353.

You can resolve the same by splitting the invoices into multiple invoices by implementing the BADI FI_INVOICE_RECEIPT_SPLIT. Implementing the BADI requires more subsequent processes consideration like Payment processes (manual or automatic), account assignment, balance sheet adjustment and BW interfacing. The details are described in the OSS note 1353125.

4.6.4 Controlling Integration

Data from billing document is also passed to the following areas with CO module

- Profit center ledger – from material data in invoice line item
- Cost center ledger – default account assignment for cost elements used in account determination
- CO-PA segment – mapping of pricing conditions to CO-PA value fields.

From VF03 (Display billing document), you can choose 'accounting overview' to see the accounting document, controlling document, CO-PA document and profit center document.

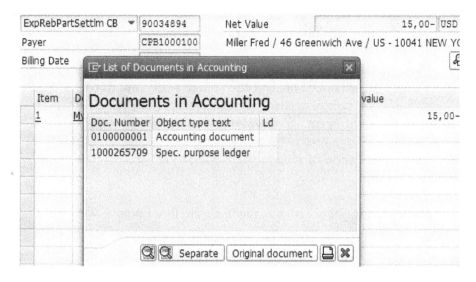

The document flow of the billing document lists the account document information.

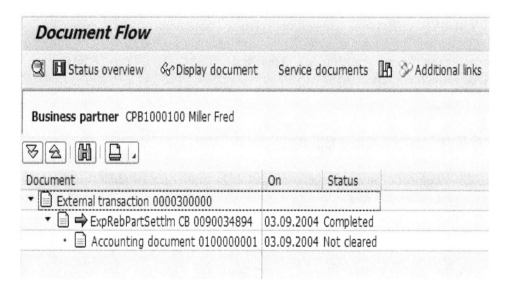

Note that you can use the function module **AC_DOCUMENT_RECORD** with I_AWTYP = 'VBRK' and I_AWREF as billing document then it returns associated FI documents. You can fetch associated accounting documents any component based on the I_AWTYP. You can use the FM **CO_DOCUMENT_RECORD** to read controlling document.

4.6.5 Revenue Recognition

Revenue recognition is another key area within invoicing. In standard revenue, revenues are recognized and posted in FI at the same time billing document is created. This can be either order related billing or delivery related billing.

There is also time-related revenue recognition. This is used for example in service contracts where the total revenue and the service period are fixed. A third type of revenue recognition is service-related revenue recognition wherein revenue is recognized based on a specific event.

In the last two types, the portion of revenue pertaining to service yet to be performed is held in a deferred revenue account.

Few important tables used in the revenue recognition are listed below:

Table	Description
VBREVAC	Revenue Recognition: FI revenue posting
VBREVC	Revenue Recognition: work list
VBREVE	Revenue recognition lines
VBREVK	Revenue recognition control lines
VBREVR	Revenue recognition: reference document

You can use the function module SD_REV_REC_DOCUMENT_VIEW to view the posted revenue recognition lines.

4.6.6 Intercompany Billing

Two common business scenarios result in intercompany billing. The first one is when a plant assigned to a different company code (legal entity) delivers the product in response to an order taken in another company code. The second scenario is intercompany stock transfers.

In the first scenario, the delivering plant is assigned to the sales org of the company that took the order. Delivery and PGI happens in the usual manner. But that delivery is the basis for two billing document. One is the intercompany billing document (IV billing type) between the company that shipped and the company code that placed the order. The second is the regular third party billing document.

The second scenario is a special type of purchase order. A delivery is created with reference to this PO and product is shipped to the ordering company code. This deliver is then used to create an intercompany billing. The ordering company would treat it like a normal receipt against a PO and proceed with the standard goods receipt process.

Enhancements

- **SDVFX001** – The SMOD enhancement enables you to change of header data in structure ACCHD. It has only one component EXIT_SAPLV60B_001 and in this exit, you can influence the header information of the accounting document. For example, here you can influence the business transaction, the time of entry, the 'Created by' entry or the transaction used to create the document.

- **SDVFX002** – You can use this SMOD enhancement to change the ACCIT customer line. It has only one component EXIT_SAPLV60B_002 and in this exit, you can influence the customer line of the accounting document. This exit is processed from the VBRK document header after structure ACCIT is filled.

- **SDVFX003** – This enhancement enables you to change of customer line for POS update and it has only one component EXIT_SAPLV60B_003. Note that for POS accounting, the customer line is filled differently. You can influence the ACCIT structure in user exit 003.

- **SDVFX004** – You can use this SMOD enhancement to change the ACCIT G/L account line. The enhancement uses the user exit component EXIT_SAPLV60B_004 to change the G/L account line. Additions for the G/L account line for example, by means of quantity specifications are possible in user exit 004.

- **SDVFX005** - This SMOD enhancement has only one component EXIT_SAPLV60B_005 that is used to enhance accruals. After all pieces of relevant data for accruals are stored in the G/L account line, you can add your enhancement.

- **SDVFX006** – You can use this SMOD enhancement to change tax line information. The enhancement has the user exit EXIT_SAPLV60B_006.

- **SDVFX007** – This SMOD enhancement allows you to change the installment plan parameters in the G/L account line. The enhancement has only one component EXIT_SAPLV60B_007. Additions to the installment plan parameters in the G/L account line are possible in user exit 007.

- **SDVFX008** EXIT_SAPLV60B_008: Change transfer structures ACCCR and ACCIT.
  After all pieces of data are filled in the accounting document, you can finally influence them in user exit 008.

- **SDVFX009** – You can use this SMOD enhancement to update the payment reference (KIDNO). It has only one component EXIT_SAPLV60A_001.

- **SDVFX010** - The SMOD enhancement allows you to influence the contents of the customer line before it is created. It has only one component EXIT_SAPLV60B_010.

- **SDVFX011** - You can use this SMOD enhancement to change of the parameters for cash or reconciliation account determination. The user exit EXIT_SAPLV60B_011 is only one component of the enhancement.
- **BADI_SD_REV_REC_PODEV** – You can use this BADI to manage customer specific event (PODEV) for the revenue recognition. The BADI has only one method GET_PODEV_CUSTSPEC. You can configure the revenue category using the transaction code OVEP and set revenue event as customer specific events (X, Y or Z). Other revenue event types are A (incoming invoice) and B (Acceptance date). SAP delivers the example class CL_BADI_SD_REV_REC_PODEV.
- **BADI_SD_REV_REC_PODEV_DISP** - This BADI enables you to display the document related to revenue recognition. If you do not implement the BADI then fallback class CL_BADI_SD_REV_REC_PODEV_DISPL will be executed. It has only one method DISPLAY_PODEV_DOCUMENT.

4.7 Dunning and Customer Statement

A dunning letter is a written request to a debtor for payment of amounts owed against invoices billed. In standard SAP, a comprehensive set of functions have been defined around dunning. Dunning notices are generated only for items that are overdue/in arrears.

As with the payment program in accounts payable, the dunning procedure contains most of the settings necessary for a dunning run which creates the notices.

The following diagram shows a high level overview of dunning process

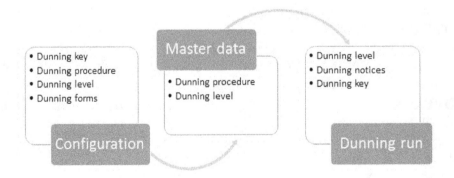

4.7.1 Configuration

The dunning procedure is at the heart of the dunning configuration. You define dunning levels, dunning forms, dunning charges and minimum amounts in the dunning procedure. The pre-delivered dunning procedure looks like this:

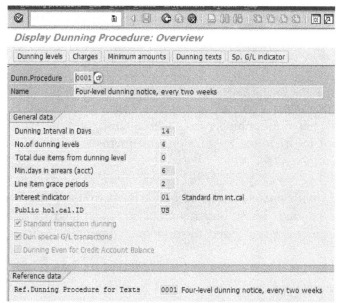

You define the number of dunning levels, and also the interest indicator if interest is to be calculated.

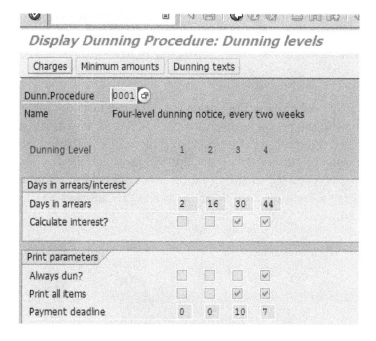

If you click on the dunning levels you will be able to define whether the customer is to be sent dunning notices, once, twice or three times after a pre-defined interval between each reminder notice. That is the 'dunning level'. Also you can define the number of days an item has to be overdue before it reaches that level. The calculate interest flag determines whether interest calculation is to be performed. The 'dunning text's push button is where the output form for dunning is associated with the dunning level. The form can be either SAP Script or Smart Form.

4.7.2 Dunning Run

The dunning run incorporates a set of steps that end with generation of dunning notice. It can be said that the dunning run is where configuration, standard code, master data, transactional information, custom enhancements such as BTE, all come together.

Dunning Run is started with transaction code F150. Parameters such as date, company code, customers are entered. These parameters act as preliminary selection criteria. Additional selections can be made based on document line item values and some master data attributes.

The dunning run consists of two steps, dunning selection and dunning printout. At this time, the system looks at dunning procedure in customer master in the correspondence tab to get all relevant information. Then it will look at the dunning level and last dunning date. This will be used in two ways. First is to determine whether sufficient days have passed for next dunning level to be triggered. Secondly, overdue items read from customer open items will be compared based on this dunning level. Only when an open item passes these two tests, it will be included in the dunning notice.

Then the system carries out the dunning printout. This is where the SAPScript or SmartForm linked to the dunning level comes into play. There is a lot of flexibility in terms of the layout and content of the dunning notice. Companies usually incorporate their logo, remit to address, contact information of their collection representative, and appropriate verbiage in the dunning letter. They also prominently indicate whether it is the first second or third notice and whether interest or dunning charges will billed to the customer.

A typical dunning run status tab appears like this

| Status | Parameter | Free selection | Additional Log |

Status
- Parameters were maintained
- Dun.selection scheduled for 04/09/15 at 21:03:19
- Dun.selection is complete
- Dun.printout scheduled for 04/09/15 at 21:12:08
- Dun.printout is complete

Companies schedule a dunning run as a batch job with 3 steps.
- RF150SMS – to automatically generate dunning run ID based on a template and date
- SAPF150S2 – to define selection section of FI Dunning
- SAPF150D2 – to print FI Dunning.

There are several enhancements in the area of dunning which are discussed in the next sub-section. The most common custom enhancement is through an user exit or BTE that enables sending dunning notices via email.

4.7.3 Technical Details

As per technical perspective, the dunning data is generated into the following phases:

- Phase 0: Read the customer master data
- Phase 1: Check and complete the MHND entries and create the MHNK entries
- Phase 2: Check for legal dunning procedure and assign credit memos
- Phase 3: check the minimum amounts for each dunning level and reassign levels and amounts for the dunning and delete entries if a dunning level could not be created and assign min interest rates and calculate interest.
- Phase 4: create the dunning data (MHNK/MHND) perform the final checks

The transaction code is F150.

Table	Description
MHND	Dunning Data
MHNDO	Dunning data version before the next change
MHNK	Dunning data (account entries)
MHNKA	Version administration of dunning changes
MHNKO	Dunning data (acct entries) version before

245

MAHNS	Accounts blocked by dunning selection
MAHNV	Management Records for the Dunning Program
T047E	Dunning notices form configuration
T047B	Dunning level control
T040	Dunning Keys

Predefined smart form is F150_DUNN_SF. You can create your smart form and define it in the dunning customization. The smart form can be executed using the FM FI_PRINT_DUNNING_NOTICE_SMARTF. The smart form change is done at BTE 1720.

You can custom fields in the dunning header record by adding custom fields in the custom include CI_MHNK. Include structure is part of the table MHNK.

Function modules

Function Module	Description
GET_DUNNING_CUSTOMIZING	Get all dunning related customization based MHNK data
PRINT_DUNNING_NOTICE	Print the dunning notice
SCHEDULE_DUNNING_RUN	Schedule the dunning run.
REPRINT_DUNNING_DATA_ACCOUNT	Reprint the dunning letter
EXECUTE_DUNNING_ACCOUNT	Executing dunning process
DELETE_DUNNING_RUN	Delete the dunning run

RFMAHN00 – You can use this report to list FI dunning statistics based on the Run date and Identification.

RFMAHN01 – You can use this report to list FI dunning based on the Run date and Identification.   The report lists detailed dunning information and it is non-ALV report.

RFMAHN02 – You can use this report to list blocked FI dunning based on the Run date and Identification.

RFMAHN03 – You can use this report to list blocked accounts based on the Run date and Identification.

RFMAHN04 – You can use this report to list dunning proposal item changes based on the Run date and Identification.

RFMAHN20 – This report enables you to list out the dunning history. This is an ALV report.

RFKKMA02 – You can use this report to output the line item-related dunning history. The output results are in the ALV. The dunning history is based on FKKMAKO table.

4.7.4 Enhancements

User Exit

SMOD F150D001 – EXIT_SAPF150D_001 is a user exit which enables users to send dunning notices by fax or by e-mail. You can use BTE 1040 instead of the enhancement. The BTE 1040 supports more parameters than this user exit.

BTEs

This section explains the BTEs used in the dunning process. There are a number of BTEs and its parameter can overlap with each other. You can use BTE based on the customer requirement and implement the appropriate BTE. Each BTE is placed in a pre-defined area and it is meant to execute particular logic. Even though BTE allows you to make additional change, you can implement required changes for the event.

- **BTE 1020** – This is a process BTE event and you can modify your dunning data and dunning header. This is before printing dunning document.
- **BTE 1030** – This is a BTE event. You can determine and override the form (defined in customization) name based on the dunning header data. You can also override the output spool name, payment advice generation flag and form id for attachment payment medium. You can get base customization information in the table T047E. The BTE is triggered in the FM GET_DUNNING_CUSTOMIZATION.
  - If the form name is smart form name then you must implement BTE 1720 to use function module FI_PRINT_DUNNING_NOTICE_SMARTF.
- **BTE 1040** – This is a process BTE event. The event is used to change output device and output parameter control. You can modify the transmission medium (FINAA) and output parameters (ITCPO) for dunning printing.
  - The FINAA-NACHA determines the transmission medium of printing dunning notice. The possible values are:
- 1 – Printout
- 2 – Fax
- I – Internet (you can set the email). To send email, then update email address in the FINAA-INTAD. If the email address is not populated in INTAD then it will get email address from the customer master record.

The dunning notice is attached as PDF in the email communication. The title is taken from ITCPO-TDTITLE. The standard text FIKO is used as the body of the email.

You can maintain the FIKO text using the transaction code SO10.

- **BTE 1050** – This is a process BTE event and it is part of the program name GENERATE_DUNNING_DATA. You can get additional data (like custom fields and other fields) for the dunning header data. You can also log any messages in this event.

- **BTE 1051** – This is a process interface BTE event and this is triggered for open customer items dunning data generation. Using the open item (BSID), you can update the dunning data.

- **BTE 1052** – This is a process interface BTE event and this is triggered for open vendor items dunning data generation. Using the open item (BSIK), you can update the dunning data.

- **BTE 1053** – This is a process BTE and is used to change sort key (MHND-CPDKY). You can log your messages.

- **BTE 1060** – This process BTE is used to change the value of Line items overdue indicator (XFAEL), Indicator (items payable, not be dunned - XZALB), Dunning Block (MANSP), Due date for payment (FAEDT) and Days in arrears (VERZN). The input parameters are Dunning data (MHND), dunning procedure and Application indicator.

- **BTE 1061** – Using this process interface BTE, you can force the dunning item data to be removed completely. The dunning line item will be removed from dunning data.

- **BTE 1068, BTE 1074** and **BTE 1076** – These events are related to IS-PS. The 1068 event will return the group interest. The event 1074 and 1076 is used to change dunning level control, dunning header and dunning item data.

- **BTE 1070** – This is a process BTE event and determines the interest rate (MHND-ZINSS), Number of days for interest calculated (MHND-ZINST), interest amount in foreign currency (MHND-WZSBT), interest amount in local currency (MHND-ZSBTR) and indicator to do no display interest in line item (MHND-XZINS).

- **BTE 1071** – Using this process BTE event, you can determine charges in foreign currency (MHNK-MHNGF) and local currency (MHNK-MHNGH).

- **BTE 1705** P/S – BTE event is for start of Dunning notice printout. You can change output parameters (SAPScript output interface). You can view the details in the structure ITCPO. The input parameters are dunning run date, ID, Customers and Vendors.

- **BTE 1710** – The P/S BTE event is triggered at end of Dunning notice printing program. You can use this event to execute any external update.
- **BTE 1719** – This is process and subscribe BTE event. This is used in dunning print program (SAPF150D2). You can do additional activities on dunning printing. The event has both dunning header and line item data. The function module can populate return code and messages. The information is used in the event
- **BTE 1720** – This is a P/S BTE event. This is used in dunning print program (SAPF150D2). You can do additional execution of the function module for printing the dunning notices. If you are not implemented this event, then the standard SAP function module FI_PRINT_DUNNING_NOTICE will be executed to print the dunning notice.

  You can use FI_PRINT_DUNNING_NOTICE_SMARTF function module to print the dunning notices in smart form. You can define the form name in the dunning customization or you can dynamically change the form using the BTE 1030.
- **BTE 1760** – This event is P/S BTE event and is used to populate application indicator based on the dunning header data. The application indicator is maintained in the table TBE11 (part of BTE component).
- **BTE 1761** – This event is P/S BTE event and is used to populate application indicator based on the dunning line item data. This is used in the multiple places of the dunning data generation.
- **BTE 1762** – This event is triggered before computing dunning level and allows you to change Dunning item data.
- **BTE 1763** – This event is to changing Dunning header data and item data in phase three of the dunning process. This is triggered after dunning level is identified by the dunning program.
- **BTE 1764** – This event is triggered only when account is not in legal dunning procedure. The event allows you to determine whether the dunning items to be dunned and change dunning header data.
- **BTE 1765** – This is P/S BTE event in collection management and you can modify the dunning line item data.
- **BTE 1770** – This event is triggered in the function module EDIT_DUNNING_DATA. You can override the edit mode to display only mode.

Most of Print program BTE events are executed only when check 'Run Open FI Events' in the selection parameter.

4.8 Lockbox and Bank Statement

The next step in the order to cash process is receiving money from customers in various forms. This section will look at various forms of customer payments and how they are applied.

A significant proportion of payments from your customers are still by checks. This where SAP's standard lockbox process comes into play. Other methods are domestic electronic funds transfer in standard formats routed through that country's payment clearing house and international wire payments through the SWIFT network. In SAP a wide variety of payment formats are supported.

In this section, we will restrict the discussion to lockbox and electronic bank statements as it relates to customer payments. This diagram gives a very high level view of how a payment file is processed.

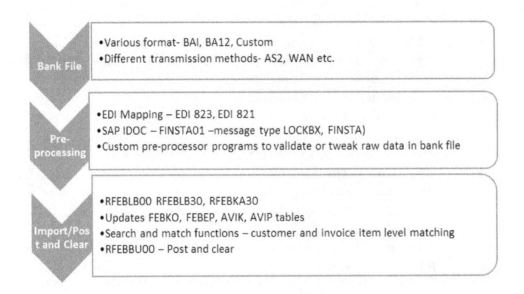

The business object types are BUS4499 (Bank statement), BUS4498 (Bank statement line items), and IDOCFINSTA (IDOC for bank statements).

4.8.1 Lockbox

The term AutoCash is often associated with lockbox. SAP has provided functionality geared towards processing payment files sent by bank.

Companies work with their bank to set up a lockbox to which their customers would mail their paper checks. Usually this is a PO Box set up in a city which allows them to minimize check transit times. A company headquartered in New York may intentionally choose to set up their lockbox in Dallas.

An actual bank account is set up for this lockbox. This is usually a zero balance account (ZBA) and moneys credited to this account are set up to be swept at end of day to the company's concentration account.

This PO box address is usually mentioned in invoices, customer statements, dunning letter etc. At the end of the day, the bank makes arrangements to pick up the checks from this lockbox and have the data input by their processing center in very quick fashion. By late evening or night each day, you will get a lockbox file in a pre-agreed format from the bank.

It must be noted that the bank account associated with lockbox need not necessarily receive credits from only check based transactions. It is quite common to have ACH, EFT and even wire transactions go into this account. It depends on the type of arrangement with your bank.

The most common format is the BAI2 format. Some companies with extensive experience with EDI will prefer the EDI 823 format which is then passed to SAP as a FINSTA01/LOCKBX IDOC. The final result is the same regardless of the file format.

BAI refers to the Bank Administration Institute and provided the BAI2 standards for reporting banking transactions. The BAI2 file contains uniform reporting codes which can be mapped in SAP. It must be noted that BAI2 standard is now replaced by Balance and Transaction Reporting Standard which is managed by Accredited Standards Committee X9, Inc.

4.8.2 Lockbox Configuration

Lockbox configuration is fairly straightforward. The bank account represented by lockbox is tied to a house bank. The two configuration steps discussed below control how lockbox data is processed. In t-code OBAY control parameters can be seen. The pre-delivered values are sufficient

The 3 check boxes here carry a lot of significance. The GL account postings flag informs the system that an FI document will be posted debiting bank and credit lockbox clearing account to recognize money received. Usually this lockbox clearing account is included in the same financial statement item as accounts receivable reconciliation account in FS version. GL account posting type indicates whether this posting should happen at individual check level or for all checks in that batch.

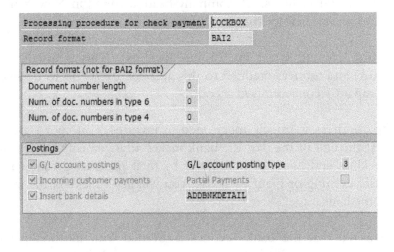

Incoming customer payment flag will post to customer sub-ledger when customer number can be determined through MICR match or invoice number match. If there is invoice number and amount match the program will clear that individual invoice line item. The flag for insert bank detail will trigger program RFBIDE00 which triggers a BDC session that will update customer master record with the bank information received in the latest lockbox file.

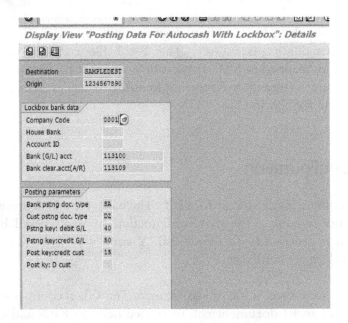

One of the main steps in lockbox set up is carried out with t-code OBAX. The origin is the bank account. Destination is the Routing/Transit number of your bank. Here is an example of how posting data is defined for AutoCash with lockbox.

The GL master record for bank clearing account has to be defined as open item managed account.

BAI2 file

Most banks provide BAI or BAI2 file to their customers. The formal name for the BAI2 file is Cash Management Balance Reporting Specifications Version 2. There is one major difference between the BAI and the BAI2 file. In the BAI2 file, the amount paid against each invoice is listed instead of a mere listing of invoice numbers and the total amount. Most companies use only the BAI2 file and we will restrict our discussion only to the BAI2 file.

Although the BAI2 file is the industry standard there may be minor variations in the file provided by your bank. It helps to have a good understanding of the reporting codes and the file structure by a careful reading of the user guide or file specifications that banks typically provide upon request.

This is the structure of a lockbox file SAP would expect. You can generate this file by running test utility program RFEBLBT2. When you try to import the lockbox file from your bank, it has to be in the following format so that standard SAP lockbox program can process the file.

```
100ABCDDESTINYABCORIGIN0402131622
5800000222 040213ABCDDESTINYABCORIGIN
6001001000060000002100005512234567 010130221 -      Check amount, check amount
4001001560100180000053 00001200000000000000GH    invoice number, invoice amount
4001001560100180000054 00001400000000000000GH
4001001560100180000055 00001600000000000000GH
4001001560900180000056 00001800000000000000GH
8000000222 04021300030002040000
9999900
```

IMPORTANT Note that SAP structure for processing a lockbox file is not necessarily the same as the structure of a BAI2 file that you get from the bank.

You need to ensure that file follows this format:
- FLB01 - Header
- FLB02 - Service record
- FLB05 – Detail header record
- FLB06 - Check record
- FLB24 - Overflow record containing individual invoice data
- FLB07 - Batch total record (Some banks process groups of checks in batches)
- FLB08 - Service total record

- FLB09 - Trailer

The end user can upload the file with t-code FLB2 (program RFBLB00). This program in turn.

You can define the program selection for the program transaction for electronic statement processing. The programs are used for the transactions under the menu option Bank Accounting -> Business Transactions -> Payment Transactions -> Elect. bank statement. The IMG configuration is stored in the table T020R.

Change View "Program selection for program transac

TCode	Program	Variant	PND
FEBC	RFEBBE00		☐
FEBC	RFEBDK00		☐
FEBC	RFEBESCSB00		☐
FEBC	RFEBFI00		☐
FEBC	RFEBFILUM00		☐
FEBC	RFEBNO00		☐
FEBC	RFEBNORDIC		☐
FEBC	RFEBSE00		☐
FEBC	RFIDSE_DUNN...		☐
FF.5	RFEBES00		☑
FF.5	RFEBFR00		☑
FF.5	RFEBGB00		☑
FF.5	RFEBJP00		☑
FF.5	RFEBKA00	BANKING	☐
FF.6	RFEBKAJ0		☐
FF.6	RFEBKAP0		☐
FF_5	RFEBFR00		☑

EDI for Lockbox

Many banks also offer lockbox data in EDI 823 format. The raw EDI data is mapped with the help of tools such as WebMethods, Mercator or Gentran which outputs data in standard SAP IDOC format. An idoc of type FINSTA01/LOCKBX is posted in SAP.

When this IDOC posts successfully, it creates a payment advice of type '05'. In this respect it is different from processing of BAI2 file. You have an opportunity to implement a custom enhancement or even a standalone custom program that calls transaction FBE2 to 'enrich' this payment advice before the next stage of the lockbox process kicks in.

At this time, several payment related tables such as FEBKO, FEBEP, AVIK, and AVIP have already been updated. You then process this data with program RFEBLB30 which is usually scheduled in the background. The next steps are common to all types of files.

Posting Program

The system submits program RFEBBU00 which performs a series of tasks. Knowledge of the functionality of this program is very useful to functional analysts and developers. Here is a pictorial representation of the actions carried out by the posting program.

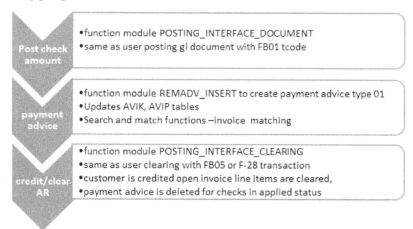

At the end of the process, a detailed spool is generated indicating how the customer match was carried out, which invoices were cleared. The user responsible for cash application would start off their typical day by going to the FLB1 transaction where a screen like this would appear:

Date	Lockbox	Batch	Checks	Applied	Part.appl	On account	Unprocess.
01/24/2001		002	163	70	7	84	2

Each status requires different treatment. Applied status needs no further attention. On account status means that program was unable to clear invoice items. You need to perform post processing for these transactions. Payment advice type 01 will be available with the invoice detail which can be used to find and clear customer open items. Unprocessed status means even the customer could not be identified.

4.8.3 Electronic Bank Statement

Electronic bank statements (EBS) can be used for multiple purposes. Companies use EBS functionality to automatically post transactions from different files representing distinct business processes. The following are some of the major areas for which EBS is configured.

- Daily Transactions –Concentration account

- Daily transactions – Disbursement account
- Daily transactions - Customer payments

EBS configuration is more complex than lockbox configuration. The following elements need to come together for EBS to generate correct financial postings and perform clearing functions as appropriate.

- ➢ External transaction type
- ➢ Transaction type
- ➢ Posting rule
- ➢ Account symbols
- ➢ GL account

The external transaction type is linked to the posting rules. The posting rules contain account symbols for debit and credit postings. GL Accounts are assigned to account symbols. It will help if you spend sufficient time understanding the meaning of reporting codes in the file from the bank. Often that can be directly set up external transaction type in EBS.

4.8.4 EBS Configuration

Here is an example of a posting rule that shows how a customer payment is to be processed from an EBS file instead of a lockbox file. Posting Rule 003 represents check deposit via interim account. This is the same lockbox clearing account you would have configured in OBAX.

Note how posting area 2 indicates that sub-ledger (accounts receivable) is to be processed.

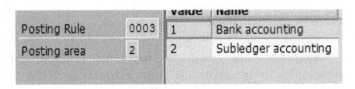

Also on the credit side no account symbol has been defined. This is intentional as the posting type 8 will cause the system to look for customer invoices to clear.

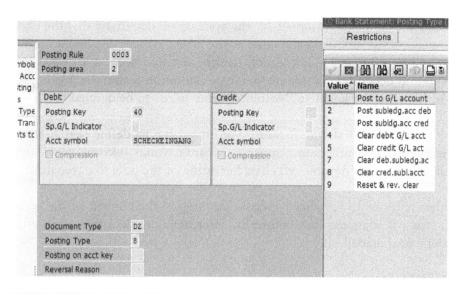

TIPS – During EBS configuration remember to create 2 posting rules, one for + and – amounts to represent unassigned transactions. This will ensure that loading of bank statement does not fail due to unidentified transactions.

Interpretation Algorithm and Search String

The bank file may be provided in different format. Some common formats are BAI, MT940, and Multi Cash. In addition your bank may have their proprietary format which may still be in a structure that could be interpreted easily.

The interpretation algorithm interprets information in the note to payee line in the bank statement and determines how that particular transaction is to be posted. You will try to use the standard algorithms delivered by SAP as much as possible before trying to use search strings.

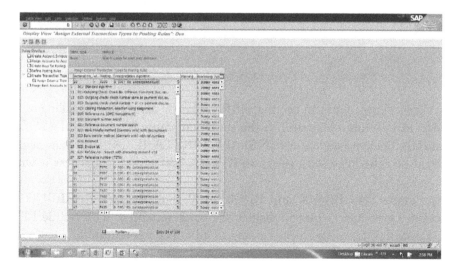

In the above example, if you pick 12- the system will determine that the check number mentioned in the bank file is the same as the SAP payment document number and the match will be complete. The check clearing account will be an open item managed account and depending on the posting type definition within the posting rule system will correctly clear the line item. Nothing further needs to be defined.

If the situation is not straightforward, you may have to define search strings and assign them to the interpretation algorithm. Search strings become necessary if characters or digits are added or removed character string of the note to payee field.

Characters such as |, +, *, have specific meaning in the context of the search string. Search string is triggered first before the interpretation algorithm takes effect when bank statement is loaded.

Processing Bank Statement

Import and processing of bank statement is a combined step and is done in t-code FF_5. The initial program is RFEBKA00. If the statement came in as an EDI 821 file, it would have already been posted as a FINSTA01/FINSTA idoc.

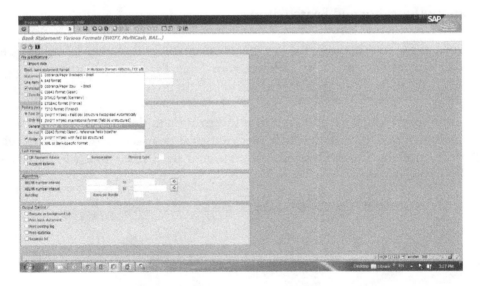

In the above screen you can see that SAP is already capable of handling several standard formats in different countries. If the statement came in as an EDI 821 file, it would have already been posted as a FINSTA01/FINSTA IDOC. In that case the processing would be scheduled with program RFEBKA30. User can access it with t-code FEBP.

Both programs RFEBKA00 and RFEBKA30, call program RFEBBU001 to create the necessary postings. You can display the bank statement with t-code FEBA. The FEBAN transaction allows post-processing of a bank statement item.

Some companies choose to only create a BDC session at the time the import process is carried out. This is particularly common in the case of cash concentration account where there could be a large number of unstructured or non-repetitive transactions that cannot be mapped with interpretation algorithms or even search strings. In such cases the user will go to SM35 and process the BDC session in foreground and manually input information such as GL account, profit center, cost center so that the FI document can post with the desired attributes.

4.8.5 Technical Structures

BAI uses the following ABAP structures.

FLB01	Lockbox Record Type 1 - Header Record
FLB02	Lockbox Record Type 2 - Service Record
FLB04	Lockbox Record Type 4 - Overflow Record
FLB05	Lockbox Record Type 5 - Detail Header Record (New Lockbox)
FLB06	Lockbox Record Box 6 - Detail Record (New Check)
FLB07	Lockbox Record Type 7 Batch Total Record (Bundle End in LB)
FLB08	Lockbox Record Type 8 Service Tot. Rec.End of all LB Bundles
FLB09	Lockbox Record Type 9 - Trailer Record (Last Record)

Tables:

Table	Description
T012	House Banks
T012K	House Bank Accounts
AVIK	Payment Advice Header
AVIP	Payment Advice Item
AVIR	Payment Advice sub item
AVIT	Payment Advice User-Defined fields
FEBKO	Electronic Bank Statement Header Records
FEBEP	EBS Line items
FEBCL	Clearing data for an EBS line item
FEBRE	Reference record for electronic bank statement line item
AGKD	Cleared Accounts
T028A	Bank statement table

Function modules

Function module	Description
BAPI_ACCSTMT_CREATEFROMLOCKBOX	Create lockbox data
BAPI_ACCSTMT_CREATEFROMBALANCE	Create bank statement from balance/check debit

	information

Enhancements

SAPLSSRV –This enhancement is used to check and validate bank account data. All components are part of the function modules BANK_ACCOUNT_CHECK and SWIFT_CODE_CHECK. The components are as follows:
- EXIT_SAPLSSRV_001 – The user exit is last check for the function module BANK_ACCOUNT_CHECK.
- EXIT_SAPLSSRV_002 – You can use this exit to check bank account data format. When you return a value in the parameter stop then stop validating the account details.
- EXIT_SAPLSSRV_003 – You can use this user exit in SWIFT code check.
- BTE 3000 – This is a P&S BTE event to validate the bank account data. This is an alternative for the user exit EXIT_SAPLSSRV_001. The BTE returns valid code and it raise invalid bank account if return code is not valid.

FEBLB001 – This SMOD enhancement is used to enhance lockbox processing. It has the following two user exit components:
- EXIT_RFEBLB20_001 – You can use this user exit to change Lock box data (AVIK) using the data AVIK and tables of AVIP and AVIK. The user exit is before inserting payment advice.
- EXIT_RFEBLB20_002 – You can use this user exit to add prefix or suffix to account number or reference number of Lock Box.

FEDI0005 – This enhancement allows you to enhance the process IDOCs of the type FINSTA01. It has the following user exit components:
- EXIT_SAPLIEDP_201 – Account statement/lockbox settlement handling of the IDOC.
- EXIT_SAPLIEDP_202 – The user exit is to do segment processing.
- EXIT_SAPLIEDP_203 – The user exit is used to make changes to payment advice of the IDOC processing.

FEB00001 – This is the enhancement for the electronic account statement. When processing the electronic bank statement, you can analyze all the transactions involving bank accounts and gain additional information. It has only one user exit component.
- EXIT_RFEBBU10_001 is only exit function in the enhancement and you can interpret note to Payee Lines of the Electronic Bank Statement. The user exit is only applicable when EBS line item's error status (of fields B1ERR or B2ERR) is empty. The custom include name is ZXF01U01. The parameters are as follows:

Name	Type	Data Type	Description
I_FEBEP	Importing	FEBEP	EBS Line items

I_FEBKO	Importing	FEBKO	EBS Header
I_TESTRUN	Importing	XFLAG	Test Run Flag
E_FEBEP	Exporting	FEBEP	EBS Line items
E_FEBKO	Exporting	FEBKO	EBS Header
E_MSGTEXT	Exporting	FEBMKKA-MESSG	Message to be displayed
E_MSGTYP	Exporting	FEBMKA-MSTYP	Message type
E_UPDATE	Exporting	FEBMKA-MSTYP	Indicator: Change data in program
T_FEBCL	Table	FEBCL	Clearing data for line item
T_FEBRE	TABLE	FEBRE	Note to Payee Reference Records for Line Item

You can implement the same solution using BADI FIEB_CHANGE_STATEMENT (as of Release 4.7). The BADI has more parameters than the user exit.

Name: FIEB_CHANGE_STATEMNT		Multiple Use: Yes	Filter: Yes
Description: Change Total Bank Statement According to Interpretation. The filter is based on the country key.			
Method: CHANGE_DATA Description: Change Bank data memory			
Name	Type	Data Type	Description
ID_TESTRUN	Importing	XFELD	Test run
IT_FEBRE	Importing	TABLE	Payment Notes
IT_FEBEP	Importing	TABLE	Line Items
IT_FEBCL	Importing	TABLE	Clearing information
FLT_VAL	Importing	LAND1	Country Key filter
ED_SUBRC	Exporting	SY-SUBRC	Return value
....	...	...	Error related parameters...
ET_FEBEP	Exporting	TABLE	Changed Line Items
ET_FEBCL	Exporting	TABLE	Changed Clearing Information
ET_DELETE_FEBCL	Exporting	TABLE	Deleted Clearing Information
CS_FEBKO	Changing	FEBKO	Changed EBS Header

Make sure that you must populate ET_FEBEP and ET_FEBCL from importing tables IT_FEBEP and IT_FEBCL to implement your changes. In user exit, these tables are used as table so it is considered as change parameter. If you return ED_SUBRC with value then it will stop the process with error message send with message exporting parameters. Changes will be updated to the database from the parameters CS_FEBKO, ET_FEBEP, ET_FEBCL and ET_DELETE_FEBCL. The entries in ET_DELETE_FEBCL will delete the cleared items from database table FEBCL.

SAP supports enhancement that change data before the interpretation algorithms. The enhancements are BTE events 2810 & 2820 and BADI FIEB_CHANGE_BS_DATA.

Name: FIEB_CHANGE_BS_DATA		Multiple Use: No	Filter: No
Description: Change the Bank Data Storage before the Interpretation Algorithm			
Method: CHANGE_DATA Description: Change Bank data			
Name	Type	Data Type	Description
I_TESTRUN	Importing	XFELD	Test run
T_FEBRE	Importing	TABLE	Payment Notes
E_SUBRC	Exporting	SY-SUBRC	Return value
....			
C_FEBKO	Changing	FEBKO	Changed EBS Header
CT_FEBEP	Changing	TABLE	Changed Line Items
CT_FEBCL	Changing	TABLE	Changed Clearing Information

As of Release 4.70, there is a Business Add-In (BADI) with the definition name FEB_BADI that is called immediately before the standard posting in program RFEBBU00. In this BADI, you can change the procedure of the standard posting or make additional account assignments by changing the tables that are to be transferred to the posting interface (FTPOST, FTCLEAR).

Name: FEB_BADI		Multiple Use: No	Filter: No
Description: Modification of Posting Data in the Bank Statement			
Method: CHANGE_POSTING_DATA Description: Change Posting data			
Name	Type	Data Type	Description
I_AUGLV	Importing	T041A-AUGLV	Clearing Procedure
I_TCODE	Importing	SY-TCODE	Current TCODE
I_FEBKO	Importing	FEBKO	EBS Header data
I_FEBEP	Importing	FEBEP	EBS Line item
I_IKOFI	Importing	IKOFI	Account Determination: Internal transfer int.
E_SUBRC	Exporting	SY-SUBRC	Return value
....			
T_FTPOST	Changing	TABLE	FI Post table
T_FTCLEAR	Changing	TABLE	Clearing Items
T_FTTAX	Changing	TABLE	Tax info
T_FEBRE	Changing	TABLE	Reference record
T_FEBCL	Changing	TABLE	Changing Clearing

			item

You can change T_FTCLEAR with your custom function module by adding row with SELFLD = 'FB' and SELVON with function module.

There are two BADIs are available for returns in Bank statement as Release of 4.7. The following two BADIs are discussed as below:

Name: FIEB_RETURNS_ADDIN		Multiple Use: No	Filter: No
Description: Add-In for returns in bank statement.			
Method: CHANGE_RETURN_CHARGES			
Description: Process returns			
Name	Type	Data Type	Description
I_FEBKO	Importing	FEBKO	Header data
I_FEBEP	Importing	FEBEP	Line item data
T_FEBRE	Importing	Table	Reference data
E_SUBRC	Changing	SY-SUBRC	Return value
E_MSGID	Exporting	SY-MSGID	Message Id
….			
C_RETURN_CHARGES	Changing	FIEB_RET_CHARGES	Return charges

Name: FIEB_RET_CHANGE_DOC		Multiple Use: No	Filter: No
Description: Add-In to change debit memo/bank statement: change of opened document.			
Method: CHANGE_BDCDATA			
Description: Add-in to change BDCDATA used for FB09			
Name	Type	Data Type	Description
I_FEBKO	Importing	FEBKO	Header data
I_FEBEP	Importing	FEBEP	Line item data
T_FEBRE	Importing	Table	Reference data
I_BUKRS	Importing	BUKRS	Company code
I_GJAHR	Importing	GJAHR	Fiscal year
I_BELNR	Importing	BELNR	Acct. Document no.
E_SUBRC	Changing	SY-SUBRC	Return value
E_MSGID	Exporting	SY-MSGID	Message Id
….			
T_BDCDATA	Table	Table	BDC data

BTEs:

- BTE 2810 - This is a process BTE event and you can validate and decide to process the bank statement line item.

- BTE 2820 (Equivalent to FIEB_CHANGE_BS_DATA BADI but executes before the BADI)
- BTE 2830 Process - Application-specific display in the sub-screen.
- BTE 2830 P/S - Transfer of the OK code to the application sub-screen.
- BTE 2840 - Application-specific display in the sub-screen which is not item-related and which does not switch off the standard display unlike event 2830. Up to five sub-screens may be included here.
- BTE 2850 P/S and process - Intervention when changing the bank data storage in post processing. This allows you to automate the filling of certain fields with the same values in post processing: If you change one field in the bank data storage, other fields are changed automatically.
- BTE 2860 - Allows a third posting (except for posting area 1 and 2) that is only possible in post processing. If you carry out this posting you should display the posted document (field FEBEP-SDOC2) in post processing. For this purpose use event 2830 (see above).
- BTE 2870 - Replace the tree or list display in post-processing. You may also replace only one of the two with a separate display. Before you implement the new tree structure, you need to do the following steps.
    - o Step 1. Create a structure ZMTREESNODE as a copy of the structure MTREESNODE. Change the component type of the component TEXT to CHAR50 and activate your structure.
    - o Step 2. Copy the class CL_FEBAN_SIMPLE_TREE (standard tree) to a customer class (in the following ZCL_FEBAN_SIMPLE_TREE).
    - o In the class ZCL_FEBAN_SIMPLE_TREE replace all instances of 'mtreesnode' with 'zmtreesnode'.
    - o Go to local definition of the class and find and replace the string 'cl_feban_simple_tree' into zcl_feban_simple_tree.

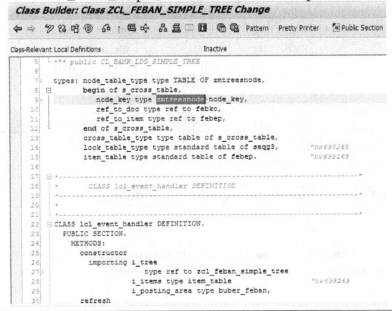

Save the class and activate.

Step 3. Make changes in the custom class and activate. The method BUILD_NODE_TABLE is building the node table and you can modify based on your requirements.

Step 4. Create copy of SAMPLE_PROCESS_00002870 and add the following code:

> e_replace_tree = 'ZCL_FEBAN_SIMPLE_TREE'.

Step 5. Activate the BTE event 2870.

- BTE 2880 - P/S and process: Replace the selection screen through with a separate selection screen.

Programs

- RFEBBU10 – Interpret Bank statement information
- RFEBBU00 – Update Account Statement/Check Deposit Transaction
- RFEBKAP0 – Print Bank statement

4.9 Reporting

As with other areas, the reporting in order to cash can be broadly classified into standard reports and custom reports. Standard reports are in the form of either summarized reports showing period balances by customers or detail reports showing line item detail. In addition, some standard reports also have drilldown options.

4.9.1 Standard Reports

The logical database DDF is used in most of customer balances and customer items report. Given below is a list of useful transaction codes for standard reports

S_ALR_87012167	Accounts Receivable Information System
S_ALR_87012172	Customer Balances in Local Currency
S_ALR_87012186	Customer Sales
S_ALR_87012169	Transaction Figures: Account Balance
S_ALR_87012170	Transaction Figures: Special Sales
S_ALR_87012171	Transaction Figures: Sales

Customers: Items

S_ALR_87012168	Due Date Analysis for Open Items
S_ALR_87012197	List of Customer Line Items

S_ALR_87012173	List of Customer - Open Items for Printing
S_ALR_87012174	List of Customer - Open Items
S_ALR_87012175	Open Items - Customer Due Date Forecast
S_ALR_87012176	Customer Evaluation with OI Sorted List
S_ALR_87012177	Customer Payment History
S_ALR_87012178	Customer Open Item Analysis by Balance of Overdue Items
S_ALR_87012198	List of Cleared Customer Items for Printing
S_ALR_87012199	List Of Down Payments Open On Key Date - Customers

4.9.2 Custom Reports

Custom reports may become necessary for several reasons. One reason could be that the format or output columns in standard report do not meet the requirements of the business. For example, the standard report may show the customer number but not customer name. Or it may not show period activity in columns in a particular report. The DSO calculation in some standard report may not be acceptable to your Credit/AR department

In other situations, the business may require that data from different areas such as SD may need to be shown in one layout. Besides showing the invoice accounting document, there could be a need to show corresponding delivery, sales order and even the goods issue document.

4.9.3 Drill down reports

Transaction Codes:
- FDI0 – Customer drill down reports
- FDI1 – Create a new report
- FDI2 – Change a report
- FDI3 – Display a report
- FDI4 – Create a Form
- FDI5 – Change a Form
- FDI6 – Display a Form
- FDIX – Delete Reports
- FDIY – Translate Reports
- FDIZ – Delete Forms

4.10 Summary

This chapter began with an overview of organizational units applicable to the order to cash process. Then, the critical elements of master data were covered. After that, the transactional flow was discussed in detail including sales order, delivery processing and inventory movements.

Invoicing and account determination were covered in a separate section. That was followed by the dunning process including an overview of dunning configuration. Possible custom enhancements in dunning were identified.

The next section covered lockbox configuration and transactions. The distinction between lockbox and electronic bank statement (EBS) was highlighted. This section also covered custom enhancements in lockbox processing.

We then covered reporting briefly including standard and custom reports. A list of useful tables and transactions were provided.

At the end of this chapter, you will have gained a solid functional and technical perspective of various aspects of the order to cash process.

List of Business Object Types

Business Object Type	Description
BUS0002	Company code
BUS0003	Business Area
BUS0012	Cost Center
BUS0014	Company
BUS0023	Functional Area
BUS1007	Customer
BUS1008	Vendor
BUS1029	Chart of Accounts
BUS1030	Cost element
BUS1112	Cost center group
BUS1113	Cost element group
BUS2072	Controlling document
BUS2075	Internal order
BUS3006	G/L account
BKPF	Accounting document
BSEG	Accounting document item
AVIK	Advice notes for payments and credit memos
FIPP	Parked document
BUS4498	Bank statement line item
BUS4499	Bank statement
IDOCFINSTA	IDOC for bank statement

List of Lock Objects

Lock Object	Description
EFBKPF	Accounting document header
EFAVIK	Payment Advice
EFBVOR	Intercompany process
EFKNKA	Credit Control Area
EFKNB1A	Customer Clearing
EFLFB1A	Vendor Clearing
EFSKB1A	G/L Clearing
EFSKB1	G/L account master record in company code
EFT011	Balance sheet/P+L
EFEBKPF	External Accounting document
E_RKBP	Invoice Document
EVBREVK	Lock object for revenue recognition

List of Authorization Objects

Authorization Object	Description
BUKRS	Company code
F_BKPF_BUK	Accounting Document: Authorization for Company codes
F_BKPF_BUP	Accounting Document: Authorization for Posting Periods
F_BKPF_GSB	Accounting Document: Authorization for Business Areas
F_BL_BANK	Authorization for House Banks and Payment Methods
F_REGU_BUK	Automatic payment activity for company code
F_REGU_GOA	Automatic payment activity for account types
M_RECH_EKG	Invoice release: Purchase group
F_PAYRQ	Payment Request
F_INVPGRIR	Authorization for Performing GR/IR Clearing
F_KNA1_BUK	Customer: Authorization for Company Codes
F_KNA1_GEN	Customer: Central data
F_IT_ALV	Line item display: Change and save the layout
K_KEPL_BER	CO-PA Planning: Authorization Objects based on operating concern
K_KEI_TC	Profitability Analysis Actual data based only by the activity.
F_SKA1_AEN	G/L Account: Change authorization based on field group
F_SKA1_BES	G/L Account: Account authorization based on activity
F_SKA1_BUK	G/L Account: Authorization based on the company code and activity
F_LFA1_BUK	Vendor: Authorization based on company code
F_LFA1_GEN	Vendor: Central data authorization
V_VBPR_BUK	Revenue recognition: Authorization for company code
V_KNKK_FRE	Customer Credit Limit: Edit sales document
V_VBRK_FKA	Billing: Authorization for billing types
V_KONH_VKO	Condition: Authorization for sales organization
F_MAHN_BUK	Automatic Dunning: Authorization for Company Codes
F_MAHN_KOA	Automatic Dunning: Authorization for Account Types
F_FEBB_BUK	Company Code Bank Statement
F_FEBC_BUK	Company Code Check Deposit/Lockbox
K_CSKB	Cost element master
K_CSKS	Cost center master record
K_ORDER	General authorization object for internal order

Important Fields to Know

Field Name	Description
BUKRS	Company code
BELNR	Accounting document number
BUZEI	Line Item
SHKZG	Credit/Debit Indicator
BLART	Document Type
WAERS	Currency key
KOART	Account Type; A –Asset, D-Customer, K-Vendors; M-Material, S-G/L Accounts
GJAHR	Fiscal Year
MONAT	Posting Period
DMBTR/WRBTR	Amount
HKONT / SAKTO	G/L Account
GSBER	Business Area
KUNNR	Customer Number
LIFNR	Vendor Number
ZUONR	Assignment number
BKTXT	Document Header`
AWKEY	Reference object
AWREF	Reference
PERNR	HR Person number
LAUFD	Payment program run date
CHECT	Check number
RZAWE	Payment method
LAUFD	Payment program run date
LAUFI	Payment program run identification
XVORL	Proposal run indicator
ZLSPR	Payment block
VKORG	Sales organization
VTWEG	Distribution Channel
SPART	Division
WERKS	Plant
VBELN	Sales order number
POSNR	Sales document item
MATNR	Material number
MATKL	Material group
KKBER	Credit control area

Index

V

W

www.ingramcontent.com/pod-product-compliance
Lightning Source LLC
Chambersburg PA
CBHW080551060326
40689CB00021B/4814